If
I chance
to talk
a little wild

If I chance to talk a little wild

a memoir of self and other

Jane Haynes

QUARTET BOOKS

First published in 2018 by Quartet Books Limited
A member of the Namara Group
27 Goodge Street, London, W1T 2LD

A catalogue record for this book is available from the British Library

ISBN 9780704374546

Typeset by Tetragon, London
Printed and bound in Great Britain by
TJ International Ltd, Padstow, Cornwall

For John and everyone else who is on a journey

Some like to let their slips and parapraxes show through, to revel in their strange behaviour: they are absolutely set on having an Unconscious.

JEAN BAUDRILLARD

I actually hate contemporary memoirs. Almost without exception, I hate the whole genre. The whole memoir genre, the comparable reality TV craze – all of it is corrupt and pathological. The more people claim what they're telling or showing is real, the further it is from the truth. People never tell the whole truth about themselves, and only ever tell part of the truth from behind the safety of a mask. Why do you think fiction was invented in the first place? A good novel is a thousand times more revealing than a memoir.

GARY INDIANA: I Can Give You Anything But Love

Contents

PLAIN JANE

After a certain age, and even if we develop in quite different
ways, the more we become ourselves, the more our family
traits are accentuated.

MARCEL PROUST

I WAS REGISTERED, THOUGH NOT CHRISTENED, AS I WAS
born into an orthodox Ashkenazy Jewish family in 1944,
with the names of Jane Angela Weiner. In contrast to the British
system of primogeniture, the orthodoxy of the Jewish faith is
inherited through matrilineal descent, which means that religious
status is passed from one wandering orthodox womb to another.

For my illiterate, maternal great-grandparents, who migrated
from a Russian *schtetl* and arrived at Liverpool docks at the end
of the nineteenth century without passports or any legible
surname, their most valuable currency was their orthodoxy. I
soon became disillusioned by my religion when the only sign of
devotion appeared to be a hypocritical gesture towards doctrine
with my family's *faux couture* display of conspicuous spending and
embarrassing hats to attend synagogue on High and Holy days.

I am told that my surname, which is a variant of the proper
noun Vienna was the sign of my paternal ancestry being lodged

in that city. I know almost nothing more of my roots than that my paternal great-grandfather was a 'fiddler'. I hope that means he played the fiddle, as he fiddled his way across Prussia, mending shoes as he journeyed. For many years it felt unbecoming that my great-grandfather was a homeless and wandering Jew, although I now realize this is an important clue in the labyrinth of my identity. A recurring theme will illustrate that the presence of bricks and mortar, windows, and a threshold do not constitute a 'home'.

Novelists are wary of acknowledging that a fictional character has the roots of his or her personality in any identifiable individual. They prefer to claim that they are random body snatchers. Marcel Proust, who occupies an insistent presence in my mind and the following pages, maintained that each of his characters required ten different keys to unlock their provenance. Writing a memoir, while sometimes a bit of a 'fiddle', does not require the provision of a key to unlock the identity of its author. My intention is to provide an often discursive and anecdotal palimpsest of identity through an inseparable broth of my personal and professional lives. I am both the rabbit and the hat. This memoir is not confined to my own foibles and fates of existence, but is also about the philosophical landscapes I inhabit and the unsuspecting cast of characters who I have dropped into my literary broth, whether it is edible or not.

I have never been curious to know more about my origins, an indifference which now frustrates my children. I subscribe to the taxonomy that seeks to ablate rather than to immortalize. I grew up ashamed of my family's peasant origins in which books and all other forms of culture were absent. They were diehard materialists. It intrigues me that while Jews are credited with acquiring material wealth from the stoniest of origins their orthodoxy insists that they must be buried naked, without even a shroud. I was ashamed that my mother's preferred tongue was Yiddish. From the moment I could read I wanted to relocate my 'self' in what as a child seemed to me to be the quintessential and cosy Englishness of Mrs Darling and Nana's nursery. Now, I know better than to be hoodwinked by Peter Pan's envious eye.

My parents liked English names – my father in particular wanted to become an 'English gentleman' – and so I was plainly named Jane. It has never given me pleasure either to be called or to answer to Plain Jane. Small and dark, I cannot think of myself without reference to Hermia's fierce tantrum: '"Little" again! Nothing but "low" and "little"!' I am also reminded of Rumpelstiltskin, who threw a similar violent tantrum on the occasion when the miller's daughter guessed his name. Names spellbind me! The dissatisfactions that frustrated me with my birth names have followed me into my professional identity where I have transitioned from the orthodoxy of being trained and named as a Jungian psychoanalyst into the indistinctly named and variegated pluralities of becoming a relational therapist. My tools are dialogue, listening and relationship but I have not thrown out the baby, aka the unconscious, with the bathwater. I am still committed to listen out for its wily manoeuvres, but I am inclined to feel that the unconscious is more likely to manifest through dreams, confusions of pronoun and gender, conversations of joy, despair or small talk. Sometimes, it will even appear through 'gossip', rather than through conforming to a Freudian, Jungian, or any other specific theory about the unconscious mind.

I hated my middle name, Angela, which led me to deny that I had a middle name. It was a source of frustration to me. Now that I am growing older, no not older but old, I understand why. It was because its signature reminded me of angels. My disappointment, which is quite different to my tantrum at being called

Jane, was because I was frustrated that its letters conjured an angel and yet I already seemed to have fallen so far from celestial grace and any previous heavenly home. I used to linger among the Victorian stones in the local St John's Wood graveyard, which was strangely attached to an orderly Victorian playground at the end of our high street, in the hope of meeting an angel – my guardian angel perhaps. But, I had fallen out of the Garden of Eden and there was not an angel to hear my cry.

I imagined myself as a blue fledgling and I had to learn to fly if I wanted to find my angel. Birds, their concealed nests, the mysteries that are hatched inside Limoges eggs, the magic of transitions between earth and heaven have always fascinated me. I am not sure why it had to be a blue fledgling, other than that the curiosity of blue tits draws them towards apertures in human life. My preference will always be for the divinity of swallows, but tits are uncommonly inclined to fall out of their nests; to require mortal if not divine rescue; and some would claim lapis to be the blue of paradise. I must also stake a claim to a lifelong obsession with the beautiful seductions of a weed, which I romanticize as Columbine, but which is commonly known as bindweed and whose creepers and the meaning of their 'double' bind, will attach to my text.

On the cusp of puberty, which I experienced as a liminal space of escape, of romantic phantasy and personal immortality, I took delight in imagining my life, in pen and ink, within locked five-year diaries where I curated lists: lists of film stars' names and their ratings as future-husband material; of dog breeds and names for my imagined children. The boys' names were 'Guy' and 'Dickon' (from *The Secret Garden*); while the girls' names were as exotic as those of the flamboyant flowers I chose to gar-land my white wedding bouquet. I would, without hesitation, have forsaken 'Plain Jane' for Eurydice, Antigone, Juliet, Leda, Persephone or Tatiana, all of whom at one time or another lent their names to my dramatic alter ego. If *Great Expectations'* Pip wanted to be 'a gentleman', I wanted to have a 'mythic' name. Now that wish stands in stark contrast to a recent epiphany in my consulting room, when I glanced into the waste-paper basket by my desk and lying there was a discarded handwritten envelope addressed to JANE. I looked down at those formerly despised letters and saw the whole of my life in a torn envelope. I liked the name. It made me think about how different it feels when I am listening to somebody talking to me in my consulting room and they speak, often in mid-sentence, my name: 'I was sitting beside my mother and you wouldn't believe Jane how hard it was for me to take her hand.' It is the insertion, which does not happen often, of my name that turns me into a named witness and not just 'anybody'.

Any complaint I had about my birth names as a child was amplified when I was forced to change my name, not by my marriage but by my mother's second marriage. I was twelve when, coerced to change my name by deed poll, I became Jane Angela Specterman and mutated from a fallen angel into ectoplasm. How did the irony of such a weird name come into existence? Who thought it up? What tribe wanted to broadcast kinship to a spectral form? I had another tantrum at having to lose my father's name, but my protests fell upon deaf ears. I was an ingrate. It was not until much later, through my own marriage, that I discarded the name, although not the spectral space that it had occupied in my adolescence. I wonder why I didn't take any earlier action, but despite the relationship problems I had with my mother, I never wanted to humiliate her. My Jewish ancestry then became camouflaged by the anonymity of my married surname, 'Haynes'.

Despite my secularism, despite my anti-Semitic adolescence, I have always felt that I am a Jew.

I have realized that while I thought I was the only child who wanted to change their name, it was far more common than I could then have known for Jewish refugees to arrive in the UK and to change, or to anglicize, their names. My anti-Semitism had its origins in my boarding-school days, when I was teased about being a 'Jew' child and the strangeness of my name. I was told that Jews were dirty and smelt. I became embarrassed by my realization that most of my relatives and acquaintances had assumed surnames derived from jewels and precious metals: Diamond, Ruby, Gold, Goldsmith and Goldman, Finegold, Fineman, Silver, Silverstein, Silverman, et al. My mother's maiden name was Finegold. I thought it meant her family wanted to find gold and that it was a greedy name. The shame has now, as my age has advanced and my knowledge of alchemy has increased, receded into a nostalgic and affectionate recognition that the despised name, Finegold, was nothing more than another archetypal expression of man's primeval longing to strike gold.

As far back as I can remember I have been obsessed with beauty, love, nature, children, animals, columbine and butterflies. I was fascinated by the mysterious industry of silkworms and the glow of the mulberries whose leaves were their diet. I longed to possess a silkworm farm. I pined throughout childhood to have a dog and to live in a house that had a staircase. I always felt, and have found it to be true, that all sorts of psychic change, – 'steps of the mind' such as the movements between hope and despair 'take place on the third stair'. I longed to slide down an ancestral banister, which I have always encouraged my grandchildren to do when the possibility arises. I think these small passions emerged to compensate for the bereavements, distortions and perversions of my childhood; a childhood that was disturbed by whispered accounts of wrongdoing, of the misfortunes of relatives who reached the United Kingdom not to find gold but to suffer the poverty and perform the petty domestic crimes necessary for survival in the East End during the Depression, before they got a legitimate foothold on the ladder to prosperity. My relatives' experience of the Snakes and Ladders of life and fate were soon reflected in my struggles with my own unpredictable destiny. I found myself parented by a father who was suffering from undiagnosed neuro-syphilis and a vulnerable mother who had developed bi-polar disorder.

Perhaps that is why my earliest memory is not of my mother or my father but of my beautiful nurse Vera, whose name I remember although I was still too young to speak it. 'Where did you go Vera, and why did you forsake me as I lay half asleep in my cot?' Vera disappeared in the middle of the night and afterwards I was told – but not consoled for the absence of her tourmaline eyes, which lit up my darkness – that she was 'a thief'! I of course had no idea what that word meant, but it remains the first exclamation that I can recall. Now, as I look back I can see that Vera stole away my trust in a consistent world. As I write these words they open up a portal of memory to sleepy eyes trying to focus on 'St Vera' who, in the dimmest of light, was emptying her drawers. With the click of a latch she abandoned our nursery home. I cannot imagine when I was at the dawn of understanding, before I could use speech to communicate, what she could have stolen that was more valuable than my trust.

Throughout my childhood it seemed to me safer to attach myself to the vagaries of nature and even to the animal kingdom rather than to rely on human nurture. Yet this is not altogether true. Despite my identification with fallen blue fledglings, I became accomplished at attaching myself to other people's families, at negotiating my own adoption. As a child I was obsessed with the card game Woodland Happy Families, with its anthropomorphized red squirrels, owls and other woodland folk, who looked so neatly groomed and cared for, and whose nests seemed preferable to my home. I felt I was either a changeling child, or Lilith of the Envious Eye* had screeched away my nursery birthright to happiness, which in my case would have been a close and loving family of origin. I remember how my superstitious mother trembled whenever anyone said something complimentary about me as a small child. I recall my feelings of acute shame as she turned her head and crudely, and she was not otherwise crude, spat on to the ground. Now *I* know, although she did not, that the belief that controlled her primitive thinking and caused her to spit out the poison of envy was rooted in the superstitious story of Lilith's 'envious eye' that has haunted nurseries through the centuries. It was the lost and unspeakable name of Lilith, Adam's rebellious first wife, whose banishment from the Garden of Eden blighted the unconscious of her Jewish womb and maternity. Lilith is to be found in many incarnations and is in part a monster-bird; indeed, she is referred in the Bible as the 'screech-owl'. It now occurs to me that she became transgendered and immortalized by J.M.Barrie as Peter Pan.

In retrospect I experienced a brutal sob for the geography of a home that although it had a postal address and refined furnishings was full of conflict and empty of consistent emotional

* There are many versions of Lilith's envious eye: La Llorona, or The Weeping Woman, is a legendary ghost prominent in the folklore of Spanish America. This myth has a tendency to assume aspects of an urban legend and is present throughout Mexican culture. According to the tradition, La Llorona is the ghost of a woman who has lost her children and now cries as she searches for them in the river, often causing misfortune to those who are near or hear her.

attachments. The experience of homesickness for a non-existent home is in every way as debilitating to the body and self as sea-sickness with its lurch of stomach and loss of balance. The main difference is that with seasickness one has no control, whereas with homesickness it is possible to create a spurious sense of control and to deny the feelings of loss. My refuge became reading and my favourite book was *The Wide, Wide World* by Elizabeth Wetherell. I found the return from boarding school for the holidays to a desolate home was worse than having been sent away to begin with. It was a walnut shell without any kernel.

Such early experiences of broken attachments to parents, or to important caretakers, can often lead to an undesirable sense of premature ambivalence in the child, which is true in my experience. The following pages will rarely escape descriptions of the conflicted experiences of a divided self. Yet there is no doubt these violent ruptures have helped me in my professional life as a psychotherapist, to understand a collective and nostalgic disappointment concerning the lost domain of home; the loss of a pre-lapsarian unity of self.

Since the isolation and disillusionment of my childhood and the absence of a stable family, I have found it difficult to identify with social or professional groups. My professional training in psychology was as a Jungian psychoanalyst and by co-incidence, or perhaps not, I have also abandoned that 'tribe' and fallen into heresy.* It makes me unusually nostalgic to remember my glori-ous training at the Society of Analytical Psychology when 'I was

* It was only after my training analyst died that I began to feel unprotected in a society whose privileges and genograms depended upon the status and power, within the organization, of the training analyst. Although my analyst was also a secular Jew, which was not a coincidence, it was unusual within the Jungian discipline to find many Jewish trainees as Jung's close associations with Nazi Germany were controversial.

young and easy under the apple boughs' of study. Now, I am a lapsed Jungian psychoanalyst who defected from my professional training society when I grew up, which is not at all the same thing as qualifying, and discovered that the institution amounted to little more than a club where your status and power base was determined by who your training analyst and supervisors had been. I have redefined myself as a relational psychotherapist who prefers to have a conversation with my patients rather than to preside as an authority professing to have spurious access to their unconscious. Dialogue is my principal tool. I spend up to eight hours a day in my consulting room listening to the stories of people who enter as strangers but often end up as familiars. I act as a midwife who attempts to restore broken narratives through a shared dialogue. Self-discovery requires the reflective mirror of an engaged and listening 'other' to be most effective. Otherwise, it is rather like the impossibility of tickling oneself and producing laughter. I prefer to think about the people consulting me as coming not so much for a 'session' as to 'a parliament of two', as entering a democracy of minds wrestling to find a shared language. Martin Buber would refer to this type of communication as 'the command of the word', by which he means the energy that moves between beings and which carries within it a possibility for transformation of the heart and growth of the soul. Even if it is not always possible for hearts to touch, there is the possibility that language can lead to change.

I laugh out loud (LOL), to use wretched text-speak, at the common misperception, or anxiety, held by many members of the public and professionals that a 'shrink' is trained to see into and through a social mask or is adept at interpreting unconscious desires. The unconscious, which is part of our subjectivity, is the most slippery part of the human anatomy and even its precise location within our brains has defied scientific research. I ask myself whether it is a curse or a blessing that the innate solipsism of human nature is impenetrable. We can never know how we are perceived by anybody even in simple ways unless they are willing and/or able to tell us.

I was recently amused when I asked a friend who is a professor of European literature to read the chapter on Proust in my draft manuscript. One of his subsequent emails surprised me when he, by chance, disclosed an opinion that did not fit in with my self-image. Ever since my earliest schooldays I have prided myself on my spelling ability and thought of myself as 'ace'. Members of my family will often use me as their spell checker. The bubble burst when I was confronted with another perception after I had serially misspelt 'Dionysius'. His email noted: 'Yes, re Dionysos (or Dionysus). Indeed, if I can don my don's hat for a mo', spelling ain't your strongest point.'

Equally, I cannot know what anybody, regardless of their status as 'patient' or friend, is thinking about anything, even if they are sitting opposite me and we are engaged in a conversation; they may use decoy strategies if they choose to remain concealed. This endorses the legacy of the insolvable mysteries of our 'animal' subjectivity. Philosophers and every 'scientist' who investigates the soul and self have tirelessly, throughout the millennia, explored the exasperating and eclipsed state – the *mysterium* – of being a human being, or any other mammal, come to that. The idea since time immemorial that man is a stream whose source remains hidden continues unchallenged. Psychoanalysts, psychiatrists and psychotherapists do not have a privileged vision into the human psyche. For most of the time they, too, despite their training, have to stumble about in the dark like cat burglars or MI5 spies, hoping their search will be rewarded. To add metaphor to simile, I think of myself as a professional magpie; indeed 'magpie' is my chosen nickname. Although I am not taken with magpies, in a sense I feel that I assume their mythic role; I am privileged to receive and even to collect all sorts of glittering and precious gems of random and sometimes unconscious knowledge while I listen to so many patterns and varieties of human nature and intention every day. It occurs that magpies steal, whereas I most commonly receive, although I do, like a magpie, collect the *bricolage* of other people's intelligence. I recollect a time in 2009 when I was introduced to Grindr. I pride myself on keeping up to date with technology and it felt like a privilege of trust to sit with my 'patient' while he inducted me into the mysteries of the app and its variety of displayed naked body parts. He chose to maintain an anonymous decorum and only displayed his forehead. Such extraordinary and variegated pieces of information, whether they are jokes, dreams, misused pronouns, or the casual name of an artist, book, film or exhibit, let alone the unsolicited photographs of a Carnac landscape of primeval stones, come my way and have led me towards the unconscious.

Perhaps that is why I do not have any inclination for hoarding personal memorabilia. I assemble so many narratives in my mind not only on a fleeting daily basis, but also on a permanent one, that I never know when flashes of a patient's genogram will return. I also have the feeling that the past has been lived and I must continue, regardless of my age, to make space for the future. If I were to die tomorrow, there would be no lofts or suitcases full of memorabilia for my family to discover. I am a shedder. I have one filing cabinet, one bedside drawer and one wardrobe of clothes. Even the contents of my bookshelves are pruned and annually transferred to Oxfam, with the exception of poetry, philosophy, art books and the books that have been written by friends or contemporary icons. And, of course, there is my laptop...

I have come to think that the rare psychic dividends, which I am privileged to listen to in my consulting room, and which are sometimes delivered as pearls of the unconscious, are the psychological equivalents of the jewels that my émigré ancestors longed to find. I also feel privileged that there are people who seem willing to trust me to accompany them on their extraordinary journey into the hinterland of what it means to be a human being in search of the holy grail of understanding. These are people who have chosen not to turn a blind eye to the random and often cruel nature of our fallen human existence, but who wish to escape, to let go of the habitual and seek out the spontaneity of new beginnings.

Any beginning, whether or not it is subsequently discarded, becomes a vital threshold moment of engagement between two people. I find that the beginning of any significant relationship, whether in a familial, social or therapeutic context, is never empty but full of expectation and an often delusory sense of freedom. Delusory, because too often we are unconsciously revolving on the inexorable wheels of a past inheritance, which may indelibly stamp the ways in which we are free to respond to the 'other'. Whether these beginnings take place in the protected and professional space of the consulting room, where one of the objectives is to overcome destructive patterns of repetitive experience, or in more random ways, they signal entry into a sacred space where two strangers meet who both hope to become more complete. Often the thought of a new beginning, which I imagine as a great event, will keep me awake at night.

Perhaps it is a rash disclosure, but I will volunteer that every time I open the door of my consulting room to a new person I also hope to discover more about myself. While I am primarily there in a professional capacity as a trained listener, if the newcomer does not bring something into the room that will also enlarge my soul, the therapy may become a failure. It feels as if I live in naïve anticipation of finding a part of myself that was lost to the world during the process of my psychic birth. Plato's image of the lost half of 'selfhood', in that it provides the answer to the isolation that I have always felt, haunts me. There is a privilege in being trained as a psychiatric midwife to help someone give birth to the undiscovered parts of their psychic identity. To be successful such an encounter will involuntarily and subtly change not only the expression on my face, as I bear witness to a story, but it will also change the rate of my heartbeat and bring some new under-standing to my soul. It is because I do not choose to separate my own processes of growth from those of the people who consult me that as I write I will intertwine some of their narratives with mine. It is also why the ancient Greek concept of reciprocity – the actions of giving, returning and receiving – will also bind my pages.

Janet Malcolm, an American journalist and writer, has infa-mously described the practice of psychoanalysis, and by extension psychotherapy, as the 'Impossible Profession'. Malcolm's com-ments on these impossible conflicts are elucidated in these pages through the unavoidable entanglements between the professional and personal aspects of my life. While ethical boundaries must be maintained that does not change the reality that in both my mind and in my writing these two branches of my life bleed each into the other. It is not a matter of being able to leave my work and the people who have consulted with me behind at the end of the day. Most of the time my professional day comes to an end at the point when I turn off the lights and lock the door, although even then one cannot lock out involuntary flashes of memory.

The reader will find these pages bring together glimpses of my emotional, social, familial, philosophical and professional lives in discursive association. I shuffle between the diversity of the interior rooms of my mind and the external physical space of my consulting room. No longer 'green in judgement', as the ancient queen Cleopatra punned, now that my salad days are over, I draw on my life and work and on a variety of influences and experiences between my own and other people's changing lives. I have become aware that historical narratives of broken 'attachments' that are either related to biological families of origin, or to more recent families of their members' own making provoke the base line of so much unhappiness. I am intrigued that so many of the people consulting me, despite the uniqueness of their suffering, can be polarized into these two groups, who are either motivated to find out as much as they can about their origins and ancestors, or to ablate them.

For the first group of 'seekers' what often begins as an Internet hobby, can mature into an obsession to become the self-curators of their identity. Its members seek to populate the parchment leaves of their ancestral trees with the historical details of past births, marriages, deaths, family migrations and long-lost transatlantic progeny. The Internet 'search', however, rarely reaches the hidden places where the family secrets are likely to be stored. Reliable facts and revelations more readily emerge from a relative's deathbed confession or from the oral histories of communities where family narratives are passed on, or gossiped about, between the elders and their children. In a society of nuclear families with frequently changing locations and constant interconnection through social media, such folk traditions risk being discarded as worthless evidence of identity. Scrapbook collections are exchanged for selfies, Instagram and Snapchat;

the latter application virtually disappears before your eyes and without leaving any trace. There are members of this group, who were disenfranchised at birth who will use the Internet as a helpful tool to begin the quest to find their biological parents or to attempt to unravel the secrets and distortions of family genealogy. More recently inexpensive tests have become available online to establish an individual's DNA.

The other group, to which I belong, is energetically committed to denying or ablating their origins. This is not an easy task. While some rebellion is a vital part of healthy adolescence, the desire to rebuild an entirely new foundation, 'Myself I shall remake', of identity is not. If I allow myself another caprice of imagination, then I emerge out of Zeus's forehead, as did Pallas Athena, the goddess of wisdom and war. I see myself arrive clad in full body armour, confrontational and ready to do battle with my life. Wholesale, have I rejected the rhythms, rituals and daily patterns of my original 'nursery', along with my Jewish socio-cultural identity? I have resisted or protested against the criteria and inheritances of my caste and clothed myself in the uncomfortable integument of difference. In part, this book will be about the ways in which, having spurned my inheritance and left home at sixteen, never comfortably to return with my bags of unwashed underwear and sheets, I have hammered out both my language and my identity on Flaubert's cracked tin kettle, while all the time I have longed to move the stars to pity.

It is not uncommon for neophytes in the psychoanalytic and psychotherapeutic professions to have been drawn from the ablation group as we are inclined by temperament to seek for new affiliations to substitute for our own family structures. Psychoanalysis is an ideology within which it is de rigeur for strict and competing training schools to bind their membership into incestuous group identities. Their teachings are then trans-generationally passed on between training analysts, their trainees and even their patients. Jung and Freud have spawned almost as many tribes as are mentioned in the Old Testament. The same pattern applies in other cults, or new religious movements, who attract initiates disillusioned with, or revengeful towards their origins.

Regardless of our conscious intention, the ineradicable past clings to the memes which line the shadows of personality. We cannot banish memory of the shrouds of children who followed the Pied Piper into his cave of no return; such deaths often leave behind a lasting legacy that has an unconscious impact on the future emotions of family members. Ever-present are the children who were named but who were not born; others who being named did not live long enough to own their names. I have found one of the most poignant characteristics of any 'developmental' story to be when the stillbirth, cot death, or late miscarriage of a sibling has been concealed as a secret within the family. Any premature infant death can become the destructive elephant in the room. The same can be true of deaths of older siblings due to childhood accidents or disease. The challenges of being born as a 'replacement' child are incalculable and particularly so when a child is born immediately after the parents have suffered a tragic loss.

I was looking after someone who suffered from what appeared to be an endogenous depression (a severe depression in which no external factors appear to be causal) which had by mid-life turned the person, despite their success as an artist and a parent, into a virtual recluse. At the time of their birth the parents had lost their firstborn, ten-year-old child to meningitis. It would not have occurred to them to seek counselling, nor would it have been available to them in the '40s, other than by a priest. Their way of dealing with the tragedy was to continue with their lives as though the death had never happened. There was one snapshot of their deceased son beside their bed. My patient never dared to ask what his brother's name was, but he grew up feeling he had stolen away his brother's life and that he must also in some unknowable way be responsible for his mother's depression. It was only when his mother was dying that she told him she had visited her son's grave regularly and revealed his name and her final instructions for him to do the same. 'This phantom that runs along behind you my brother, is fairer than you; why do you not give it your flesh and bones?' [Friedrich Nietzsche]

A woman consults me who has been wounded by multiple premature deaths in her family. She cannot expel her fixed idea that there is already someone seated in my room. A phantom precedes her who has usurped her place. She never fails to cross 'our' threshold from the street into the inner sanctum of her emotional life without being followed by the thought that she is going to find a usurper seated on the sofa; her sofa. She tries to take rational possession of herself as she enters the room, which she feels to be occupied by a spectral other. She fears she will find her doppelgänger waiting to steal her life. Her mother lost a full-term male child at birth but she does not know any details of the death of her sibling except that it preceded her birth, although she has suspicions about the context. My 'imposter' writes me an email:

> My jealousy of the 'other' I fear to be in your room when I arrive is not a specter but a real person with a prior, better (or bigger) claim on your attentions – somebody else who fills up space in your head and heart and suddenly makes me feel, 'Where is my home?' This isn't of course the rational thought,

but a sudden 'shameful' feeling. The word 'family' makes me feel the child in the dark seeing the light spilling out of the door to a room that I cannot enter.

I am often asked what the difference is between 'shame' and 'humiliation', which are two critical building blocks of emotional development that can demolish self-image. When we experience shame we may recoil or shrink, like a crouching cat behind a shoulder bone, into a visceral memory of something as insignificant as an item in the wrong place: 'You've got some green rocket stuck between your teeth,' or, 'Your skirt is caught up in your knickers.' Shame causes us to feel embarrassment and when we are embarrassed we are liable to feel unmasked and fragile. Some of us blush beetroot with shame. Shame is an active emotion as demonstrated by the often-used phrase, 'I am ashamed of myself.' I was ashamed that I wet my pants when I was a child. Usually, the 'shame' is something we have inadvertently taken upon ourselves and it is easier than humiliation eventually, and across time, to delete or to forgive.

Humiliation is different: it is often intentional, cruel and even sadistic. We are most likely to experience ourselves as being its passive recipient. Humiliation is most commonly something done to us by another. For example, the child suffers humiliation through the gaze, which accompanies the humiliating admonishment of their act of enuresis. In childhood we are most vulnerable to small but indelible acts of humiliation, which can impact on or permanently reduce our selfhood, sometimes forever. Sometimes, it will be with violent consequences. Both in literature and through my clinical casework I see the consequences of even small words like 'stupid', 'dirty' and 'clumsy' being impossible to erase.

I shall always return to literature to provide more convincing explanations for human pathology than doctrinaire theories, many of which amount to no more than hidden authorial confessions, camouflaged into a hopeless attempt at the objectivity of science. This does not, however, disqualify their partial relevance as a contribution to psychological knowledge. Working as a therapist, I know that it is crucial I observe my self-reflexivity as the basis of a hypothesis to test another person's experience, but, at the same time, I do not make the mistake of assuming that the meaning of our responses will be similar.

Literature does not pretend to have objectivity and respects the phenomenal powers of language: The impact of those small words I referred to which can cause such permanent damage to an immature ego. I have learnt never to underestimate the power of infant humiliation and its enduring and unpredictable power to influence adult trajectories of sexuality, sado-masochism and power. A child may experience the smallest act of Oedipal humiliation as a morbid wound. Such actions can be so small that they pass unnoticed, except by their victim, as the novelist William Golding described in *Darkness Visible*. Here, Oedipal triggers exist that have been lost from memory or repressed, but which become conduits that contribute to the descent of the beautiful eleven-year-old twins, Sophie and Toni into adult sociopathic and perverse sexual lives:

> ...having babies that Daddy would want the way he didn't want the twins, his twins and nobody else's... Sophie knew it couldn't happen, couldn't be allowed to happen. All the same that was no comfort and she couldn't get her mouth together to blow but it went wider and wider and she began to cry. Even the crying was all wrong because she was exhibiting it before

Winnie and even worse before Daddy, and thus informing him how important he was, it got mixed up with rage.

The consequences spawned by, in this instance, 'Daddy's' Oedipal humiliations, are experienced viscerally by the twins, and become the possible basis of unspeakable acts of female terrorist revenge. In part, these acts spring from repressed origins in what at first appeared to be insignificant actions, and their genesis has passed unobserved except by Golding's twins. Sophie and Toni are possibly the first female terrorists of literary fiction. What becomes critical to Golding's narrative is that the origins of their forensic psychopathology, as has so often been the case with other notorious forensic acts of revenge – the example of the protagonist of Hitchcock's *Psycho* springs to mind – lie in the infantile humiliations experienced within the family locus.

From what backwater did the verb 'spawn' emerge, I wonder? My heartbeat stumbles upon an enchanted puddle of frog's spawn, which brings with it related memories of a lost childhood. My migrant-Jew childhood transition from bomb-shattered London and spooky graveyard to a Christian boarding school, St Hilary's, in the Surrey countryside becomes encapsulated in the pastoral idyll of the reproductive cycle of tadpole and newt. I waited with patient appetite for the spring term to come round with the pink of cherry blossom and those astonishing transformations of mud, tadpole and newt. I mourn what has revealed itself to be the lost patience of my childhood. In spite of a co-existent unhappiness, it was the deracination from my urban identity that drew me towards the English countryside and the wonders of nature that I discovered as a peace-time 'evacuee'.

Yesterday, I was reading *Milly-Molly-Mandy Stories* to my youngest grand-daughter Annabelle (or to me, the privilege of 'Bell').

Nobody read them to me so possibly it was the first book that I learned to read for myself. The stories seem now to be about a time so long past that they are, not of real village life but of Arcadia. Bell had scant patience with Milly's quaint activities, with the rhythms of community, its obsolete words and unfamiliar fruits of the season. I found myself performing not an explanation but a translation of words like 'skein', 'aniseed balls', 'tadpoles', 'nasturtium', 'parlour', 'forge', 'jam jar', 'frock', 'farthing', 'brook' and 'meadow'.

> There was a time when meadow, grove, and stream,
> The earth, and every common sight,
> To me did seem
> Apparelled in celestial light,
> The glory and the freshness of a dream...
> The things which I have seen I now can see no more.

FROM 'Ode: Intimations of Immortality
from Recollections of Early Childhood'

Wordsworth's nostalgia for Eden resounds with a Proustian obsession that any lost domain or home tucked away in the obscurities of the brain can sometimes be tempted or triggered back into consciousness. My memories chime too with a regret both for what never existed and for my inevitable decline. Death is never an option.

The ways in which children first encounter the concept of death are varied and curious. Inevitably, it is less traumatic if the acquaintance is symbolic rather than premature and morbid. The chronology of understanding what it means 'to die' can take place anywhere from the age of two depending on the child's intellectual development and symbolic understanding. I remember the moment when my firstborn grandchild, Daniel, realized that death is irrevocable. He was not yet three. We were walking down a garden path when we came upon a large and edible French snail that was crushed and mushy. Dan stared down: 'It won't be alive any more.' One memory invites another. When I remember Dan's beginnings I think of a small boy taking his first steps and falling over with an indignant expression of surprise. I remember him being hungry as a little gannet, and how he astonished us all when he knew the names of more than twenty seabirds before he was twenty months old. I remember him in his red-felt duffle coat looking with awe at a large red letterbox at the end of the road. I remember how quickly he protested that it is the girls and not the boys who always have the leading roles in fairy tales.

Twenty years later I am in casual conversation with four-year-old Bell about an unframed photograph beside my bed:

BELL: Look, here is a picture of you and me and Dido [My dog] Granny. When you miss me you can look at it.

ME: I do often but I don't miss you although I do think of you all the time.

BELL: Not all the time, Granny.

ME: A lot of it.

BELL: When you are dead, Granny, then you won't be able to think about me any more.

ME: No, you are quite right, but by then I hope you will have so many happy memories.

DADDY: Bell! Come on, time for school!

BELL: Do we really have to go to school?

DADDY: Yes, we do.

Bell comes running back into my room despite her father's urgency.

BELL: Granny there is only one person in this family who knows about death.

ME: Who is that?

BELL: Danny Dog [Our boxer had died in the summer]. Yes, only Danny knows what it is like to be dead. When you are dead you lie down on the floor and you cannot get up again, not ever but only Danny knows what happens to us next.

A memory of the first time I fell in love surfaces. It is of a small child of perhaps nine who has been in boarding school since she was six. She has a friend called Jennifer, who is the daughter of a housemaster at the boys' school, Charterhouse, which was close to our Holloway Hill. I remember a golden afternoon when Jennifer's parents invited me home to tea for toast and ripened blackberry jam. I entered into the glorious shabbiness of their Milly-Molly-Mandy house, with battered couches, antimacassars and that exquisite smell of birth, of fragile fontanelles, coming from a golden basket of curled-up cocker pups. Not holding, but almost suffocating one of the golden pups asleep in my arms, I wanted it to be forever.

Ever since it has been the small acts of human kindness and connection, of animals, birds, children, my 'patients', my family, my friends – and not angels – that have been my consolation for a life-pendulum that has swung between euphoria, contentment, fulfilment and pain. It is a life that has been passed over, even if I have absented myself from the Passover, with herbs both sweet and bitter; it is my life. A life that has never ceased to challenge me with its uncertainty of being, its bolts from the blue, its random chaos of joyful forms; its suffering. Dark thoughts dance together with tender memories in the consolation of speaking what I feel and not what I ought to say.

2

O MOTHER, MOTHER, MOTHER! WHAT HAVE YOU DONE?

Blest the infant Babe,
(For with my best conjecture I would trace
Our Being's earthly progress,) blest the Babe,
Nursed in his mother's arms, who sinks to sleep
Rocked on his Mother's breast; who with his soul
Drinks in the feelings of his Mother's eye!

WILLIAM WORDSWORTH, *The Prelude*

MY MOTHER HAD A NERVOUS BREAKDOWN WHEN I WAS around six. I didn't understand what had happened to her, but only that I was not allowed to see her. I was doubly confused because I had heard the term applied to cars and the Automobile Association. I must have overheard incoherent and forbidden bits and pieces about her having shock treatment (electro-convulsive therapy [ECT]). I thought that I was responsible, in some obscure way, for her 'shock'. I knew that she was in a nursing home called 'Greenways' in Avenue Road, St John's Wood, which sounded very green, but what I didn't know was that it was a private psychiatric nursing home for people who had to be 'sectioned'; in her case, because she was at risk of doing harm to herself. I was not allowed to see her because the only person she wanted to see was her famous Viennese psychiatrist, Dr Joshua Bierer.* When she left the nursing home a young and pretty American woman called Louise, who never left her side, accompanied her. Louise must have made a deep impression on me to remember her name in the same way that I remember Vera's name. Louise, I reflect now, was an influence – although she only resurfaced when I wrote the word 'Greenways' – in my later becoming a therapist. I was told she was my mother's 'special' friend. Louise explained to me that she had come all the way from America – Chicago, I distinctly remember – to learn more about unhappiness. For a long time my mother only seemed to smile when Louise was by her side. I wonder now whether she was a psychiatric nurse, a medical student or Dr Bierer's mistress. I thought she was so beautiful when she smiled that Chicago must be a magic place which had something to do with exporting a cargo full of smiling kindness.

Although my mother recovered to some extent from her suicidal tendencies, it was soon clear that she was suffering from the beginnings of a full-blown bipolar condition, which in those days was known as manic-depressive illness. I lived in fear of giving her another 'shock'. By the time that I was a teenager, in spite of her creative success in the fashion world, my mother survived

---

* Dr Joshua Bierer was born in Radautz, Austria, to a distinguished family in which all male members for three generations were medical doctors, his great grandfather was court physician to the King of Serbia and a great friend of Theodor Herzl, founder of the Zionist movement. Joshua later founded the Marlborough Day Hospital in London, which was the first of its kind. He was a man of great knowledge, charm, charisma and entrepreneurial sense.

(Extract from Dr Joshua Bierer's obituary in *The Times*, 22 November 1984.)

on nembutal, lithium and her favourite barbiturate 'bluies', to which she became addicted. Even the suspense of Wimbledon's Men's Finals was too much for her without self-medication with one of her 'downers'. Yet her favourite quotation, as well as the song she was most inclined to sing to herself was Gershwin's *Life Is Just a Bowl of Cherries*. She might have been a character in a Tennessee Williams play. Williams commented that, 'Life is one long nervous breakdown', which was true for my mother, whose ancestry included a lineage of gorgon mothers all without a maternal bone in their anatomy. The malign pattern was broken at last when she discovered her deeply buried maternal instinct in a magnetic field of devotion between herself and my daughter, Tanya.

Dr Joshua Bierer, along with the enchanting Louise, were the unconscious role models for my decision to become a therapist. Ten years later I was destined to read *The Divided Self* by R.D. Laing. This book became the catalyst in my decision to give up my career as an actress at the equally seductive Royal Court Theatre. I have never regretted this decision. I wanted to work with its author, R.D. Laing, the infamous psychiatrist, existential therapist and guru who, through the prism of time, is best remembered as one of the most important twentieth-century philosophers on the subject of selfhood.

Laing, like Peter Pan, and myself, felt a great deal of frustration with mothers. I have an image of him sitting cross-legged on the floor, gazing around a room of 'disciples' and friends and provoking us with the question: 'Whose womb would you like to have been born from?' By which I understood him to be reflecting on the critical responsibilities of motherhood and regretting both his own genesis and the fact that, as we cannot chose our parents, the business of genes and maternity is essentially a lottery.

The poet Eileen Myles' *Afterglow: A Dog Memoir* [Grove Press, 2018], has an interesting riff on Laing's question:

> When two people meet and engage in the act of fertilization simultaneously a million pictures are surging in their brains. Think of your parents making love if you will. Pay attention. An academy award, a cavalcade of thoughts of pictures is coursing through their heads. Yes, right up here. You are one of them.

I think our son, Alexander, was precociously aware of such a question, although he did not apply it to his maternal but rather to his tribal origins. As a boy of less than eight, who was requested to attend Westminster Abbey as part of his schooling, he used to protest, notwithstanding our heathen household: 'But, I came out of a Jewish womb!' Laing's question provoked our group to gaze around the assembled females and to reflect on menus of the 'Great Mother' and on our uterine lives. As ever, Laing was a scientific generation ahead, with his interest in and curiosity about the consequences of maternal and neonatal psychological health in relation to the emotional and hormonal conditions in the womb, which is our first 'home'. His premature interest pioneered what is now reflected in the current and 'hot' interest in epigenetics and the growing body of literature supporting the hypothesis that prenatal environmental exposure – including the influence of the mother's psychological and hormonal based alterations *in utero* physiology – can have sustained psychological effects across the lifespan of the individual. While many of the old wives' alarming tales about the dangers of a hare crossing a pregnant woman's path are scaremongering, there is increasing medical evidence relating to the consequences on our emotional lives of external trauma interfering with inter-uterine foetal development. Whereas, the consequences of post-natal depression had been under investigation for years, this was the first time that I heard anyone reflect on the impact of the intra-uterine environment on subsequent emotional life.

I have contemplated Laing's question for many years and I feel that its perversity, as some may perceive it, must be tempered by the fact that the women sitting at his guru-feet were all victims of ambivalent if not ruinous relationships with their mothers. One member of his audience was an exceptionally beautiful young woman who might have been Virginia Woolf's double. She possessed an equivalent intelligence that would allow her to write a ground-breaking book that spanned philosophy, myth and psychology. The wounds inflicted by maternal filicide in her nursery were still so bloody that it was almost impossible for her adult self to finish a sentence about the past without the intrusion of crimson blushes which were reflections of internal shame; a historic shudder which was the involuntary sob of a humiliated child. It is also an archetype of childhood phantasy for many children who, while not directly answering such a question, will convince themselves that they must have been born out of another more exalted womb and that they are changelings who find themselves trapped in the wrong family.

I have a flash memory of my daughter Tanya's childhood and teenage years when such an unsettling question, albeit differently proposed, was popular. I remember how all her friends who came for sleep-overs kept an unwritten inventory of mothers – who was 'in' and who was 'out', which usually but not always translated as who was the most indulgent. Later on, this interest in mothers among her adolescent friends morphed into which of them had the 'hottest' mother.

Despite his addictive and unpredictable Rabelaisian personality, it is Laing above almost all clinicians who continues to influence me and act as an internal supervisor. How often do I hear his clipped Glaswegian accent: 'The World Health Organization [or whatever, or whoever] cuts no ice with me!' – his invariable response whenever he was confronted by dogma. I don't know if Laing knew that Proust shared his dislike of impermeable boundaries: 'A work in which there are theories is like an object that has the price tag still attached to it.' And yet theories and the techniques they promote are, to begin with, an inevitable skeletal necessity for any disciplined learning, whereas neither creativity nor imagination can be taught. I am not convinced that motherliness can be taught either. Yet, there can be no doubt that the Maternal Way will always be more challenging to travel if the principle motivation is to do everything differently from one's own mother.

When I gave birth to my daughter, Tanya, and became a mother at twenty-four, I had no desire for any status other than to be her mother and a wife. My experience of the first year of motherhood was spent feeling as though heaven now existed on earth; not only did I understand Wordsworth's lines but I experienced the mutual sensations he described when he wrote: '[The Babe] *who with his soul/ Drinks in the feelings of his Mother's eye!'* I would wake up in the night and sit beside our sleeping child in awe of her 'blest' perfection. When she was awake there was nothing I liked to do more than return her gaze of love.

In a painful parenthesis, this meant that I was ill-prepared for the acute post-natal depression that hit me with the birth – seven years later and four miscarriages on – of our second child, Alexander. As an inadequate compensation for my harrowing experiences of multiple foetal miscarriages, and before Alexander unexpectedly arrived, I had, through private study, acquired enough O and A levels to be accepted at Bedford College, London University. The English Department was still situated in the privileged Inner Circle Regency villa, The Holme, in Regent's Park, now long sold and refurbished into one of the most expensive private stucco residences in London. I was euphoric and triumphant. Disappointment followed when I discovered that the brilliant Shakespearean scholar, Ann Barton, who had interviewed me, barely survived her first year as Professor of the English Department. Before I arrived, she fled back to All Souls, Oxford muttering, a bit like Hamlet to the gravedigger on the topic of England, that in London all the men are mad.

I became intoxicated with the privilege of studying Mantegna's paintings of herons and learning of his influence on W.B. Yeats at the same time as looking out from the cardinal-red walls of the Great Ballroom's windows onto Regent's Park lake and watching live herons preen. I remember the first time I saw a single black cormorant perched unobtrusively among their graceful shapes.

If Tanya's birth was to bring heaven to earth my second experience of maternity might, despite the immediate and passionate maternal bond of love I felt for my son Alex, have been likened to God's descriptions of the hoary frost. Icy conditions froze my maternity into a post-natal depression. Even worse than the maternal experience of depression is not knowing what the maternal torpor is doing to the baby. I am still tormented by memories that often led me to suicidal thoughts – the recurring urge to hang myself in an impassable forest. I have searched and searched, without success, for the name of a famous film star who, in the early seventies, took that route through the woods of her despair and hanged herself; she was someone with whom I dangerously identified.

It became impossible for me to continue with my studies and enjoy the luxury of intellectual discovery until I had recovered my emotional health. I took sabbatical leave from Mantegna and the herons, if not the cormorant. I was between having finished a Freudian therapy and beginning my Jungian training. I did not believe anything, or anyone could help me. Panic attacks, sweats and night terrors immobilized me for a year. Reluctantly, my husband persuaded me to see his own psychoanalyst whose response was odd. I was 'Fine. It was baby blues'. Whilst temporary 'baby blues' are normal in the first weeks after birth, they did not explain my situation. I remember our GP told my equally panicked husband, who had become afraid to leave me alone, 'She will be fine once she gets back into her studies, she is not meant to be in the kitchen, or a full time housewife.'

One particular day I returned home to find my baby unresponsive in his cot. He had been suffering with a gastric virus and our nanny assumed he was just sleepy. I knew at once that all was not well. Gathering Alex up, my husband and I rushed to our GP, who within minutes had referred us to Great Ormond Street with a limp-limbed baby possibly suffering from meningitis. The journey seemed to take forever but as we drove into the hospital forecourt Alex opened his sleepy eyes and, looking up into mine, for the first time ever he said 'Mummy'. He had recovered from a carelessly prescribed overdose by the GP of an anti-emetic. His recognition of my terror and the expression of his love happened at the same moment as I, through relief from the traumatic imagination of his loss, regained my desire for life and motherhood.

Current research has shown that boys are more vulnerable than girls to the impact of maternal depression. We cannot know what despairing feelings the child absorbs from the torpor in his mother's eyes. The impact of my illness on Alex's infancy was certainly ameliorated by the fact that his father, John, played a major role in his earliest care. Since the time of my illness there has been more research into post-natal depression and the various possible effects on the child. The engagement and presence of the father in the child's daily life is one of the most significant contributory factors to subverting any long-term legacy.

Retrospectively, my own experience has privileged me to understand better some of the people who come to see me for help with post-natal depression, and also others who only discover years later what it was they were suffering from. Sometimes, the woman is still trying to make sense of her ambivalent maternal relationship, which may be influenced by a mysterious and lasting sense of guilt that has become repressed in her unconscious. This guilt is no longer accessible to her as an explanation for her current feelings of inadequacy and depression. (There may of course be other reasons for her maternal ambivalence, such as fallout from a 'replacement' pregnancy for an aborted foetus or stillborn child, a traumatic pregnancy and/or birth, or an abusive relationship with the father while the baby was still *in utero*.) Whatever the genesis of her feelings, it is one of the most painful experiences imaginable to sit with a young mother who cannot understand why the vulnerabilities of the child, her baby that she longs to nurture and protect, seem to provoke such unspeakable feelings of dread, terror and ambivalence. It is as though a cormorant and not a friendly stalk has delivered the child into her chilly care. In non-psychotic contexts I have never heard a mother talk about killing her infant. Her pain is manufactured out of her inability to protect and nurture her child. It is not uncommon for the devoted parent to have suicidal ideation in relation to her despair, her exhaustion and her guilt. It is always vital to remember that sometimes it is biology and genes and not maternal ambivalence that lie at the root of these problems.

I have already described the birth of my daughter as being among the most joyous days of my life but my joy did not preclude an obsessive maternal over-attachment escalating out of control. Her birth precipitated the repetition of my nocturnal fears of maternal abandonment. An attachment anxiety developed in both mother and baby and I soon found myself a weekly visitor to the famous Anna Freud Well Baby Clinic in Maresfield Gardens, Hampstead, which was then a unique and independent mother-and-baby-support service. Anna Freud's close friend, Dr Josefine Stross, ran the Hampstead clinic. Josefine had accompanied Anna and her ailing father on their challenging journey to England when Sigmund Freud left Vienna in 1938. Freud's own doctor Max Schur was prevented from accompanying them by appendicitis.

Dr Stross put my husband John in mind of Lotte Lenya playing the spectre agent in *From Russia With Love*. I have never seen that or any other James Bond film, but her Birkenstocks, tweeds and hairy calves bemused me. She had collaborated with Dr John Bowlby and James Robertson in the early days of the Tavistock Institute, when they were studying the effects on young children of temporary separation from their parents through the war and hospitalization. She was an iconic and devoted if terrifying paediatrician. I lived in mortal fear of Josefine and trembled every week when my baby was ceremoniously placed on the manual scales to check that she had gained the statutory ounce.

In her later years, her shaking hands seemed to suggest that Josefine was suffering from unacknowledged Parkinson's disease, although she continued to administer Tanya's booster injections! It is also alleged that when attending Freud on his nocturnal deathbed – when Max Schur was once again absent – she administered a third and terminal injection of morphine.

I both trusted and feared her scalding tongue: 'Why do parents insist on taking their toddlers abroad when all they need is an apple tree and a sandpit in the garden?' Tanya, as a small girl, was equally terrified of her, which made for a degree of incompatibility between them. But it was Josefine's decision to refer me for a Freudian analysis which was financed by Anna Freud's Hampstead Clinic to deal with my separation anxiety.

I had already achieved my ambition to work with R.D.Laing and after being a constant visitor at Kingsley Hall I became his PA during the preparation and execution of the Dialectics of Liberation Conference at the Round House in London in July 1967. I was introduced to the radical philosophies of the various contributors, mainly from the United States among who was the ground-breaking anthropologist/social scientist Gregory Bateson of the 'Double Bind' theory; at that time I could not have imagined how important his theories on the ecology of the mind would become to me.* Other participants were the Beat poet, Alan Ginsberg, the director of The Living Theatre in New York, Paul Goodman, who was one of the original philosophers of Civil Liberty and 'Queer' theory; and Herbert Marcuse. Also present was the indescribably handsome and charismatic

---

* A double bind is an emotionally distressing dilemma concerning communication, in which an individual (or group) receives two or more conflicting messages, and one message negates the other. This creates a situation in which a successful response to one message results in a failed response to the other (and vice versa), so that the person will automatically be wrong regardless of response. The double bind occurs when the person cannot confront the inherent dilemma, and therefore can neither resolve it nor opt out of the situation. Double-bind theory was first described by Gregory Bateson and his colleagues in the 1950s.

Civil Rights black-power campaigner, Stokely Carmichael, who, after delivering his subversive rhetoric and readings from Frantz Fanon's *Black Skin, White Masks,* was banned from returning to the UK. I was responsible for finding and renting a large house in Fulham where the organizers and the invited speakers all lived throughout the week-long conference and where we ate, smoked and debated into the breaking dawn. I was too young to understand the unique qualities of the intellectuals and activists that Ronnie had gathered around him. The goodness and intelligence of Gregory Bateson shone through the volatility of the collective outpourings of these societal discontents like an indomitable beacon of balance and restraint.

In 1968 our two families became further linked through sharing the experiences of parenthood. Jutta, Ronnie's mistress and later his wife, had given birth to their first son Adam several months before Tanya was born. Inevitably, many contentions and philosophies around parenthood and, in particular motherhood, were the frequent source of our midnight conversations. I cannot recall the responsibilities of 'fatherhood' ever being discussed by Ronnie with the same fervour as 'motherhood', if at all.

Ronnie was violently opposed to circumcision, which he thought was equivalent to primitive body mutilation. When I became pregnant the first time the circumcision issue caused me immense conflict, as I knew that if I gave birth to a male child and did not have him circumcised my mother would not accept him or speak to me. As it transpired, and to my great relief, our first-born turned out to be a daughter. All the males in our family – except for my grandson – have been circumcised. It was all the rage among non-Jewish parents when my husband was born, because at the time the medical elite regarded the foreskin as a 'dirty thing' and a contributory factor to the dreaded risks of masturbation. For our son Alex, who was born seven years later than his sister, by which time I was less dramatically influenced by Laing, the obstetrician performed the procedure very neatly by applying what looked like an inoffensive little bell, which fell off after three days. We had avoided the crisis of a ritualistic ceremony of circumcision by the sharpened knife of the Jewish *mohal*. In view of Alex's later expressed innate perception of the obligations of origin, it turned out to be the right decision. I don't think he would have forgiven us if we had denied him his covenant with 'Yahweh.' It has been left to my grandson, whom, with Ronnie's voice once again resurrected in my ears, I beseeched my daughter not to mutilate, to challenge us: 'Why am I the only male in this family to have a foreskin?'

Ronnie, in a second riff about birth also challenged society's disquiet and fear of the placenta. Conventional medical practice still condemns the placenta praevia as a contaminated piece of flesh that must be dispensed into an incinerator with a precipitate speed for fear of it spreading infection. How strange it is, Ronnie would reflect, that an organ of life that only a few minutes earlier has been the source of existence so quickly becomes transformed by medical opinion – which until the middle of the twentieth century was exclusively paternalistic – into something treacherous? In many third world counties the placenta is treated with respect and ritually buried into the earth, while being accompanied by various mythic narrative ceremonies of gratitude.

Although the placenta contains microbes and bacteria, the growing practice of placental encapsulation has started to change its reputation, which would make Ronnie smile in his grave. There is no conclusive research evidence but there are an increasing number of midwives in both the US and the UK who will prepare a woman's placenta into capsules for her exclusive use as the ingestion of placental products are currently perceived to be prophylactic against postnatal depression. Ronnie was always questioning the ways in which our bodies and their waste products could move so quickly between socially received perceptions of good and bad.

Laing was by then using LSD to gain access into both his own and some of his patients' unconscious processes. Hitherto I had not seen the idea of a drug-induced transcendent experience as being compatible with motherhood. I had listened with great interest to accounts of other people's 'trips' and was acutely aware that for some it had not been a taste of a Huxley heaven but of Huxley hell; It was clear that there was no knowing which way the drug would take its effect until it was too late to turn back. On one occasion, however, my curiosity won over my maternity: When invited to submit under Ronnie's wing, and with the knowledge that the substance was pure lysergic acid; temptation got the better of me. The time seemed propitious and another opportunity of a Laing-assisted trip might not be on offer. Accompanied by music from a clavichord played by Laing, I swallowed the nectar from a glass phial and my maternity dissolved like morning dew. Had the Pied Piper appeared and piped Tanya away across the fields, I know that, unlike the mythic earth mother, Demeter, I should not have moved one inch away from my rapturous enjoyment of the enchanted world I had entered.

I was sitting with my family and older grandchildren – who are past university age and experienced in the world of recreational drugs – when I shared this story. They listened in fascination, while my daughter listened in horror. 'What! You mean you took LSD when I was a little girl, in front of me, and you didn't feel guilty?' No, strangely for someone who is over-burdened with responsibility, I didn't feel guilty. Her father was present while I had this experience of a transcendent reality and how it felt has continued to feed my imagination ever since. It was just one brief absence, in an entire life-hood of being a mother, from maternal responsibility and the anguish and joys that motherhood thrusts upon us forever. I have had endless thoughts about what 'motherhood' has meant to me, and conducted many thorny debates and questions around the merits of unconditional versus conditional love, a subject that concerns every parent, child and lover. This is a question that never ceases to provoke argument between Tanya and myself. Although we cannot agree, I do have the consolation that when she first became a mother, regardless of our differences, I was still trusted to become her guide. We continue to be inclined to arguments which have been a feature of our intense relationship. This book was prompted by one such conflict, or knot of difference. A book that I had no intention, or preconceptions of writing. Our disagreement had been a fierce one; although now I only remember the intensity rather than its subject. I returned home in agitation, tears and self righteous indignation and found myself announcing, in defiance, to John and the world, 'I shall write a book.' John nicknamed my early efforts, *Daughters Beware Daughters*!

We are still locked in one unresolved debate about the existence of 'unconditional love'. I know that in the first years of her life I loved Tanya unconditionally, but that was due to the fact that we were a symbiotic nursing couple. She loved the 'milk', at first literal and later metaphorical, that I gave her. She never suffered from colic, infantile reflux and breast-feeding was one of the highlights of my life. It is the subject of the only recurring dream I have been gifted: the dream of my breasts responding to the sounds of a child stirring from sleep to be fed. But, that is now a long time ago. I wake disappointed.

Tanya tells me, but does not accuse, that I am a conditional person who subscribes to Talion Law. I think that is true and I do not like the fact that although I like to give, I do privately find it hard to give without thinking about the return. She tells me – and I don't need to be reminded – that she still loves her demanding, if enchanting, adult children unconditionally and without any expectation of return. I think of my daughter as a mythic pelican who tears the flesh from her breast in her attempt to keep her children safe in the chaos of a random world. Her desire not only to protect, but also to indulge, comes from an understandable need to compensate for the irreversible loss of their father. It requires no insight to conclude that her feelings spring from the racist murder of her children's father, Jay Abatan, that took place between one random second and the next. Jay's unsustainable head injuries turned Tanya's young and insouciant world into an unpredictable and threatening space in which I was required to share with her my Athenian armour. Due to the complexities of Jay's murder and the incompetence of the Sussex Police Force, it took a further thirteen years before it was possible to have an inquest; the verdict it returned was one of 'Unlawful Killing'. By this time, our two small children who Jay had been forced to abandon, had grown into young adults, who could no longer be protected from objectifying facts and the harsh reality of his murder, but who chose to attend the absurdly delayed inquest; they saw the footage of the violent injuries and heard the indelible recording of post-mortem reports.

Sometimes, I reluctantly find myself at further odds with Tanya; in contrast to her devotion and desire to compensate her children for their father's wanton murder, I cannot help remembering there was nobody present in my childhood to compensate for my experiences of 'soul murder'; I had only the kindness of strangers. I was propelled into a harsh world without a safety net. I was forced to make the prematurely valuable discovery of my own agency and to discover the truth of Aristotle's maxim that acting is preferable to suffering, act to potentiality, essence to accident, knowledge to non-knowledge.

At last, I have realized there is no right or wrong way when it comes to child rearing, or much else... and mostly hold my tongue. But where I cannot hold my tongue is in my observation that I have a daughter, who is also a senior psychotherapist, who has refused to become disfigured by Fate, despite the fact that she, her children and our whole family will carry the wound and consequences of Jay's murder with us in different ways for ever. Her courage, her optimism, the lightness of her being and attractive nature remind me of an unassailable, bright star.

Another reason why our opinions about child-rearing practices differ could be that Tanya felt herself to be unconditionally loved by us, her parents, from when she was small until and beyond the passionate eruptions of adolescent sexuality. Perhaps this experience, even if transitional, of unconditional love predisposes the recipient to be able to express it in turn thereafter. I never felt unconditionally loved, although my husband John has been an unconditional rock of patient love in enduring the many vagaries of my difficult personality. I think I must be a bit like Goldilocks to live with. (Goldilocks was, in the Elizabethan era, a nickname for the 'coronet' signs of venereal disease.) Inspite of this appellation, *Goldilocks and the Thee Bears* still remains one of my most referred to, if not favourite fairy stories, with its insistence on 'things' or in my case, 'something' being 'just right'. I don't want my morning coffee or afternoon tea to be too hot, or too cold. I want to be soothed by the small elements of domestic life and for them also to be 'just right'! In the same way, I will frequently use the story of *The Princess and the Pea*, with its problematic mattresses to help someone who is struggling with the romantic frustrations of social media to understand the challenges, disappointments and game-play of apps like Grindr and Tinder. I grew up as feral as any fairy tale: a manipulative, enigmatic, if not a psychologically robust, child, who had to become an expert in trading places and binding myself into adoption by other families in order to survive.

An alternative rejoinder to Tanya's complaint of my addiction to the 'conditional' could be supplied by the French sociologist, Marcel Mauss. In his iconic book *The Gift*, Mauss explores primitive societies where a common societal practice existed, and still exists, of 'gift exchange' as a means of keeping the society in balance and harmony. This concept of reciprocity goes back to the ancient Greeks and possibly beyond. During the Renaissance, the artist Botticelli immortalized images of love in his *Primavera*. His Three Graces may be seen as a dancing enactment of the actions of reciprocity, as revealed in the triple gestures of giving, receiving and, most importantly to my conditional mind, *returning*. I cannot deny that as much as I enjoy giving, and my children would describe me as generous, I do get bitter when our argument degenerates to the equation that Tanya sports the unconditionally maternal while I am seen to limp in second with the conditional. The venom in this hornet-sting is that my conditional nature corrodes my desire to be generous: the more generous I am, the greater is my expectation, my need for it to be acknowledged and responded to.

There are however exceptions to my 'conditionality', or wretched ambivalent nature that happen whenever I hold a contented baby in my arms and sniff its fontanelle, when I am in the company of my dog, when I am watching a changing landscape like the sea, or when I have begun to understand somebody or something other than myself. On the threshold of dusk, I walk down our street and hear twelve different passages of blackbird song.

For me to begin to understand someone else's suffering I have to be able to inspire them with the courage to open up their warrior wounds to my sympathetic attention. As a therapist my success, if there is any to speak about – and it would be immodest of me not to say there often is – is linked to the Greek concept of reciprocity. I am frequently asked how come that, working as many hours as I do and following a principle of being available to the people who regularly come to see me on a 24/7 basis, I am not burnt out. The answer is that I receive so much from the people who consult me. They present me with their 'lives' just as Salome was presented with John the Baptist's head on a golden platter. Or, it sometimes seems like that! If I am able to receive what I am given, and there can be no advance guarantee, then there is the possibility that I can return an alternative path towards the *mysterium* of selfhood. Without collaboration, I am as likely to be taken advantage of as Humbert Humbert did with his naïve psychiatrists:

> I discovered there was an endless source of robust enjoyment in trifling with psychiatrists: cunningly leading them on; never letting them see that you knew all the tricks of the trade. Inventing for them elaborate dreams... and never allowing them the slightest glimpse of one's real sexual predicament.

VLADIMIR NABOKOV: Lolita

My clinical work and life is always informed by the contribution of poets and writers, especially Shakespeare, Proust, Keats and Tolstoy, who were not attempting, except through the transcendent magic of language, to cure wounds of the body and soul. It would be unconscionable of me to consolidate my thoughts on certain topics without consulting literary sources. For example, in tackling one of the subjects of the next chapter, child sexual abuse, I am compelled to draw upon Nabokov's treatise on hebephilia.* It is so full of insights that only with great restraint have I succeeded in limiting my quotations from *Lolita*. It is a novel, along with *Death in Venice*, that should be compulsory reading for all professionals involved in child protection.

It is not only R.D.Laing and Barrie's Peter Pan who blamed mothers for mankind's universal ills. In an emotional crescendo of tragic recognition, Shakespeare's warrior hero Coriolanus howls, 'O mother, mother, what have you done?'

In this Roman tragedy, we witness not only martial violence but also a tornado of maternal manipulation. As mothers, rarely can we predict what, with hindsight, we will discover to be the consequences of our maternity. Volumnia's 'double bind' clenches on her son's actions and precipitates Coriolanus's fall from the honourable status of renowned warrior into the humiliation of eternal and infantile notoriety. Shakespeare leaves his audience in no doubt that it is Volumnia's manipulation of her son's conflict between the maternal and the civic that not only destroys him but also causes him to destroy his 'mother' city, Rome. Torn between his filial duty and his warrior's code, he abdicates the soldier's *vertu* for infantile maternal bonds: 'There's no man in the world/More bound to 's mother; yet here he lets me prate/Like one i' the stocks.' At the opening of the play Coriolanus has returned to Rome triumphant from

---

* Hebephilia, in distinction to paedophilia, is the strong, persistent sexual interest by adults in pubescent (early adolescent) children which is typically ages 11–14.

foreign victories but he then refuses to follow Roman custom and modestly to expose his bloody wounds to his citizens in the public forum. (You will find descriptions of these wounds in *Plutarch's Lives*, but no known record exists of the overgrown Oedipal neurosis that binds him to his mother's will, in defiance of Roman custom.) Shakespeare provides his audience with a novel dimension to the historical narrative that now focuses on Coriolanus's destructive relationship with his mother. The tragedy reveals both the accomplishments of a great warrior and the shame of a son who is bound to and destroyed by a malign and binding maternal attachment.

Shakespeare is not keen on mothers and they are most conspicuous in his dramas by their absence. He does not manage 'a good enough one', let alone a loving mother, anywhere. Hermione in *The Winter's Tale* almost succeeds, while Queen Elizabeth and Margaret take the justified prize for calling down curses in *Richard III*. It is only Queen Constance in *King John* who, driven to the edge of sanity by the murder of her child, Prince Arthur, is a mourner in the tradition of the archetypal Greek mother, Niobe. 'Young Arthur is my son, and he is lost / I am not mad: I would to heaven I were! / For then, 'tis like I should forget myself, if I could, what grief should I forget!' *King John*, Act 3, scene 2

Queen Constance's overwhelming grief, in which she is not consoled, in spite of her pleas by the fugues of madness, reminds me of another myth of maternal calamity. It is one of my favourite myths and is the story of the Greek goddess of the seasons and the harvest, Demeter and her grief at surrendering her daughter, Persephone, to the god of the Underworld, Hades. In this ancient myth of birth and rebirth, Persephone's adolescent attachment to her mother must be ruptured for the universal and biological cycle of reproductive fertility to continue. It is one of the finest metaphors myth has provided us with for the vagaries of the mother/daughter trajectory from childhood dependency to sexual independence. Hades representing the interloper, the 'other', as well as phallic potency, falls in love with Persephone as she is playing in the cornfields. He snatches her away on his powerful 'charger', or pricked steed, into the Underworld and so *transfers* her from one developmental stage to another. Hades must, in the service of individuation and growth, become the catalyst who cauterizes Persephone's Oedipal attachments and triggers her desire to relinquish dependency on her mother and to leave childhood behind. A similar story can be found in the Bible:

> Before he had finished praying, there came Rebekah with her water jug on her shoulder. She was the daughter of Bethuel son of Milcah [Milcah was the wife of Abraham's brother Nahor]. Now the young woman was very beautiful. She was a virgin; no man had ever had sexual relations with her. She went down to the spring, filled her jug, and came back up.
>
> GENESIS 24: 15-16 ET SEQ.

Rebekah will become the wife of Abraham's son Isaac, and there is another biblical story of movement from child to pubescent, from adolescent to young adult in Ruth who 'stood in tears amidst the alien corn'. These are challenging rites of passage to which every mother and daughter must negotiate and adapt to. The mother, or the parents, may begin to lose control of their child when emerging hormones, or a sexual intruder challenges them. The pubescent child may become obsessed with all sorts of subversive imagery from outside the home, often announced through a new interest in rock icons, both male, female and gender fluid, who represent independence from family mores.

Those Botticelli locks that mothers loved to brush and plait are appropriated. The daughter may insist that ringlet and curl are exchanged for a trendy bob or androgynous trim. It seems there is something archetypally innocent about a child with flowing hair. Despite protests about tangles, the mother may experience a deep maternal satisfaction in brushing her daughter's hair. I know I did. My promises not to hurt, as I tried to smooth away tangles, always brought to my mind thoughts of mermaids sitting on coral rocks, grooming each other. I still keep a pink Mason Pearson's soft-bristle hairbrush in my bathroom cupboard for the occasions when I highjack Bell and persuade her to allow me to brush her silky hair: 'Granny never hurts me when she brushes my hair.'

A mother's delight in her daughter's beauty may contain positive and negative spectrums of narcissism. Where it is lodged in a demonstration that the beautiful child is an object to be displayed, or primarily to be seen as an extension to her mother's beauty, or alternatively as a compensation for an *absence* of maternal beauty, then the invisible umbilical threads are at risk, along with adolescence, to be ruptured. It is often mothers *who have not themselves been objects of beauty* who may be inclined to bask in their children's beauty and then come to resent, consciously or unconsciously, men starting to regard their 'child' as a sexual object, while at the same time the mother starts to fear that she is no longer sexually visible or desirable.

It is essential that any daughter – initially through her Oedipal love, or later through the sexualized love of an interloper into the family triangle – abandon her primary attachment to her mother. It becomes even more difficult for a daughter to experience the developmentally healthy separation from the mother – as Persephone was forced through capture to endure when she was snatched from Demeter – as she moves between puberty and sexual maturity, between dependence and independence, if she cannot feel comfortable in her evolving sexuality in front of her parents. (In the following chapter I shall be exploring more about father/daughter relationships.) Persephone's tragedy is that she has to disappear into the darkness of the underworld if she is to sever the passionate maternal bonds that hold on to her like bindweed. Her emotional life is compromised between sorrow for her grieving mother and her overwhelming instinctual and erotic desire for the dark, handsome stranger who must *transport,* or transfer, her from one developmental stage to the next.

Throughout the complexities of the adolescent quest for a separate identity, and individuation from the family of origin, it is critical that the adolescent does not feel elements of maternal retaliation or envy; that she is not forced either into compliancy or into a hyperbolic rebellion. Some conflict is always required to usher in the processes of growth and individuation, but ideally, it is a conflict without fear of retaliation or abandonment, both of which can be devastating to a daughter's self-esteem. Maternal retaliation, which may be unconsciously exhibited in a mother grieving for the absence or waning of her own fertility, may lead to an extended feud. Hades' phallic potency also embraces the possibility of a frightening alchemy which turns mothers into grandmothers and can frighten their hair grey overnight.

Vain mothers, absent mothers, wronged mothers, helicopter mothers (who are a twenty-first-century viral strain), impinging mothers, if they are tainted with pathological narcissism, can all do a good job of suffocating their children's personal composure and self-esteem. The important and numerous populations of 'good enough' mothers rarely get any mention, but in the pages of literature good fortune invariably takes a back seat. Fairy stories always feature toxic stepmothers. The archetype of the 'devouring mother' is not a fallacy, but it is important to remember that good enough mothers also exist.

I was returning to London on Eurostar and was indulging in one of my favourite occupations – eavesdropping on families. During the journey I became aware of a grandmother, mother and small daughter sitting at the parallel table engrossed in a game of cards. I soon identified it to be a French version of Happy Woodland Families, which I still love to play. The mother also had a newborn baby in a Moses basket beside her, whom she breastfed on demand. Whenever the baby's cries intruded on their game and distracted the mother's attention away from her small daughter, the grandmother tactfully absorbed the frustration by entertaining her granddaughter with improvised games that involved the passing scenery. It was a long journey but this three generational tribe of women passed it in touching and simple devotion. My nostalgia was aroused for the happy family of childhood that never existed within my family of origin but which I hope my own children have experienced, at least from time to time. Nostalgia relates not only to the memory of what has been lost and cannot return but also to what has never been.

No sane person can deny that being a mother is an impossibly challenging task and how often in my consulting room do I quote the words of Philip Larkin: 'They fuck you up your mum and dad / They may not mean to but they do.' Not so much in anger do I recite them but acceptance. Oh! As a small and lost child how I longed to have a mother whose maternal engagement resembled Mrs Darling's; but as an adolescent would I have wanted a mother rummaging around in my underwear drawer?

The nature of 'good mothering' is constantly shifting and always needs to be age appropriate.

> Mrs Darling first heard of Peter when she was tidying up her children's minds. It is the nightly custom of every good mother after her children are asleep to rummage in their minds and put things straight for next morning, repacking into their proper places the many articles that have wandered during the day. If you could keep awake (but of course you can't) you would see your own mother doing this, and you would find it very interesting to watch her. It is quite like tidying up drawers. You would see her on her knees, I expect, lingering humorously over some of your contents, wondering where on earth you had picked this thing up, making discoveries sweet and not so sweet, pressing this to her cheek as if it were as nice as a kitten, and hurriedly stowing that out of sight. When you wake in the morning, the naughtinesses and evil passions with which you went to bed have been folded up small and placed at the bottom of your mind; and on the top, beautifully aired, are spread out your prettier thoughts, ready for you to put on.
>
> J.M.BARRIE, *Peter Pan*

Who does not, at times of heightened vulnerability, long for the nurturing mother of their dreams; a few may even have had the good fortune of having one. Peter Pan never stopped wanting his mother and in Wendy he found an idealized Oedipal substitute. It can become even more threatening for male adults to recall the intense attachment and dependence they once felt for their parents.

I have been working with a man for several years who has a dutiful and respectful relationship with his mother but who has obstinately insisted that 'duty' and not love is the operative word in his portmanteau of memory. I am aware that as his mother's health deteriorates she figures more frequently in our sessions, but only ever with respectful acknowledgement. Now that she is approaching her mid-nineties her son spends more and more time not only visiting her but talking to me about the fact that she will soon die and that he wishes he could have become closer to her. In comparison with some of the other patients, I consider him to be a positively attached and respectful son, although he complains that he does not really like the 'smell' of his mother. He explains that he has always found it impossible to embrace her vulnerable body. He has complained about how remote she was during his childhood when, overwhelmed with homesickness, he had to endure the loneliness of boarding school. How distant, both physically and emotionally, he always felt from his parents. He has never linked these acute memories of homesickness with the word 'love' and he protests vehemently if I try to. One morning, comes the 'Aha!' that I have long been anticipating. Today, he is talking about his ambivalence in agreeing to a boarding-school education for his two sons; once again he recollects his own intense childhood unhappiness. Unconsciously, he now introduces the word 'love' as he indistinctly mutters: 'I loved her so much.' I tell him that I have never heard him use the word 'love' about his mother before and at once he protests that he did not. I gently insist that he did. He has so often talked about his experiences of homesickness and his despair that she did not understand him. Now, I 'know', because I have been listening out, that this is the first occasion on which he has actually spoken of a long hidden store of childhood love. And longing. At last, I feel we will be able to witness his grief before the end of his mother's life arrives. Perhaps, he will even find the courage to take her withered hand into his.

This reluctant declaration of love for his mother reminded me of a brilliant and extraordinary documentary, *The Condemned* (first shown on BBC 4 in 2013), about 'lifers' in a Russian high-security prison, whose incarceration was based on having committed at least two murders, or multiple rapes and murder. Its director, Nick Read, writes: 'My intention was to make a film about a community living on the very edge of the known, civilized world – to point a torch into their dark corner – and explore the concept of evil.' What entity did these murderers allude to and express nostalgia and longing for? *Their mothers.* Some of these forensic monsters confessed that their heart's desire was to be buried, after their execution, in a plot beside their mother's grave.

The death of one's mother, whether she is beloved or feared, and at whatever life-stage it occurs, will become a moment of epiphany. When a mother dies, or abandons a child prematurely while they are still physically dependent, although her memory and voice may fade, the abandoned infant's physiology will never cease to register the trauma. I have witnessed such phenomena many times and these painful occasions are not confined to my consulting room.

I was sitting in the hairdresser's and being attended to by a young stylist whom I did not know. We quickly got into conversation about his family and he referred to his father's divorce and remarriage. Because he was positioned behind me, his face was reflected in the mirror in front of me. I asked whether his mother had also remarried. Before he could reply: 'She passed away when I was seven,' I observed the involuntary flush of rising blood pressure spread across his cheeks as a sign of his fleeting sadness; then an embarrassed expression at being so affected by mention of his loss passed through his eyes. He seemed to gulp, then he sneezed, and we were diverted from his visibly repressed pain while he turned away to blow his nose and recover his professional composure.

Laing's question as to which womb would be a desirable prenatal habitat has remained indelible. When I was pregnant medical scanners did not exist and it was almost impossible to visualize prenatal development. Today, patients, both men and women, will often show me astonishing three-dimensional images of developing foetuses on their smartphones. These images, which in the earlier stages of development remind me of exquisite Leonardo da Vinci cartoons, while towards the beginning of the last semester they are already 'children', remind me of Laing's medically precocious conviction that hormonally related emotional states, and the psychological repercussions of a pregnant woman's experiences, cannot fail to make an impact on her unborn child's developing psycho-biology. Laing's question of which, or whose, womb would be most desirable continues to be a free-floating counterfactual at the back of my mind.

The poignancy of Laing's question returns when I am working with patients whose narratives feature early ruptures of attachment, emotional impingement or repeated inconsistences of care which have gone on to distort their lives and present repetitive emotional hurdles. Sometimes, although I no longer practice as a classical Jungian psychoanalyst, patients will arrive in my consulting room that have had previous long psychoanalyses. In view of that, they may reflect: 'Ah yes, I now understand all the reasons as to why I have had, and still have, emotional distress. It has become clearer, but I still *feel* the same. I still feel as though I have never had the mother or father or the lover that I wanted, dreamed of, or needed. I still don't know how to *feel* better'. On these occasions I often recall and paraphrase some of Jung's words from his Afterword to *The Secret of the Golden Flower*. I might suggest that there are some insoluble problems, some traumatic wounds that never heal. And yet, sometimes, one has to be able to *let go* without resolution of the problem; to let go of the persecutory thought that one was not blessed to have the relationship with the idealized mother, father, sibling, child or lover of one's dreams. One answer is to attempt to channel or to sublimate this unanswered longing into some higher goal or horizon and to find a symbolic equivalent. The question of how we learn 'to let go' has become a core preoccupation of my clinical work in this the latter part of my life.

I only have scarce and scarred memories of being nurtured by my mother. I spent many lonely hours crying for her in the long watches of the night way beyond infancy. I pause, to ask how she is remembered? Strangely, it is her handwriting that I shall never forget; despite leaving school at fourteen she wrote in a glowing copperplate script. Her biscuit gestalt is always cloaked in a waisted, fashionable camel-hair coat, which I do not like but which flatters her honey colours. Her ankles are elegantly turned. Her eyes still retain the opalescence of a frightened doe. I see her raven halo of hair and interpret her sad-eyed expression as a testament to thwarted expectations. She has a charcoal natural beauty spot below her left eye and slightly towards her nose, as velvet as her sad eyes and soft as a moleskin paw. Her image is distinct and indelible.

3

OH DADDY!

If by chance I talk a little wild, forgive me;
I had it from my father.

SHAKESPEARE, *Henry VIII, Act 1, Scene 4*

I LOST MY FATHER, WHO DIED FROM SYPHILIS, OR GENERAL paralysis of the insane, when I was too little to know what it felt like to be fathered beyond infancy. My two oldest grandchildren, Daniel and Portia, lost their father at similar ages. I have observed how their lives have also changed for ever in ways that are gender specific, but which are not appropriate for comparison, as they would not wish me to perform a public autopsy. My littlest granddaughter, Bell has a wonderful father, Alex, who is our son. As I have seen two generations of fathers die prematurely, it requires a disciplined focus to believe that there are others who are here to stay. Life has taught me that tragedy skulks around every bend in the road. In order to stay sane I remember to celebrate the sweet herbs of the Passover feast of gratitude.

I have recorded elsewhere* my memories of my father's disease, his descent into madness and his subsequent burial

---

* Jane Haynes, *Who Is It That Can Tell Me Who I Am?* , Constable, 2007

in an unmarked communal grave so I shall not repeat myself. Different memories are surfacing that contribute to this version of 'Fatherland'. I loved my father unconditionally before his behaviour began to frighten me. Now I cannot help wondering whether there was some inappropriate conduct taking place within the parameters of paternal 'Love'. I remember, in my mother's absence, one possibly perverse example, or possibly it is an innocent memory. Each morning while my father was shaving – but my memory becomes opaque as to whether he may or may not also have been defecating – he invited me into the bathroom to talk to him during his morning rituals. I liked the feel of his lathered chin, which was different from the rougher texture of his prematurely balding head. I hear his disembodied voice: 'I have to go to work and I won't see you again all day,' and received from him a handful of wrapped boiled sweets. It was always in the bathroom. When I think of his hands, I remember how he always proudly displayed them clad in leather driving gloves. Can these be 'true' memories, or did I construct them out of some childhood confusion and curiosity about orifices?

The window opened. She thought she was asleep but she did not know. Perhaps it was a dream? She did not know. Perhaps Vera had come back to find her, or an angel. She heard a screech owl although she had never seen one. She heard the ringing of curdled bells but she could not tilt her head, or cry out, or reach towards the comfort of her Goodnight Bear. She could do nothing. She was alone in the dark. She was not alone. There was a halo of light. A man was standing at the end of her bed and staring at her, except he did not have a face. He did not have a mouth. He had eyes. He was crawling. He had eyes for her. He was wearing a tobacco suit and he smelt

of smoke. He stood up in the dark and smiled again, except he did
not have a face. She did not know who he was except she smelt, or
did she feel, the rough weave of his tobacco suit against her cheek.

My father delighted in our new garden; it was a Hampstead garden with a death-dealing hedge of yew. A largely forgotten myth proposes the roots of the yew to be so fine that they can grow through the eyes of the dead and prevent them from seeing their way back towards life. My father liked to collect yew berries for me to take to the Nature Table at school. We gathered puffballs from the hedge, laburnum pods and lupins. I remember a sadistic squeezing of snapdragons that I thought would stop them breathing. There was larkspur; I don't think I had seen a lark in those days but the name seized my imagination. I had no idea that it was the July flower of my birth, or that it was poisonous and its origins were pregnant with myth. My father's gifts were recognized as amounting to a poisoned chalice that was not welcomed at Sarum Hall – my preparatory school in Hampstead – and they were never displayed on any table except the one at home in our front hall. The allegations of poisonous berries alerted the Social Services of the day and an investigation resulted in my father being 'sectioned', and his daughters removed into 'care'. For me, it meant I became a boarder at St Hilary's School on Holloway Hill in Godalming, Surrey in the autumn term of 1949.

The problem with memories of my father is that through the embarrassed hearsay and whispers of my extended family they have become contaminated with shame. Years later, R.D.Laing talked to me about his school days in Glasgow and his encounters with anti-Semitism. He had grown up believing a common urban myth that 'Jew' boys smelt differently, horribly so. At all costs one was to avoid sharing a desk with them. I only remember my father smelling of shaving soap. And tobacco.

My father's illness, or my childhood experience of professional misunderstandings of it, led to my developing a phobia about needles. Without any conclusive medical knowledge in 1948 as to how briefly the spirochaete bacteria remained infectious (which is now known to be less than three months) the doctors summoned me for a battery of Wasserman blood tests. These were performed with blunt needles and accompanied by internal examinations. These piercings and invasions left my body as petrified of needles and white coats as if they meant the end of the world. And that is what it felt like when the indomitable matron of Holloway Hill announced that we were due for our annual immunization. I lived in terror of injections into maturity. I still suffer from acute 'white-coat syndrome' and whenever a doctor approaches me my soaring blood pressure throbs like a fire alarm. Back then I wanted to find somewhere to hide from matron, and just like Peter Rabbit I escaped into the 'Out Of Bounds!' school vegetable gardens, which were at the farthest and muddiest point of the perimeter. We were forbidden to venture there unescorted because of someone called 'The Flasher'. Regardless of prohibitions, I would keep away from matron for hours in a state of mortal terror at such times. Ever since 'The Flasher' had been detected behind the periphery of beech trees, the vegetable gardens were designated as out of bounds. There was a teacher called Miss Knight, who was in charge of the kindergarten, and when her spinster hysteria demanded action be taken, the police were called to investigate reports of 'The Flasher'. They interviewed all the boarders, but as none of us knew what 'flashing' meant and nobody seemed willing to explain, it was a pointless exercise. Miss Knight (it was rare to find a Mrs amongst our teachers as so many of their fiancées had been killed in the war) was a woman of a certain age, with a hair-netting of white chignon, who made no bones of telling me: 'Plainly speaking, Jane, you are a child with choices to make. You will either be very good or very bad and I would not like to take a bet which, but always remember you had the choice.'

Where have all those repressed 'flashers' gone? I noted that, in his autobiography, David Hare writes about a schoolboy memory from the fifties of other flashers and how he was required by the police to attend an equally ineffective identification parade. Perhaps, the flashers are now variously occupied flashing and rubbing their cocks away in front of Internet porn rather than lurking in the undergrowth in the traditional way. Those well-manured beds of vegetables, caterpillars and wild flowers, like old-fashioned vetches and clover, were my dugout. With my surname still at 'W', I was always destined to the suspense of being the last on matron's list. I trembled as I tore away at daisy petals waiting to be unearthed, not like Peter Rabbit by the ears, but rather by my hair, as I muttered: 'Live or die, live or die...' every bit as unhappy with my mortal coil as Hamlet.

When I reflect on fathers collectively, through a clinical prism, I conclude that they enter my consulting room more frequently in relation to their emotional impact on their sons than on their daughters. Which is not to say that daughters do not equally require the gleam of love in the paternal eye to fulfil their earliest lineaments of self-esteem. There are so many constellations of paternal relationship and types of emotional attachment that how could a father not influence his daughter's future choice of sexual object and partner? If I pause to make a three-hundred-and-sixty-degree survey of my female clientele, there are some women who might compare their fathers to Neanderthals and regret that they were disappointing monosyllabics who preferred their Blackberry to speech, but otherwise they mostly seem to forgive the limitations of benign paternal discourse.

I do not share Freud's opinion that the dangers, or *bondage*, of the Oedipal relationship are as hazardous to navigate as the terrors of Scylla and Charybdis. I prefer to go along with Jung, who lived among the Swiss pastures, where the mysteries of fertility were not as secret as they were in strait-laced Vienna. Except, if statistics in *fin-de-siècle* Vienna are to be believed, ninety per cent of the male population was infected with venereal diseases. In pastoral Switzerland the birds and the bees, and the beasts were procreating in the pastures before young Jung's curious eyes. Jung theorized that most children, except those who experience humiliation or who are otherwise abused, do, with time, and generally through boredom, recover from falling in love or violently out of love with their dad or mum. They grow up only too willing to escape the endogenous family bondage for something new, something different.

As a therapist, and without any conscious processes of selection, or intentional avoidance, I have not cared for patients who were suffering from the aftermath of incontrovertible sexual abuse by family members, or strangers, with one exception. There have been several women who have shared memories of small intrusive incidents where, like me, they wonder whether they happened or were imagined. The inappropriate uncular fondle of budding breasts, the slither of a too-enthusiastic greeting-tongue, or a housemaster's misplaced enthusiasm. Reports from the young women consulting me, who use public transport daily, about anonymous sexual intrusions of penile erections or molesting fingers into personal space, are daily fodder, especially in the summer. However, my professional experience does not illuminate the painful frequency with which many male siblings, cousins, stepfathers and fathers are liable physically to abuse their sisters or daughters.

My only experience of explicit female penetrative abuse has been of a young woman whom I am permitted to name because she has recorded her experiences in a book first published in South Africa, *Indescribable*, from which I have permission to quote. Candice came to see me twenty years after her stepfather was imprisoned in South Africa for invasively abusing her between the ages of eight and fourteen on every available piece of antique furniture in their colonial drawing-room. At our first meeting I was struck by her exquisite yet childlike and diminutive appearance, which was dominated by her eyes, inset like sapphires, beneath a brow of seductive raven curls. Her innocent appearance was at odds with her striking self-composure.

That Candice knew what she was looking for in a therapist became evident when it was clear that she would not be fobbed off by any attempt at a quasi-therapeutic approach. Towards the end of our first session I surreptitiously, or so Candice experienced my gesture, glanced at my watch. I was concerned that we were so engaged in her story that my inner clock had lost its sense of time and the session had overrun by several minutes. Candice stared: 'You know, I would prefer it if you want to look at your watch that you did it openly; it would feel better.' There was a long silence while I considered how to respond, but I did know it was an important test. 'I will try not to do that again but it is helpful to know how you experienced it. Thank you.' The deal was sealed and Candice continued to consult me for almost two years, until, after fifteen years of marriage and a romantic weekend in Provence, she and her husband Jonathan joyfully conceived their daughter. It is hard to imagine that a young woman, who is both subject and object of the following account, was able, despite some inevitable and continuing psychosomatic challenges to her body, to make me feel that a rainbow shone whenever she entered my room.

> I can hear Dad walking up the stairs. I pretend I am asleep and quiet with my breathing. He walks into the bedroom and I smell cigarettes, wine and I smell desire coming out of him.
>
> Dad strips down to his pubic bone. I am not facing him but I know his thing is hard as stone. It's not going to go down until his blood pressure is released and since I am the only nurse available, I am the one who will have to relieve the pressure.
>
> He lies next to me.
>
> 'Are you sleeping?'
>
> I don't respond. He comes closer.
>
> 'Are you sleeping?'
>
> I groan to let him know I am deep in sleep. His smoky hands begin touching my hearts, then they move under the hearts and visit my soon-to-be-hairy. He opens my legs, I try to be stiff but I am flexible as a cat, as loose as a rag doll. He turns me over with so much ease.
>
> 'Now you're awake.'
>
> 'I guess I am.'
>
> 'I love you, I love you so much.'
>
> Hard and horny Daddy loves me.
>
> 'Don't worry Candice, God understands.'
>
> CANDICE DERMAN, *Indescribable*

I cannot decide whether what took place between me and my stepfather should be named as sexual abuse or not. In comparison to Candice's experience it was a mere caprice and has not left any wounds, except for my contempt. I was almost twelve when my mother remarried and when her hitherto 'beau', the shabby and benign Uncle Mac, who had no interest in children but was intrigued by French carriage clocks, was replaced by 'Uncle S', who was destined, before my twelfth birthday, to become my mother's second husband. It surprises me now that the inherited objects that remain in my household today, aside from my most precious inheritance, the antique pearls that my father gave to my mother on their wedding day – 'these are pearls that were his eyes' – are gifts from Uncle Mac. I remember him as a travelling salesman who was always accompanied by a battered suitcase stuffed with synthetic wool samples. Although I felt ashamed of his poverty, it is these gifts that continue to live on in our home: an antique French carriage clock and a hand-painted, worn and wobbly French antique table with a secret drawer. He must have had an aesthetic awareness notwithstanding his shabbiness.

Uncle S insisted, despite my tearful protestations, that once he married my mother I had to change my name by deed poll. It does now occur to me that perhaps my mother was anxious for her daughters not to carry more paternal shame into the world, or her world, through the birthright of their name. A few days after Uncle S moved in to our cramped flat, I cannot bring myself to write 'home', my sister's new budgerigar died. I did not and do not like budgerigars because their 'blue' seems garish compared to the gentler plumage of my fledging blue tits. I should have preferred a golden canary, except I have always detested the sight of a bird in a cage; it is something that always puts me, as well as all heaven, in a rage. The budgerigar fell off its perch on the same day that my stepfather fell off his pedestal. We had been living in an ugly brick post-war council flat in St John's Wood that seemed to me such a shameful alternative to the home my father built for us in Hampstead. It was early morning, my mother had already gone out to work and I was alone in the house with the 'Specter'. I walked into the kitchen to get breakfast and found the bird, which had been purchased as a gift, or bribe, for my little sister, dead on the floor of its cage. Perhaps, it was even in triumph that I entered the 'parental' bedroom to announce to my new 'father' that the bird had budged off for ever. I even hate the word budgerigar; it has nothing going for it with all those b's and g's.

It was early enough for me to be in my nightdress and to begin with I was flattered by the ardour of my stepfather's desire to console me for the avian bereavement, even by the zeal of his embrace, until a small transgression occurred. His hand wandered beyond the bounds of consolation and beneath my nightdress until I budged *him* away forever. My mother worshipped the Specter until the day that she died. I did not want to disillusion her and she would not have believed me anyhow. In the greater scheme, it was a fallen and over-enthusiastic but not forensic gesture.

A madeleine crumble of memory begins to surface. I remember that as I entered the bedroom I wanted to compete with my mother for the attention of this unfamiliar consumer of Eau Sauvage that was now sharing her bed. I like to think, although I cannot be sure, that I was innocent of the predatory form the attention might take. After all, I had an important announcement to make, tolling the knell for Cock Robin, if not for the budgerigar. I didn't know, or perhaps I already did, that a man's hands could wander wanton into the tabooed space of childhood.

I do not want this chapter to morph into a paper bullet about sexual abuse but its omnipresence in our society, along with my own indistinct experiences, provoke so many conflicting thoughts, particularly now we are living in times that I feel, perhaps unfairly prejudiced, have become an equivalent of a McCarthy-style witch-hunt. It has become almost impossible to differentiate between actions of sexual abuse between unprotected and powerless children or *raped* adults and others who do have the agency and education to speak up for themselves but for whatever complex reasons have hitherto chosen not to. My politics are at odds with the current tides of bulimic revelations from adults who, unlike children, are privileged with a developed capacity for agency and selfhood. These dramatic declarations galvanize the media into a repeated frenzy and are at risk of distracting society from the tragedy of gross child sexual abuse. There seems no discrimination to be made between forensic crime and titillation.

And have times changed? I remember how aggravated my mother was in 1962 when I told her that I was joining the Royal Court Theatre in Sloane Square. She did not approve at all, but her approval had never been of any consequence. She appealed to a distant family friend who, it turned out, was the theatre's landlord. He summoned me to his offices in Park Lane, which almost intimidated me. When he could see that I was determined, he ended our conversation with the following words: 'Well, I have only one piece of advice left for you. Don't ever be tempted to lie down on anyone's casting couch and don't let me hear you have married a *Yok*. (The word, which means a non-Jewish man, always made me cringe. But I met John at the Royal Court Theatre – a yok – and yes reader, I married him.)

Sexual abuse is a subject of epidemic proportion but one that turns even professionals into shrill hysterics who believe the law must always prosecute and isolate. Child abuse has existed through the centuries. Deprived children, serfs, slaves and

adolescent servants, as opposed to the current epidemic of con-
fessing celebrities, have always been the invisible victims. Ancient
Greek stories of literal and metaphorical rape reach out to us
through the ruins of their visual imagery and the myth-making
stories of their gods. I have used the *Rape of Persephone* as a
metaphor to describe a crescendo, or epiphany, in the mother/
daughter trajectory, but that is only one example of many tales
of transgression and, in some instances, growth to be found in
one of the most imaginative and profound books ever conceived:
Ovid's *Metamorphosis*.

Today, sexual abuse is more visible, more virulent, financially
rewarding and ubiquitous, with the global grooming possibilities
provided by the Internet, chat rooms and other social media
platforms. All seem to have no conscience. Whilst the malign
exploitation of growing numbers of unprotected minors who
are asylum seekers or refugees exacerbate the possibility of
even more commercial exploitation in the service of abuse
and slavery.

Since Nabokov's Humbert made his confession of hebephilia, and of the irresistible elements and sexual titillation of
untrammelled childhood innocence, society and its media has
continued to exploit these qualities as commodities by which
to pedal consumer wares. The twenty-first century's cultural
proliferation of sexualized images of pubescent children being
marketed as commercial products exacerbates and amplifies
any wayward tendencies of sexual fantasies into a pandemic of
Humbert-like obsession.

I do not condone sexual abuse in any shape or form. But the
idea that it is something performed only by socio- or psychopaths
is naïve. Sexual abuse is more disturbing than most individual
forensic crimes because the compulsive desire to commit abuse

appears to be an inerasable part of human nature that has nothing
to do with social class systems, absence of education, or money
and power. It has always existed in every culture and I fear it
always will. We must now, with the proliferation of such dangers,
educate our youngest children to become aware. Such violations
are lived out through subtle as well as the most brutal gestures of
physical transgression. Yet, suspected sexual abuse committed by
friends, professionals and colleagues remains a topic about which
it is almost impossible for most adults, whether professionals
or not, to have a measured conversation. Sexual abuse does not
only take place at the bottom of the deserted vegetable garden or
through grooming by criminals and perverts on the Internet. It
happens in every society, organization, family home, school class-
room, church, orphanage, convent, and hospital, *et al.* Wherever a
group of educated and responsible people is gathered in animated
discussion about the dangers and prevention of sexual abuse, such
abuse, I both fear and suspect may be going on, albeit invisibly,
somewhere in their midst. Compulsive sexual abuse exists in both
florid and subtle forms and while being a tragic perversion of
human desire it is, equally tragically, endemic in society. Among
the most disturbing and objective statements that Freud made
was his observation about the waywardness of human sexuality:

> Do you not know how uncontrolled and unreliable the aver-
> age human being is in all that concerns sexual life? Or are you
> ignorant of the fact that all the excesses and aberrations of
> which we dream at night are crimes actually committed every
> day by men who are wide awake?... We dwell upon the evil in
> human beings with the greater emphasis only because others
> deny it, thereby making the mental life of mankind not indeed
> better, but incomprehensible.

I was reading a clinical draft of this chapter to a group of colleagues when I noticed that one member of the group had become increasingly withdrawn from the discussion. He was looking grey. At the end of the meeting he could not wait to get out of the room, which he did without coming anywhere near me to say 'Goodbye', which felt insulting. Later on, I telephoned to ask him if anything was wrong. He confirmed my sensations of his 'loss of balance' and explained that during my reading he had started to have flashbacks of an earlier time when between the ages of twelve and fourteen he was forced to submit to piano lessons. Although he tried again and again to tell his mother that his teacher was moving his hands off the keys on to the teacher's horny erection and patch of wetness, he was vehemently reproved and told that it must all be in his imagination. For whatever reasons, there are some mothers like those of Candice and my colleague who prefer to turn a blind eye to what may often be taking place in the respectable comfort of their drawing rooms. While there are many sexual abusers who are not family members, the tragedy is that far too high a percentage of them are the father, brother, cousin or professional guardian of young children. Oh Daddy!*

To deny that there exists an innate capacity in the male mind for sexual abuse is naïve. One only has to think of the collectively instinctual, even bestial, acts of any pillaging army, or the pre-Revolution estate owners' treatment of their serfs in Russia, or worldwide colonial equivalents. Women are not exempt from committing such acts but statistics suggests that female perversions are more rare although when they do happen they may become even more perverse and violating than the male

---

* NSPCC statistics for 2016 record that one in four children are sexually abused and ninety per cent are abused by someone already known to them. Most sexual abuse remains unreported.

manifestations. Sexual abuse is a problem subject of epidemic proportions and one that drives even professionals into shrill debate on how and whether the law should prosecute and isolate. Child abuse has existed throughout recorded civilization and neglected children and adolescent servants, as opposed to the current epidemic of media confession, have always been its invisible victims.

A critical and challenging distinction must be maintained between an individual obtaining a private, albeit perverse, pleasure from looking at non-violating images of infant or pubescent imagery and without the intention to harm, and the compulsively malign actions of grooming with intent to commit abuse. Unfortunately, there are also too many recorded examples of tragic and brilliant professionals who are expected to be examples of continence and conscience that are also the victims of such unholy compulsions. I would go so far as to argue that there are two victims in every private act that does not involve sex trafficking. The child requires protection from criminal transgression but their perpetrator also needs to be understood, if not forgiven. Once again there is an important distinction to be made between adults who are drawn towards using their professional skills to work with children because they want to heal, protect and care for them – tragic individuals whose originally loving and mentoring impulses to educate or heal have turned into mutual tragedy – and rank criminals.

In December 2014, Dr Myles Bradbury, a dedicated Consultant Paedicatrian, who was looking after children suffering mainly from cancer, was sentenced, as reported on BBC News, to 22 years imprisonment for conducting 'criminal intimate examinations' upon 18 children at Addenbrookes Hospital in Cambridge. The parents accompanying their sick children were invited to sit in the same examination room, but were then screened by a curtain, preventing them from seeing what took place. Dr Bradbury abused his victims, secretly filming the physical examination by using a spy pen. His computer was seized, revealing over 16,000 indecent images of child exposure. The exact number of his victims will never be known as he disposed of his computer's hard drive. Recently, there has been a tribunal concerning another consultant who was allowed to remain in post after being discovered to have a computer collection of indecent images of children, because evidence was provided that he was an outstanding and devoted professional about whom there was no evidence of acting out any sexual indiscretions. Inevitably, there are many and varied routes towards the tragedies of compulsive sexual abuse which are enacted by all members of society. If the statistics are correct in demonstrating that male relatives are responsible for a large proportion of the thirty per cent of recorded cases of sexual abuse which are committed by family members, a question arises as to whether such early illicit experiences of adolescent abuse and illicit sexual arousal may not act as a trigger to a permanent blueprint or potential desire to commit compulsive acts as adults. I remain unconvinced that in such tragic cases prison can ever be the answer.

I recall a distinguished professor of forensic medicine, who was also a psychotherapist, telling me that he had given up working psychoanalytically in his private practice with convicted sexual abusers to whom he had devoted many professional hours after the failure one day of what he had considered to be an optimistic therapy session. This incident persuaded him that he was helpless to change such entrenched compulsive behaviour. As he opened his front door on a bright summer's morning, to let his male patient out after their session, an attractive woman, who was scantily dressed for the sun, was pushing her toddler past the door. The psychiatrist felt his gaze involuntarily move to her provocative breasts. At the same time he observed that his patient's involuntary gaze had moved blindly past the woman to focus steadfastly on the child. My colleague realized that where such entrenched roots of sexual desire existed, mere words, his therapeutic words, had no power to 'cure'. Democritus, the pre-Socratic philosopher is reputed to have plucked out his eyes because he could not look at a woman without evincing desire, which he claimed distracted him from higher thought processes.

The challenging question remains as to how best society can address these disturbing facts and statistics. If it is true that adolescent sibling abuse is a common phenomenon, professionals may be wise to consider what the habitual and perverse consequences may become of these early actions of incestual sexual exploration, which may either have been consensual, or experienced as actions of bullying and sexual abuse. To return to Nabokov's protagonist, Humbert, it is clear from the first paragraph of *Lolita* that his subsequent adult perversion with 'nymphets' had its origins in an innocent experience when Humbert was on the cusp of puberty. The first page of the novel reveals that Lolita's precursor, the pubescent and idealized child, Annabel, 'a few months my junior', who Humbert fell consensually in love with, died in a distant accident shortly after their 'consummation': 'Did she have a precursor? She did, indeed she did. In point of fact, there might have been no Lolita at all had I not loved, one summer, a certain initial girl-child. In a princedom by the sea.'

My modest attempt to answer this challenging question recommends that the focus be less on cure than on prevention. Parents and educators need to teach very young children to learn to 'read' their bodies in the same way that they must learn to read books. Sex education needs to begin in the nursery and not only at pubescence, or puberty, which means that some parents, who may find such matters challenging and distressing to discuss, will also need educating. One of the earliest indications of sensual pleasure in children, even as young as babies, is visible in their innate desire to self-soothe themselves through the comfort they experience in the repetition of rhythmic actions, which may, or may not lead on to infant masturbation. Babies have varying responses as to how quickly they derive pleasure from accidental stimulation of their premature sexual organs through nappy changings, etc. Such behaviour often confuses, or even disturbs parents, as well as nursery school and reception class teachers. Children need to know that it is not shameful to want to touch and explore their own, or with consensual negotiation, each other's bodies, which they have anyhow done since time immemorial by illicitly playing Doctors and Nurses, although the politics of such games are now threatened by political correctness.

Children need to be educated, as soon as they can understand language, that their body needs to be respected and protected and that while it is acceptable to do some things, like masturbate, or hold on to their sexual organs in the privacy of their bedrooms, it is not acceptable and even provocative behaviour to do so in public. They need to be educated that there are right and wrong, or good and bad ways, in which their bodies can be touched and excited, and by whom. These discussions into the rights and wrongs of their small bodies need to happen both within the family but equally importantly, in view of the statistics, as part of the curriculum, in the kindergarten, reception and subsequent classrooms where teachers need to be trained to become alert and sensitive to a distinction that must again be made between children's naïve use of descriptive and novel phrases of collective exclamation such as: 'He's a paedo!', and subtle communications that arouse concern. As soon as children can understand language and are able to share their thoughts and fantasies they need to learn that it is OK and even essential to feel able to discuss – in a public forum and ideally without shame – the languages of their bodies and a shared reality of the existence of feelings of physical pleasure. Such a discussion needs to include the unpalatable truths that such feelings can also be violated. When such sensitive discussions take place within a familiar and contained group of children, they are more likely to be received without heightening anxiety.

It is hardly surprising that R.D.Laing also held unconventional and advanced views on the treatment of sexual offenders and their child victims. Among his more controversial claims, which contributed to his notoriety back in the sixties, was a recommendation that there needed to be a greater understanding of and a more sympathetic treatment to the confused emotions of child victims of sexual abusers once their abusers had been identified and arrested. Laing considered that in some cases, where a symbiotic, albeit perverted, relationship developed between the abuser and the abused, there was the risk that further abuse could be inflicted on the child by the sudden and unnegotiated disappearance of their abuser. This idea continues to be a taboo subject among many professionals, although Candice would give the idea her imprimatur. Baroness Helena Kennedy expresses a similar view in her book, *Just Law* (2015):

> If society were to decide that in the interests of victims, establishing responsibility for sexual abuse and rape was to be followed not by the punishment of imprisonment, but by a

diagnostic and therapeutic response for the abuser, then we could contemplate a different process. But since most people would never accept such a radical reform, we should continue to struggle for more cautious improvements.

Laing maintained that the situation between abuser and abused was sometimes more complex, more subtle, than either the public or the professionals were prepared to acknowledge, or to evaluate. He claimed that many of the victims were children or adolescents who were already invisible to society and who had become conditioned by their 'carers' to abject physical neglect and emotional abuse.

> Now and then I took advantage of the acquaintances I had formed among social workers and psychotherapists to visit in their company certain institutions such as orphanages and reform schools where pale pubescent girls with matted eye-lashes could be stared at in perfect impunity remindful of that granted one in dreams.
>
> VLADIMIR NABOKOV, *Lolita*

Laing hypothesized that this sorry state of affairs could have the effect of complicating the child victim's distorted reactions to sexual abuse. He suggested that in many cases the social neglect was already so extreme that a child might even come to 'love' or harbour mixed feelings of erotic attachment and gratitude towards their abuser, however unpalatable that reality might be to society. Laing felt that not to take this into account in designing a treatment plan that negotiated for a total separation after arrest might unwittingly perpetuate the feelings of blame, shame and trauma in the young victim who may have felt, albeit spuriously, valued for the first time. What continues unspeakable, even among many social workers and therapists, is the idea that there can be contexts in which a child may have enjoyed the sexual contact and attentions of their abuser. In such cases, as Candice would vouch, the un-negotiated disappearance of the perpetrator may lead to more confusion, more grief and even unwarranted feelings of blame and a misdirected sense of responsibility in the victim. This is not to suggest that the perpetrator should not be punished for their crime but an informed professional consideration should be given to the immediate, following arrest, processes of attachment and separation.

It is questionable whether the compulsion to groom and to abuse, when it exists in explicit and compulsive form, can ever be cured, although its origins may be understood with sympathy. It is critical to remember the immeasurable differences between someone having perverse or even predatory fantasies, or thoughts, and someone sexually violating a child or young person. We are not, nor should we ever be held responsible for our involuntary thoughts however unwelcome they may be to us, whereas we are always responsible for our actions. 'My brother kill'd no man: his fault was thought' (words of Edward IV, from Shakespeare's *Richard III*). Therapists, perhaps above all professionals, must make this critical distinction when listening to concrete confessions as distinct to phantasy.

The French cinematographer Louis Malle in his exquisite film, *Au Revoir Les Enfants*, provides a perfect example of this critical distinction. The film, which is often autobiographical, takes place during the Nazi occupation of France and is set in a rural Jesuit boarding school. There is a moment when the school's principal tenderly bends over the wounded knee of his innocent and seductive pubescent pupil, Julien. His face becomes animated by desire and longing and I waited, in suspense, for an act of inevitable abusive transgression, but instead, the teacher virtuously exercises restraint. His expression falters and becomes sad as he resists the temptation to enact his tangible desire, merely instructing the boy go to the matron for treatment.

Shakespeare's insights into the vagaries of the human mind never fail to astonish me. I want to use one of these insights into human psychology, dramatic and scientifically ahead of its time, to illuminate another insidious methodology of malign emotional abuse, which in this example is paternal. Shakespeare had a chilling and intuitive insight into what was to become Gregory Bateson's indispensable psychological theory in the twentieth century. The 'Double Bind' happens, as I have already described, whenever an individual is caught between two irreconcilable authorities. I have already explored – without identifying Shakespeare's employment of it – the maternal double bind that existed between Coriolanus and his mother. Volumnia's actions of *binding* her son into a double tragedy are dramatically imitated in the tragic paternal relationship between Polonius and Ophelia in *Hamlet.**

Any individual may become the victim of a double bind if they fall prey to or become trapped in a situation in which they are confronted with two irreconcilable demands, or have to choose between two conflicting courses of action. This dilemma becomes the tragic destiny of the motherless Ophelia who, in love with Hamlet, confides her exalted emotions to her father: 'My lord, he hath importuned me with love in an honourable fashion/… and hath given countenance to his speech, my lord,

* Bateson's theory of the double bind offers us a paradigm for Ophelia's tragic inability to find a solution to preserve any coherence or integrity other than to commit suicide.

/ with almost all the holy vows of heaven.' Polonius's cynicism shreds Hamlet's holy vows of intention into 'mere unholy suits', thereby plunging Ophelia's mind into the torment of two conflicting imperatives: 'In few Ophelia, / Do not believe his vows, for they are brokers / Not of that dye which their investments show, / But mere implorators of unholy suits, / Breathing like sanctified pious bawds, the better to beguile.'

Ophelia is caught in a psychological bind between her duplicitous father and the lovesick Hamlet. The conflict between her father's crude sexual prohibitions and her love for Hamlet precipitates a morbid disillusion and melancholia in her fragile adolescent mind. In filial obedience to her father's will she is unable to mediate, or to console Hamlet's distraught and heart-broken reactions to her inexplicably sudden changes of heart. The integrity of her being is further compromised by her father's murder, when her morbid despair can find a solution only through suicide.

Shakespeare's continuing deployment of Oedipal conflicts in his exploration of intense father / daughter relationships – that are often enacted in the unexplained absences of mothers – long precedes Freud's startling 'discoveries' of childhood sexuality and seduction. In *The Tempest*, Shakespeare illuminates the awkward Oedipal quandaries between Prospero and his daughter Miranda. More boldly, he pens the idea of explicit paternal incest in the less well-known play *Pericles*. In *Pericles*, set in the ancient city of Tyre, Shakespeare uses the device of a *Prologue*. Using the dramatic persona of the medieval poet John Gower, the audience is, without apology or warning, informed of King Antiochus's paternal incest:

'This king unto himself took a peer,
Who died and left a female heir,

So buxom, blithe, and full of face,
As heaven had lent her all his grace,
With whom the father liking took,
And her to incest did provoke…
But custom what they did begin,
Was with long use accounted no sin.'

Shakespeare knew the unquantifiable difference between thoughts and actions and that however strange, perverse or unwelcome they seem, they are harmless as long as they remain inside our minds as metaphysical ideas. We are not responsible for our involuntary thoughts, which like our dreams can be received as welcome or unwelcome gifts that are delivered to us, unsolicited, from the unconscious. The leap between involuntary thoughts and any compulsive action is immeasurable. Abuse occurs when the subject's thoughts, through a compulsion to leap out of control, are propelled into actions without restraint or respect for society. They mutate from order into criminal disorder, from thought to transgression. Any anti-social thought that begins as a symbolic metaphor but translates into concrete action is dangerous and will turn its victim into a criminal. As a psychotherapist I have the burden, as I listen, as must any teacher, of trying to distinguish between harmless fantasies and rogue thoughts of abuse, and the intentions of their concrete and forensic enactment.

The compulsive personality inhabits a mental space of regression and in some instances is possibly another victim of childhood humiliations that have grown into adult perversions. As already argued, it is easy to underestimate the consequences of childhood humiliation. A distorted and tragic version of self may then emerge in the adult that in some instances has consciously been motivated by an original desire to serve society while simultaneously that integrity is being sabotaged by unconscious, involuntary and compulsive forces. There are, as already provided, historical and contemporary examples among politicians, doctors and many other professions, to confirm this hypothesis. In such tragic states of compulsive perversion of the self, the desire to serve, protect and to mentor society may like the branches of a tree, reach as high above ground as the roots of any compulsive and forensic 'fall' will be spreading involuntary toxins of perversion underground.

I remarked that fathers have not been my thing and I have had little exposure to victims – other than Candice – of florid sexual abuse in my consulting room. This does not preclude me from seeing men and women who have been, sometimes unwittingly, emotionally abused by their fathers. There are other seemingly less violent forms of abuse caused by bullying and/or inconsistent parenting that can have as profound and permanent an effect on the personhood of the developing child and their future sexuality as florid sexual abuse. Boys are particularly vulnerable to emotional paternal abuse. A substantial part of my client list has consisted of emotionally abused 'Lost Boys', both gay and hetero, whose experiences of their inconsistent, absent or bullying fathers are a source of obstinate emotional wounds. I have too often seen the consequences to young men who have been traumatically abused by their fathers, although emotional abuse is a less vibrant media subject than its sexual equivalent. An adolescent boy's experiences of the phallic power of his father to abandon or humiliate him are infinite and often indelible. I have listened to instances in which grown men who have been such recipients turn into lost boys as they remember multiple rejections and moments of rank humiliation.

It is on the whole true that men do not incline towards 'The Talking Cure' but repeated statistics demonstrate that contrary to popular opinion, males are more vulnerable to clinical depression, suicide and premature mortality throughout their life cycle than females.[*] Perhaps that is why almost all primitive tribes have such complex and extended rites of passage which are intended to change boys into men, who must learn to bear extreme physical and emotional pain without the comfort of Marcel Proust's good-night kiss, the rituals and tribulations of which were so carefully detailed by the French writer.

A taxonomy of manhood has emerged in my consulting room of young men who are the sons of charismatic yet abusive fathers. I am thinking of two men, Chad and Max, with whom I worked for several years and who, although biologically unrelated, are psychological twins, albeit not of the identical variety. They are both the sons of sixties' fathers, and both were emotionally wounded by their fathers' narcissism, and by their repeated experiences of tantalizing love in their unreliable fathering. These two symbolically 'homeless' men have illustrated how hard it is to overcome childhood feelings without succumbing to an adult status of victimhood in an irrational, irretrievable nostalgia for a secure 'home'. Oh, Daddy!

Their fathers were both, by coincidence, artists who had acquired international counter-culture reputations in early adulthood, but who were blinded by their premature media fame. In both instances my patients were eldest sons, although there was an essential difference. Max's parents had separated before he was born and his father was never present as an interruption to

---

[*] Statistics confirm that male genes seem to be more susceptible to mortality throughout their life cycle. There are more spontaneous early miscarriages of male fetuses recorded, more male infants die in the first year of life, more male adolescents are killed and more men will commit suicide than women. Worldwide, slightly more males are born than females. [wikigender]

Max's Oedipal longings for his mother's undivided attention. Max is the only son of his mother, while his father helped produce eight half-sisters. Chad is the oldest child in his father's tribe of six. Unlike Max, he experienced what he now remembers as an idyllic early childhood and a lost domain of transitory boyhood perfection until his father left to create another family; whereas Max's father always tantalized Max with his capricious paternity.

Max's father was one of the coolest, hip members of the sixties underground. He was also falconer to the Saudi Royal Family and an Egyptologist who would enchant Max with stories of the Pharaohs and his theories about the Pyramids. He would appear, without warning, to scoop Max into a van, with less than an extra sweater for luggage, and set off on another unpredictable and exciting falcon expedition to the Welsh mountains, at the end of which Max would be returned, or 'dumped' home without any idea as to when his father would return. Max seemed to shrink amidst his extraordinary accounts of his father's publicly archived life and visibly to lose oxygen. It was not surprising to discover that he had suffered from frequent and acute asthma attacks as a child. He recalls being wired-up to oxygen and rushed to hospital as one of his most secure, if ironic memories of 'attachment'. Historically, Max felt a need to puff himself up with the fabulous and to try and turn his own life into an equivalent fable.

Chad's feelings moved between admiration and love for his father and sadness and anger at his inconstancy and neglect. During our association he became intrigued by Shakespeare's work. Sometimes, he metaphorically identified with Hamlet in his confusion of paternal emotions. He compared his father's early protectorate, before his departure, to Hamlet's idealization: 'That he might not beteem the winds of heaven'. He also resonates to the disillusion and contempt Hamlet felt about his step, or shadow-father, Claudius. For Chad there is the nostalgia of lost ideals, while for Max there is the hunger of longing. Chad has since come to have a more benign understanding of his father as someone whose adult life unfolded prematurely. With this ever-growing sense of understanding, Chad corrects my harsher description of his father as abusive and prefers to perceive him as 'immature and confusing'. As a father himself, he is resolute in his consistent and mature attachment to his children. Chad remembers, once too often, being put into a taxi and left to find his way, with a stifled stillborn gulp of anguish, from a deserted countryside railway station. 'No one left and no one came on the bare platform'. He will never allow this premature experience of separation to happen to his children.

Another coincidence was that both fathers worked from studios that were located amid the recondite and illicit energies of sixties' Soho. Their sons recollect these independent spaces as private domains where their fathers displayed their collections of 'erotica', underground comics, magazines, record covers and other aesthetic interests. Chad remembers his father's studio as carrying a more intoxicating whirl of the premonitions of adult sexuality than the sterile conformity of today's graphic Internet porn. These studios were private spaces of idiosyncratic sensibility and erotic refinements that left the adolescent boys feeling a sense of awe. In Chad's instance it was his discovery of: 'My first exposure as a young boy to those erotic images of women. Their perfection was both arousing and daunting to me.' Max was sexually intimidated, angry and aroused.

Max met with me several times a week over many years, but the frequency reduced and finally ended, as he recovered. The recent death of his mother and the difficulties of triangulation between his own emotional needs and those of his adored but demanding children have caused him to raise a *cri de coeur* for some temporary counsel. I do not consider that either of them used me as a habitual crutch, but rather as their consistent reservoirs of memory of past unhappiness and anxiety about their challenged trajectories into adulthood. As a psychotherapist I do not want to become what Ernest Geller described as 'a facile pedlar of hope' but rather to help them come to terms as far as possible with the unhealed wounds of historic traumas, and although I am not convinced that such indelible wounds ever fully heal, they can fade.

When I asked Chad for permission to use this material he remonstrated with me: 'Why do you suggest such wounds should ever heal? I am not sure that I want mine to heal. I want to observe and understand them as souvenirs of painful experiences in my life.' I love the way he spontaneously produced the word 'souvenir', which not only means a keepsake but also, in its Latin origin, means something that has come into mind. I resonate to Chad's attachment to a souvenir of a past suffering but where the psychic abscess has now been drained of active toxins.

That I have chosen to write about lost boys, rather than lost girls is of relevance. Girls, where a functioning ego or a public mask remains intact, are inclined to grow up more resilient than boys. Like Wendy, they incline to be more socially competent. That is why J.M. Barrie observed that it was Wendy, not Peter, who needed to teach the 'lost boys' the narrative skills to help them recover from their traumas and suspicions that they did not matter to their parents. There are many other adults who enter into therapy, or more frequently into life, who feel that they have never mattered. 'Matter' is everything around us; matter is everything that takes up space. For a healthy attachment history to develop it is not enough that a child matters to its parents. Children viscerally need to know that they have *consistently* mattered.

When I reflect on why it happens to be a tribe of lost boys, of which Max and Chad are but two heterosexual examples, rather than lost girls who have gravitated towards me, I do not have any answer other than that as I have not had a brother, or a father of any longevity, perhaps I am unconsciously drawn towards difference, and I am intrigued to understand better the male psyche.

This does not mean that I do not also 'enjoy' working with young women. I have a sub-group of three young women who happen to be between twenty-five and thirty. I glow because although they are often at odds with authority, they trust my alternative embers of wisdom enough to employ me as a confidant. Their circumstances could not be more different from those of the 'twins'. One element of their shared dilemma is that they each have fathers who are not at all like the impatient Mr Darling, but who are men more like Prospero in their wish to protect their daughters from any approaching danger. These three young women come from large and secure families that in a moment of crisis would provide safety nets. It is the presence, both physical and as internal critics, of their confident, loving and consistent fathers, singularly married that contributes to their daughters' existential dilemmas. These fathers find it hard to understand the alternative 'mappings' of their daughters' lives, which do not follow the clear ordinance-survey-type maps of their own career paths.

This beautiful 'trio of protest' knows that while I respect their parenting, I will not privilege the social conformity of their families but will prioritize their struggles through the opaque labyrinths of individuation. I think of them as 'young girls in flower', to borrow another of Proust's phrases, even though there are many psychic knots to untangle. When I reflect on these young women, whom I have come to know rather well, usually it is with the gentle smile of love. I love the bouquets they toss into my lap full of their sweet and bitter wild herbs of existence. I like to conceptualize them as individually decorated mosaics or luminous *tesserae* in a *Book of Becoming*.

Tessera Number One arrives after a rush-hour journey on the tube. She is the only one who holds an executive position while all the time she pines to find another professional route where she can exchange organizational bureaucracy for her undeniable creativity. She has become stranded in anomie and the famine of an incompatible professional responsibility in the public sector. She arrives with an urgent question, or a confession, of nocturnal dread. 'I wake up in the early hours of the night and ask myself what am I doing with my life? I guess I wake up not questioning myself, but having the question forced on me by the night and the darkness. I don't end up there in my thinking – the terror of the thought shocks me into wakefulness from my dreams, as shockingly as if I've had cold water poured over my head – or heart. Sometimes, in the early hours of the morning, I feel as if I am in a waking nightmare where I am being swallowed whole by habit. A bit like Prometheus chained to his rock. I am the space between nothing but I don't have fire. As it happens, I am a bit of a pyromaniac, I love sitting before and dreaming into a fire. I challenge myself, "Is this the life that I want to live?"' Our work together, in part, is to find out whose life this is and what her life feels like.

Tessera Number Two arrives with her ritual of bringing us both a coffee from Pret which I never drink but which she insists on bringing me. She accompanies her coffee with a brownie whose crumbs she ignores. In fact they are welcome guests as she has recently been discharged from an in-patient unit for an eating disorder. It makes it easier to find myself on my hands and knees with a dustpan after she has left. (I have, anyhow, already reached a reluctant stage of resignation regarding some young people bringing in snacks or snatched lunches, even checking IPhones. My dustbin seems to be constantly full of banana peel.) She has been her father's principal confidant since her mother died of a bowel cancer, when the home finally became more like a hospital ward. Recently, despite her father's protests about her own health, she has managed, with support, to leave their country house and begin an MA in London. It was a difficult decision to leave her father alone but a necessary one. It is exactly a year since her mother died and over the weekend her father told her that he has joined a dating agency. This information has emotionally dislocated her and left her feeling ambivalent and worried that she might retaliate by regressing into her anorexia. Tonight, there is much to deconstruct and share.

Tessera Number Three is a deft juggler of multiple identities and mood. Sometimes I open the door to Rosalind, but other times I find it is Celia waiting for me. It might be Lizzy Bennett. Sometimes it is Woolf's gender-bending Orlando who strides into my room. She has had a phantasy about what it would be like to be reborn into her father's skin. His moth-eaten school uniform still loiters at the back of the family cloakroom. She would like to dress up in its stiff collar and gown and roam the city, just for a day or two.

Whether one is born into the world as a son or a daughter, it is a gift from the gods to have a loving and engaged father as a consistent rock, whose symbolic resources will survive through memory and beyond physical death. Human nature is, I consider, born with an archetypal longing for the gleam of recognition described in Wordsworth's account of the infant at the mother's breast. With time, the infant will also want to seek out the proud gleam of paternity. Fame may become one substitute, and 'selfies' another, but there cannot be a substitute for the golden energy of *consistent* recognition in the parental eye.

It has grieved me more that my two oldest grandchildren are without the protectorship of their father than any of my memories of the cabbage-patch disgrace of a diseased paternity. I take a morsel of comfort from the fact that my oldest granddaughter, Portia fell in love with the pearl necklace my father gave to my mother on their engagement the moment her small and curious eyes focused. Precious little fingers caressed the shining beads. Portia covets this symbolic gift of innocence. 'Those are pearls that were his eyes.' They will become Portia's pearls. I know that my father loved me during the distorted nursery years that we shared. After his death I became a changeling always seeking out other families who I could admire. My father lies buried in an unmarked plot outside of a Victorian institution for the insane, which has long since been redeveloped into luxury homes. He was not privileged to have a burial stone where I could lay Rosemary for remembrance.

> Full fathom five thy father lies;
> Of his bones are coral made;
> Those are pearls that were his eyes;
> Nothing of him that doth fade,
> But doth suffer a sea-change
> Into something rich and strange.

SHAKESPEARE, *The Tempest*

4

THE POLITICS OF FRIENDSHIP

*Let us be grateful to the people who make us happy; they
are the charming gardeners who make our souls blossom.*

MARCEL PROUST

T HERE IS PARADOX IN PROUST'S GRATITUDE BECAUSE
equally he saw friendship as an obstacle, which wasted
energy that could be focused on the industry of 'Art'. Another
paradox in the 'Politics' of this chapter is that its focus is not
limited to social friendships but includes reflections about the
people who consult me professionally and who, according to the
Ten Commandments, 'Shall Not', must not, be called friends.
My earlier statements regarding the entanglement between the
professional and personal aspects of my life will be enlarged
upon. Proust's words have a special resonance for me in that
so much of my personal and psychological fulfilment takes
place in my consulting room, where I conduct 'professional'
relationships.

It might be argued that professional and personal relationships
do not mix and yet at this late stage in my career it seems that
without the possibility of 'friendship' being a silent ingredient
of the therapy there is less chance of any profound and healing

change of attitude taking place. Maybe, I equate friendship with kindness, but there is a difference. I try, although I may sometimes fail, to extend kindness to everyone who enters my orbit. It is a *sine qua non* in my professional work. Friendship is more intimate and moves beyond kindness. Some people who consult me complain that their previous therapy failed because they felt like an alien in their therapist's 'life'. They could not even imagine another context in which they might have become friends.

It is almost the end of the summer break and I have stopped by at my favourite butcher's in Marylebone. I am fumbling for a credit card when I hear someone call my name: 'Hello, Jane.' I look up and see a young man, casually dressed for the sun, who has a regular Thursday slot at 11 a.m. in my Marylebone consulting room. It is Thursday and the time happens to be 11.05. Taken by the happy surprise and our extended summer absence, my body moves forward towards the ritual of a fond embrace until my mind interrupts. We confine our greeting to a warm exchange of words and exclamations of surprise at our random meeting over the butcher's bloody counter.

As I grow older finding extended time for friendship and in particular the cultivation of new friends becomes more difficult. Friendship is a greedy consumer of time and I am not certain that I have always been good enough at it. Yet, wherever there has been a historic connection of genuine friendship its memory cannot be extinguished, although in many ways it is the failure of friendship that lingers longest in the memory. I have had a shared falling out with two close female friends about whom it would be impertinent to write. I introduced them to each other and often fantasize that they have become 'best friends'. I wonder if I am 'the enemy', or if they remember the good times and mourn the loss of friendship as I do: 'Let him who wishes to kill his opponent first consider whether by doing so he will not immortalize his enemy within himself,' counsels Nietzsche.

I have only one friend who has been my close companion and muse since childhood – Gala Mitchell. She grew up in a Cheltenham mansion under the guardianship of her grandfather and she now lives alone in a trailer in the unkind wilder-heat of the Arizona Desert. I fell in love with Gala as dramatically as did Dante with Beatrice when I first caught sight of her on the Christopher Wren staircase of our school, the Arts Educational in Tring. I became an instant and lifelong supplicant to Gala's mysterious and introverted beauty. Later, she became a psychedelic, wilful and reclusive muse for the inspirational designer Ossie Clark, while the filmmaker Ken Russell cast her as Jane Morris. She intrigued Warren Beatty, and Michael Jackson insisted to his plastic surgeon that he use Gala's retroussé nose as the model for his own reconstruction.

Because my earliest 'best friends' were girls, the historic friendships that I shall explore in this chapter are between women. All things change. Today my closest friendships are with men, whom I find to be more separate, less competitive, envious and definitely less 'bitchy'. Someone should write a treatise on the usage of the word 'bitch', which in simple terms means a 'female dog'. Frankly, volatile female dogs on heat are preferable to bitching females. The saddest thing is that the 'bitching' technique starts early on in the feminine psyche. If you go into any playground where reception-class girls are playing you will find splendid examples of the bitching mentality. Last week a patient texted if her nine-year-old daughter, who was feeling horribly sad, could join our session. They were, in fact, already on their way. I also felt despair when the sad-eyed child revealed that two alpha members of her class, (or bullies), kept a register in which class members were marked as 'cool', 'medium' or 'lame'. She believed them when they ticked her off their register as lame. Sometimes she felt so humiliated that she thought how it might be easier 'Just not to be.' Why is the appellation of 'cool' such a captivating, demolishing and yet desirable label?

Men, unless they are suitors, are less demanding and less passionate as friends; less preoccupied by intimacy and also less curious about the minutiae of daily life. Woman are often white witches in disguise who spin spells as they peel away onion skins of 'self', or share domestic gossip in the 'market', rather like the nineteenth-century women who worked in Bavarian weaving mills.

Friendship is not a consistent thing but can be invaded by ambivalence and horrid moments that may or may not last when admiration is drowned by envy, jealousy and competition. I listen to Bell already preoccupied as to whether she is X,Y or Z's best friend; as an only child, she seems expert at being in the middle. I can still remember my childhood 'best friends' and I want to call up their names.

My first best friend was Jane Goldsmith, not quite five, who like me was a pupil at Sarum Hall Prep in Hampstead. I thought that Goldsmith, like goldfinch, was a beautiful word to have as a name. Her golden ringlets, and the fact that she told me that her father was the King's doctor impressed me. (I have just consulted Google and found that my memory of her father's medical status is correct. He was King George VI's ophthalmologist). That is all I can remember about Jane until another memory surfaces, which may be why I still remember the surname of Jane's distinguished father. Something strange was happening to my father's face that has left me with a lifelong sensitivity to squints and uncoordinated eyes. My father's eye had started to wander and it frightened me. I loved his eyes, which were as green as any cats; I covet hazel-green eyes. I did not then know, and neither did most others, that his wandering eye was a sign of his undiagnosed venereal disease. I must have imagined that if Jane's father could make the King's eyes better then surely he could do the same for my father.

Next on my list is Birdie Haig, whom I settled for as best friend only as a compromise for she had a Celtic-hag temper. She shared my Holloway Hill School dormitory and I used to pull her long fair plaits until we were forcibly separated like a pair of conjugal foxes. I cannot remember any other friends at Holloway, where I boarded from six until twelve and where my constant companion was Orlando, the flea-bitten ginger tomcat, who ruled my bed.

And then… then there was Gala, about whom I could write a novel. To begin with she tolerated me as a handmaiden; subsequently it was her family, to whom she had introduced me, who informally adopted me. I still do not understand how the adoption happened but it was one of the epiphanies of my life. Gala and her younger sister Susan, who sometimes slept with her dogs in the stable kennels (like Francis Bacon and Lucien Freud), had been delivered, until they were sent away to school, into the exclusive care of nannies. I was welcomed in, however, and now felt loved by a family for the first time since I had been separated from my father. I was unofficially adopted into a chaotic but exotic Cotswold quasi-aristocratic and bohemian household who found me loveable and changed my life forever.

Gala's mother Billy was a blonde bombshell, a southern beauty from Texas. She met 'Mitch', Gala's father – who was the most handsome and most silent man that I have known – when he flew into Texas as a Spitfire pilot at the end of the war. He returned with his unsuitable eighteen-year-old and pregnant bride to the family mansion in Cheltenham. His father had, since the 1890s, part owned Mitchell and Butler's Brewery. Mitch's mother was a Seventh-Day-Adventist-invalid-recluse who lived in a 'cell' behind the croquet lawn. Mitch, in the English tradition, had grown up in an attic nursery with a moustached nanny in uniform. He rarely saw his parents and, like a bird that does not learn to sing at the appropriate developmental stage, Mitch had never learnt how to hold a conversation. He grew up into a silent but thoughtful Apollonian introvert, who compensated for his silence with displays of physical courage. He was always clearing his throat. He was another beautiful and athletic 'lost boy', both an eternal *puer* and an archetypal Apollo. He fell in love with Billy, a firebrand of Dionysian energy, who would later flay him alive metaphorically. Billy was to become the unofficial 'Queen' of the island of Mustique, where Oliver Messel designed her home. She was 'courtier' to Princess Margaret while Mustique was still a rarefied desert island that was plagued only by mosquitoes. I kept a framed picture of Mitch beside my bed. I fell in love.

I still do not understand why Billy found it easier to be a mother to me than to her two beautiful daughters. Perhaps it was because I was her Jewish 'orphan' who, unlike her daughters, unconditionally always adored her. I was exceedingly grateful for even crumbs of her interest. The family had never seen a 'Jew' before. Concerned for my happiness, Billy championed me years later when John baulked at the thought of marriage and prepared to set sail to Asia. Neither of her daughters ever forgave her for abandoning them to draughty Cheltenham nurseries and inferior boarding schools, while she sailed across the oceans for months on end with Mitch, even braving early Atlantic crossings with him in their yacht.

Every month we came up to London from Cheltenham to lunch with Gala's grandfather at the Ritz. I travelled with her parents as far away as possible from my own family. The first time that I flew in an aeroplane was on 18 July 1960 when we went to the West Indies. St Lucia and Mustique were still without hotels, but offered unspoilt sands, flocks of pink flamingos and Colin Tennant's pet elephant, Bupa. 'My' flawless family romped naked across deserted beaches, while I blistered and burned. It was there I stopped being afraid of black skin.

22 JULY 1960

Never before have I experienced such a unity of mind and content. The coloured children are proud of their school tunics. The island's outlook on the colour bar has helped me to form new views about this unfair situation. Here there is a wonderful co-existence – one exemplary to the world – though I occasionally find myself differentiating between the percentages of colour. I like 'niggerhood'. It is my birthday – I don't give a damn except I shall no longer bear the humiliating secret of my paltry fifteen years.

We stopped off in Trinidad, where Billy had an unspeakably handsome and athletic black lover called Harry Baird, who became a minor film star in the sixties, and where she opened a nightclub. While Gala entranced a mesmerized audience, serpentine, as she danced and skimmed the limbo, I sat on a bar stool and read out erotic poems; our favourite was Christopher Logue's *Lithe Girl, Brown Girl*. We were sixteen. The unknown poet Derek Walcott was in the audience.

How did these two precocious girls, one as lithe and exotic as Titania and the other as 'little and low' as Hermia, become lifelong friends?

∾

We met on a staircase designed by Christopher Wren that was destined to be the point where our lives crossed. Before it was converted into our school, another eccentric family, the Rothschilds, had owned the house, but we were still ignorant of Wren, the Rothschilds or each other. I did not know that you were Jewish. I was not even sure what a Jew was. In fact, you were the first Jew that I, or my family, met, and you were the first anti-Semite too. When you gazed at me spellbound, or should I say blindfold, on that stairway you didn't know anything about me beyond I was threatened with expulsion after I had cut my skirt up to my crotch with my nail scissors. People called me mute but I was not interested enough to speak to anybody; and they complained that I won the pianoforte prize although I was never heard practising anything. We were both thirteen.

We didn't get to *know* each other until we were performing in a school production of *A Midsummer Night's Dream*. I was playing, or was it better described as displaying, Titania and you were Bottom – that boring bellows mender. How anybody could have cast you as Bottom I still don't understand. You were always being mistaken for less than you were but perhaps that wasn't surprising in a school that was designed for will o' the wisp anorexic butterflies. Our roles demanded that we kiss. Yes, our first kiss took place in front of an audience. It felt good. It felt too good. Looking backwards across, or is it beyond, time, it was my best kiss, ever. Unlike you, I grew up to keep an international-celebrity kiss-list. Now I prefer poetry. The taste of your breath was pure and your teeth were playfully sharp like kitten-sting claws. Nobody knew it was a tongued kiss, without there being any sense of performance or rehearsal. Nobody ever knew that it was full of sensation, without being sensational. Later on, I seemed to lose any capacity for sensation but by then I had become a psychedelic seventies genie of the sensational. You were jealous and our relationship fell into jeopardy in our twenties when I kissed another girl. The boys never counted but she was as fair and frivolous as you were dark, serious and shy.

There was silence and a rift that lasted even after she died, but it wasn't only her that I loved, you jealous fool. She died tragically. She was one of the creative prodigies of our generation, another version of Sylvia Plath, and she was a founder of the British Pop Movement; she didn't want to die. Cancer hates creation and hers fed off the hormone stew and increased blood circulating through the fulsome beauty of her pregnant body. But this is not to be her story, not hers and mine. Thank God most people don't know how cancer can, when it chooses, misbehave like the Lord of Misrule and turn a beautiful body, or any body, inside out.

And then Puck enters, '*Offstage Left*'. I thought that he was speaking in riddles. The lines sounded like riddles to me but his couplets turned out to be an insight that I have struggled with ever since. Puck's lines have taken me a lifetime to unscramble. 'Love looks not with the eyes, but with the mind, and therefore is winged cupid painted blind.' Yes, it has been a lifetime's experience for me to understand that couplet, and only now do I fully understand it in the seclusion of my Arizona desert trailer. I was a mute recluse until you stalked me. I took after my father. With your schoolgirl love of psychology we tried to unscramble

Puck's aphorism while we truanted on a bank of thyme in the rose garden.

Now, too late, I understand the meaning. Proust puts it plainly: 'Love is a striking example of how little reality means to us.' When you gazed at me were you looking for yourself, for that invisible and missing part of 'You'? Was I destined to become the Dionysian complement to the plainness of your Jane? Did you ever suspect how tragic the random gift of beauty that has not been inhabited by self-esteem can become? Now, through the rags and tatters of my life, I have also come to understand Yeats's prayer for his daughter, which you loved to read to me. 'May she be granted beauty and yet not / Beauty to make a stranger's eye distraught...'

My beauty blinded you, whereas I wore it like a curse. I don't suppose you knew, as I accomplished the fatal and broadest sweep of the final Wren stair that your eyes, your gaze had very little to do with the moment that you fell in love with me. It really was not *with* me. I was just the peg for you to hang your projection on. I understand everything better now. My flawless symmetry stirred something that had already been lost deep inside you: a sense of your self as desirable. We were psychic untouchables. You smashed my malignant mirror. You hooked yourself leech-like into my genes. I still have the copies you gave me of the first words you wrote in your locked journal.

SUNDAY, SEPTEMBER 7TH 1957. DORM.

'Hello, You.'

Her spine is indolent, yet taught and positioned in space like a leaping lemur, or a reticent black stork, and her neck arches on to an equator between past and future. The inimitable ways her white aertex shirt flips her collarbone to reveal a supple forearm of dancing muscle.

I am thirsty for perfection. I can only find it in beauty and nature. And poetry. But she is my perfection. I want to cannibalize her. I want to gaze into her violet eyes drenched in cruel disdain for ever. There is a mole that draws me into the enigma of her brow; I should not want to call it a beauty spot for that would be too vulgar. My mother has a beauty spot. The bell is ringing for prep and I must depart.

PS. I don't know if she reminds me more of the stork, or of a velvet gazelle. No! She is an impala. I love that word, impala, it makes me feel as though she could impale me on the flourish of a wrought-iron railing where I would die of love. She will be my impala forever, I wonder if I will ever dare to tell her.

PPS. Moles are so important to our sense of identity. Shakespeare knew that and Imogen had one too.

'Hello, You, again!'

   Lights out. The Dorm

   I don't know what it is about her that gets me. The distance between her legs, and the way that when she walks she almost manages not to touch the floor, or is it just my imagination, mesmerizes me. She doesn't lean backwards, nor does her head advance in front of her neck, she has perfect posture as well as pitch; the balls of her feet seem to levitate. She grows with each step. Her eyes are dawn violets wrapped in gossamer. I wish I could steal them. Why am I so obsessed by her beauty? Is it an escape from my own flat feet, or are my feet just another expression of my dull spirit, and my fallen earth body? I read that Jews are supposed to have feet like the devil and that they smell different. I hope that I don't smell. I must remember to buy some more deodorant. I would do

*anything to see her come around an unexpected corner, to watch
her clean her teeth and stand sentinel with her toothpaste, or for
her to open a door and not know that I was waiting for her in
a seizure of joy on the other side. I fear that my obsession with
Beauty is like a magpie's attraction to objects that sparkle, and
that I am superficial, I don't understand why but when I gaze at
her everything feels better. I am just a plain 'Me', but when 'She'
smiles something happens, I become an autumn of butterflies, a
fluttering of goldfish tails, an industry of hungry silkworms, I will
do anything at all to make her smile.*

I stopped writing my diary once I had seduced Gala into being
'Best Friends'. I remember the first time she took me back from
school to her house, or rather the chauffeur Sutton collected us
in the Daimler and I was carsick. It was the stuffy smell of walnut
polish and leather, but I am still afraid of being carsick. Gala had
never spoken to me about her home except that it was called
Glen Fall. It seemed almost as large as our school, but grander,
and there were still servants to answer when we tugged the bell
pulls. I liked the cook who was called Priscilla and guarded her
pantry like a Rottweiler. There was a loudspeaker telephone in
the larder. Her parents were abroad. They always seemed to
be abroad. I was in awe of the polished gong in the front hall
that was sounded before meals, even when her grandfather was
alone. He intimidated me. He changed for dinner every night
although he dined alone. Grandfather seemed lonely and he
spent hours looking out of the window and gazing towards
the horizon with his binoculars. Glen Fall had its own time and
the hours were announced only by the grandfather clock in the

vestibule. Grandfather did not wear a watch, which made it easier for the maids to ignore Greenwich Mean Time, and often the gong for dinner would sound at premature hours so the staff could finish early. Grandfather loved his roses and I fell in love with his rose garden long before I came across T.S. Eliot. I had never seen bottled water, which was bottled from the glen-fall. Everything was magical. There were swans on the lake just like Yeats described, and in those gardens peace did come dripping slow and the evenings seemed to be full of linnet wings. I have never since been happier.

Grandfather was austere but kind. When I was sad because I had to go back to my family he would pick me roses, which he wrapped in sodden newspaper. I had never had flowers picked for me and clutched them all the way back to London. Sometimes he would send for Sutton and take us to London to lunch at the Ritz, where we got the giggles. Afterwards we visited the Colnaghi Gallery in Bond Street where he would negotiate another Dürer print for his collection. He called me 'Lapis', his little Jewess, and he took us both to Georg Jensen where he bought us lapis-lazuli eternity rings – I have never forgiven myself for losing mine – although our love has endured regardless.

After I was married and Tanya was born there were other friends who were less glamorous than Gala. These friends commonly had children of the same age as Tanya or Alex. Among the most carefree times of my life were those I shared with Jutta Laing when we were both new mothers. I remember our days being filled with light and love as we proudly pushed our babies across Primrose Hill and how every ivory tooth that appeared was a small miracle. The most precious antique object that I own is a mother-of-pearl reliquary, which perches on my mantelpiece and is crammed with the milk teeth of my children and dogs. Together, we met the small challenges of our children's lives: threadworms, nits and fevers. It was a love-fest of motherhood and friendship that we doused in patchouli and psychedelia while our pride in our maternity shone brightly for all to see. We cared nothing for feminism or burning our bras, had we worn any.

Later, under Ronnie's hawk-eyed guidance, we believed that childhood should be unfettered by rules and boundaries and everything was a haze of weed selected from a psychedelic smorgasbord. We smoked, wore afghan coats, let the bathwater overflow while the children splashed. Our babies slept safely beside us while we talked the nights away. Jutta often sang and Ronnie played Scriabin and Rachmaninov. I could not imagine that a day would come when I would find something else that I wanted to do with my life as much as to look after my golden daughter... but all things change.

All things change and my friendship skein seemed to unravel. My heart has never recovered from the rejection I suffered at the hands of the woman to whom I next became closest and whose amazing daughter was also my daughter's best friend. We became each other's confidante and emotional complement; we were Helena and Hermia. She was tall, leggy, dreamy and fair; she didn't seem to know how to negotiate the world; while I was small, dark and streetwise. We embraced the world as if it consisted only of Shakespeare, music and poetry. She refused to tell me how old she was but once when we had to rush to Accident and Emergency I saw her date of birth and had a shock. We went to a boring parents' evening at North London Collegiate, our daughters' school, and something that one of the pompous teachers said sent us into fits of insuppressible giggles. In front of our mortified daughters, and a group of stunned parents, we collapsed on to the floor in a helpless tangle of uncontrollable and hysterical tears of anarchic laughter.

In spite of such laughter, or because of what it hid, our glorious relationship died at the same time as her husband's sudden death. Once upon a time we had shared all our secrets but with his death I became the embarrassing depository of past confessions. We had shared each other's darkest secrets and knew every corner, *almost*, of each other's lives. Her husband had a sudden embolism and died. Overnight, I became a funerary urn full of toxins. Friendship was sacrificed. I pleaded, I cried, but my tears fell on deaf ears. My family never could understand our compatibility, nor do they believe me when I repeat that I have never recovered from her banishment. I have not felt comfortable sharing dark secrets, or intense friendship, with another woman since our relationship's demise over twenty-five years ago. I do not want to listen to confession anywhere; I do not want to be anybody's exclusive confidante *outside* my consulting room for that way danger too often lies.

Friendship is a controversial subject when it comes to the practice of psychotherapy and what really happens in the consulting room. If you are a psychoanalyst or exclusively psychodynamic therapist, it must be focused on the 'transference' of the patient's emotional and familial past, even their palaeontology, on to their therapist. Ideally, where 'transference' is the principal tool of therapy, and it is no longer my principal tool, the analyst is present as a blank screen on which is cast the patient's projections and transference of unconscious communications.

While I no longer practise as the Jungian psychoanalyst I was trained to be, it has happened that about seventy per cent of the people consulting with me once or twice a week in the psychoanalytic tradition have continued to do so for between five and many more years. Sometimes, I ask myself, and them, if these inordinate lengths of time signify a failure of practice. I asked a stubborn woman, a medical professional, stubborn in the sense that at first, as a matter of principle she rejects anything that I say, and everything, why she continued to value therapy: 'I have my brain and my body but therapy is like making the invisible mind visible and finding the right questions for the body-brain to answer. I have a challenging professional life where I am responsible for life and death decisions every day and it helps having you to witness my anguish and to remember my successes and my failures. I feel you are beside me.'

I feel very close to these regular 'visitors'. (I have an ongoing problem with nomenclature – whether I address people as patients or clients and wherever possible I prefer to use the noun 'people'; but this can become confusing in the context of a book. I have come to dislike the word 'client'; as the Latin origin of the word 'patient' means 'to suffer' and as suffering is one of the main ingredients of both psychotherapy and life I have now settled on the title of 'patient'.) The remaining twenty-five per cent of my practice consists of an ever-changing population who require time-limited therapy to deconstruct a particular knot or symptom. One fifth of the appointments in my diary are flexitime for people who 'come and go talking of Michelangelo'.

I imagine this cast of characters as lost 'knights' who are on a quest to individuate and explore alternative destinations. At the first consultation, I silently pose the question, more to myself than to the person sitting opposite me, 'O what can ail thee knight-at-arms, alone and palely loitering?' Perhaps it is no coincidence that on one wall of my consulting room there is a paper inset of fragile butterflies, which are insects that intrigue me still. Their existence on my wall celebrates my childhood glimmers of joy. Today, they have a different significance as they morph into emblems for these men and women who consult me on their paths towards individuation and emotional autonomy. Part of my challenge is to assist these 'knights' to emerge out of their chrysalises or cocoons of anxiety and feel a greater freedom to roam, or even to fly for a little while, unfettered in an often disgusting and random world.

One of the many problems of the 'impossible profession' of psychotherapy is that after seeing people over such extraordinary spans of time and with such frequency, they become not only my patients (or clients) but also my 'familiars'. I cannot say 'friends' because I receive money in return for the specific professional services that I provide. These actions are not reciprocal and must always be shaped by ethics. Such relationships may sometimes feel symmetrical but because of ethical boundaries they are not; although they risk becoming meaningless unless we each give and receive a unique emotional commitment that cannot be measured fiscally. I must become a reservoir of reliable memory, attention and listening engagement for everyone who consults me. They have no responsibility towards me except cooperating in improving or healing their emotional health and settling their monthly account. In contrast to my reservoirs of information, they will have limited access to the fabric of my life outside my consulting room, unless they care to Google, which will only provide them with some 'public' facts.

Some people are curious about my life, while others express no overt curiosity and I sometimes imagine that even if I came in with my head concealed by bandage they would not be disconcerted. I exaggerate, but there are other ways in which it is possible for people to discover elements of my 'private', although not my 'secret', life. Shared biography is only a small part of any relationship. Other elements are composed from invisible alchemies of compatibility which range from smell, eye contact, mutual consideration, or argument, colour, intuitions, linguistic pleasure in shared metaphors and difference in matters of aesthetic preference to name but a few. There are 'patients' who tease my sense of humour that is always *en retard* and know that it will take me a minute too long to get their joke. These are the utensils of intuition that can leave me feeling as close to some of the people who consult me as I do to my friends and my family, which is still a difficult and uncomfortable thing for me to negotiate, contain, understand or communicate.

I feel that the kernel of my existence, as I have grown older and my children have become independent, is lived inside my consulting room. Too often I arrive home tired or too spent to want to eat the delicious dinner John has thoughtfully cooked. I do not have energy spare to recount the anonymous emotional complexities and variegated stories that may have flowered or withered, during my extraordinary day. I want to explore further the complex politics of emotional fusions, attachments and boundaries that happen to me in my consulting room. John Bowlby, the high priest of human-attachment theory, wrote:

> Intimate attachments to other human beings are the hub around which a person's life revolves, not only when he is an infant or a toddler or a school-child but throughout his adolescence and his years of maturity as well, and on into old age.'
>
> BOWLBY, 1980

I make it clear from the beginning that I do not believe any psychoanalyst or school of therapy holds a Royal Warrant of

Access to the Unconscious, although John Bowlby's theories of attachment history, which explore the critical importance of the vagaries of our early attachments to our later lives are always at the base of my theoretical thoughts.

When I am away from my consulting room and thrust back into the often untimely and untimed demands of domestic or social family life, I think of it by contrast – despite the surges of emotional pain that often thrust like whirlpools of frantic energy into the spaces between the leather couch and my chair – as an uninterrupted locus of engagement. It is a space where the most privileged dialogue and debate sometimes happen. I like to indulge myself by filling the marble fireplace with Phalaenopsis orchids, flowers whose moth-weird whiteness helps me to absorb pain mores subtly than the ubiquitous white Kleenex tissues, but which also irritate me because they are cruel and cultivated. Timely confessions, salt tears, numinous dreams of flying and of torture; the nature of these conversations sometimes elevate the twilight room into an enclosed garden of love, albeit the darkest shadows lurk close by. I try to be observant, not to become inflated by the spells of intimacy that sometimes allow me to feel as though I have been led into a sacred grove of the trees of life.

It is not a secret that I come to 'love' many people who consult with me. I do not mean that I want to have an explicit sexual relationship. I will not wander off-piste here to deconstruct the many meanings of that defiant and trickster word 'love' which many philosophers and writers have spent their lives commenting upon. The 'love' that I feel is not romantic love but neither will the Graeco-Christian concept of *agape* suffice. Its erotic boundaries are patrolled by ethical considerations which forbid me to exercise any improper influence, either fiscal or sexual, upon its objects and which insist that I always exercise probity, reflexivity and emotional continence.

This is a love that is born out of a deep engagement, or 'intimate attachment', with another sensibility. It may provide a gradual access to the recesses of someone's psychic habitat that is not otherwise available for inspection. My contribution to this 'love' is dependent on, or grows out of, my memory and the heightened quality of my listening – knowing when to listen to every word, when to seem as if I am almost not listening, and even when not to listen at all, or at least not too hard, but only to eavesdrop upon reverie. These sensations or gestalts of another life that are transplanted in my mind, are a vital ingredient that cannot be compensated for through conscientious 'note taking'. The people who come to see me over long periods of time depend on my memory. They do not depend on me to remember their last session, or the one before; they depend on my memory being able to hold on to a living and coherent gestalt. A reservoir of emotions, fantasies, interactions, dreams and family genograms is tucked up inside my mind, and remains constant perhaps long after physical bodies depart.

I have fallen in love many times in my consulting room, far more times than outside of it, but within the unusual genre of a chaste love, whereby I am privileged to recognize and greet the beauty of an emerging and unmasked self. Wantonly, I fall in love with the angle of an arched foot emerging from a brogue that I have become so familiar with I could sketch it, blindfold. I fall in love with the snowdrop-green beginning of a smile; the clenched, wrung or extended hands spread before me that are as beautiful as any Dürer etching. I do not want my blush of vulnerability and these wounds of love to be invisible if the person has the prism through which to perceive them. Sometimes, when I am listening to someone share the pity of their history, I feel like Desdemona who fell in love with Othello's stories:

> My story being done,
> She gave me for my pains a world of sighs
> She swore, in faith, 'twas strange, 'twas passing strange,
> 'Twas pitiful, 'twas wondrous pitiful:
> She wish'd she had not heard it, yet she wish'd
> That heaven had made her such a man...

Othello, ACT 1, SCENE 3, WILLIAM SHAKESPEARE

As I reflect on these politics, I do not know how else to describe the following paradox of a professional interaction other than as one amongst the most energetic connections of my life. It took place within the despotic fifty-minute 'Freudian' hour, during which, although I was a paid participant and not a friend; what I experienced was the unforgettable trust of friendship. I have been meeting with a late-middle-aged man, whom I shall name 'the Pianist', for several years. Our first meeting took place when he was about to be discharged from hospital after a period of treatment for acute panic attacks. He was educated at Cambridge and then he entered the international world of law where he achieved formidable success. He is a modest and shy man who grew up far away from his family, who lived in an isolated region of India. As their eldest son, he was educated from the age of ten in boarding schools in the UK, while his siblings remained at home. He has never found it easy to express his emotional needs, and his material needs remain modest. Early and planned retirement brought with it personal challenges as to how to live his life, how to use his wealth, how to individuate beyond the needs of his family. Music was one of his passions and we have come to agree that throughout his early life it linked him, albeit unconsciously, as a small, overseas-school-boy, (he was ten when he left India) with his absent mother. She had been an exceptional pianist. We discovered that aural memories of her practising and performing to the family had accompanied his childhood homesickness across oceans and continents.

We have talked, and talked together about music. I knew that he practised the piano every day and learnt his chosen scores 'by heart'. It will not surprise that he is a perfectionist. His practice, although heartfelt, was always work in progress; it was frozen into a rehearsal that never had the satisfaction of becoming a performance. His tyrannical perfectionism meant that nobody had ever witnessed him perform, but only overheard the repetitive sounds of him practising. He described how his heart would beat too fast at the thought of a public mistake, or the horror of losing his beat. He convinced me that his playing was not only mediocre but also incompetent. He tormented himself with memories of his confessed mistakes as if he was St Jerome. I remonstrated that his ideals of performance sounded like torture instead of play. I protested that all performance, if it was not going to remain rehearsal, required an audience. I am not sure how the exchange happened, and that is one of the astonishments of therapy: One is never quite sure how anything happens; one can spend months, or even years talking about something without there being any signs of growth or change.

A random day arrived when I discovered that the 'Pianist' had made recordings of two performances, which he unexpectedly brought to our session. I was taken by surprise when he arrived with a complex device that looked more like a bomb of some sort than a recorder, along with two sets of Bose headphones. We attached ourselves. The first piece was a performance of a

Rachmaninov *Fantasia,* which was followed by an arrangement of Bach's *Air on the G String.* It was extraordinary to have the Pianist's heart and emotional life opening out like a lotus flower, not in front of my eyes but into my ears. Music was flowing as a connected experience directly into our neural pathways. I thought that he might sound like a student enthusiastic to accomplish Grade 8 but I was listening to a performance that made my heart and mind escalate with joy. Had it been less accomplished but just as enthusiastic, the shared act of trust would have created an equal effect of delight. The Pianist had become brave enough to leap beyond the confines of theory and the masochism of repetitive rehearsal into an accomplished performance in which he was joining me as both the unself-conscious audience and a celebrant of 'himself'. Understandably, I had some anxiety about submitting this portrait of him for approval which objectified his emotional life. His response was surprising. He asked me why I had gone to such lengths to conceal him; he commented further that he did not understand why it was such an important memory for me: 'Once I had taken the decision to play for you and to bring the equipment, I never gave it another thought.'

Similar challenges and creative risk-taking are also required for the compositions that I want to undertake as a therapist. The Greek word *theoria,* in its literal sense, takes us beyond the squabbles of different professional societies with the dissonant scores of their competing doctrines and, as Montaigne described, is derived from a verb meaning: 'to witness a spectacle. The practitioner, or seeker after knowledge, is deemed to gaze with eyes of the soul upon "eternal truth".' Apollo, the music maker, and the soul of the Pianist had visited my consulting room.

When I think about the history of theory and its relationship to the technical risks and challenges that are provoked in my understanding of the complications of professional 'friendship', it is the brilliant but maverick and flawed Hungarian psychoanalyst, Sándor Ferenczi, who floats towards me across time. He was Freud's controversial colleague who broke away from the 'nursery' of psychoanalysis, as did many of Freud's associates and members of the notorious Monday Club. Ferenczi, in defiance of Freud, encouraged his 'analysand', or patient, to become a co-participant in the healing encounter by the creation of a symmetrical dyad. He passionately believed (with an inflection of irony on the adverb 'passionately') that the self-disclosure of the analyst could be an important reparative force. I agree with him. Ferenczi was convinced, in defiance of the abstinence at the heart of Freud's lodestone of transference, of the need for transparent disclosure and a mutually emotional encounter between analyst and patient. The analyst was actively to be encouraged to discuss content from his/her own life experiences and thoughts if it could advantage the patient.

This was in violent contrast to the Freudian imperative of abstinence, the concept that the analyst must remain a blank screen in order to facilitate the 'transference process', that the analyst should never be seduced into revealing any aspect of his or her personal life. Subsequent schools of psychoanalysis, in a failed attempt to make the profession scientifically respectable (but the unconscious is not interested in such matters), have set down their interpretation of Freud's rules and regulations as rigidly as if they were the Ten Commandments, or preparations for a cultural revolution. While one of Lenin's more famous lines was, 'without theory there cannot be a revolutionary party,' soon after making that assertion, he wrote to his mistress, Inessa Marmand: 'But theory is a guide, not Holy Writ.'

There are, however, other documents that testify to Freud's frequent displays of idiosyncrasy and even spontaneous expressions of, and need for, affection in his consulting room. In her *Tribute to Freud*, the poet H.D. describes her analysis with him in Vienna in 1937 in which she records occasions when he defied the stern portrait his disciples have imposed upon us:*

> The professor himself is uncanonical enough; he is beating with his hand, with his fist, on the dead-piece of the old-fashioned hair sofa that has heard more secrets than the confession box of any popular Roman Catholic father-confessor in his heyday... 'The trouble is – I am an old man – you do not think it worth your while to love me.'

Ferenczi could not accept Freud's patriarchy, but he dramatically lost the plot when he decided that kissing his female patients could become mutually therapeutic. On 19/20 December 1917, Ferenczi wrote revealingly to Freud following the suicide of his former patient, Frau G. 'She came to me – a very poor, very beautiful, very intelligent, affectionate girl – a year ago... I happened to be in a period of vacillation with respect to Frau G. – her youth and charm enchanted me – I gave way to a kiss.' [Brabant et al., 1995, p. 253]

As shocking as it may seem, it has become common knowledge that the suicide of patients being analysed, or subsequent to having analysis, by the Freudian school in Vienna was not uncommon. There are also instances of professional psychoanalytic

---

* This is Hilda Doolittle's account of her two periods of analysis with Freud. As Ernest Jones, who was Freud's gatekeeper, reviewed the book most favourably in the *International Journal of Psycho-Analysis* (1956), the reader can assume that her report is accurate although it defies the stereotype of Freud's blank screen.

members of Freud's *Monday Club* having breakdowns or even suicide as a result of their internecine wars, envy, broken friendships and rivalries.

I have never kissed a patient erotically but it is not uncommon for me warmly to embrace or even to hug people if they signal a wish for physical contact after an agonizing, or an emotionally gruelling session. I am also committed to the idea that to achieve results there are some occasions when it is helpful for patient and therapist to become mutual confidantes and for the therapist to make relevant self-disclosures. A small and random example occurred yesterday.

I was sitting with a seventy-five-year-old woman whose elegant repartee and gorgeous blue eyes are brimming with wit and intelligence. She is wearing skinny blue jeans that are accessorized by stiletto sandals that must be five inches high and which balance upon nothing bigger than a five-penny piece. I am in danger of being distracted by the thought of how she manages to balance without a disastrous fall. We are talking about her impossibly dependent and capricious daughter. She already knows that we have daughters of an exact age. During her conversation, which is a buzz of articulacy, irony and, on her part, corrosive wit, there are many moments when the grist to her mill – the ambivalence between mother and child – reminds me of my maternal housekeeping. After another comment about her conflicted state of maternal love, I decide to share with her that her provocative metaphor regarding 'a safe deposit of love' in her relationship with her daughter elucidates some of my maternal dilemmas. Before my sentence is complete she jests, or rather she thrusts: 'I hope I am helping you as much as you are helping me.' She is.

Ferenczi's sexual abuse of his young patient, Frau G., conforms to a pattern that is not as uncommon as one might hope.

In Luis Buñuel's film *The Exterminating Angel*, there is an ironic and historical allusion to doctors kissing patients, which is then accompanied by ironic dismissal in a comedic reference to Freud's concept of transference. My mother provides me with another less malign if controversial example. At the time of her first breakdown, she obediently fell in love with her Viennese psychiatrist Dr J.B. who had an irresistible and charismatic personality. He had been there to console her after her experiences of electro-convulsive therapy, which was then applied without anaesthetic and left the patient in a state of traumatic dread. When I was showing an early adolescent interest in Freud and pleading with my mother to abandon her 'uppers and downers' and to consent to psychotherapy, she disclosed that what had helped her to recover more than any psychological treatment were the occasions when Dr J.B. would collect her from the Greenways Nursing Home, during her convalescence, and take her up to Hampstead Heath at dusk where he would console her dread with a kiss. It removed the stigma of her illness and instead she felt special and desirable. They remained lifelong friends and I believed her when she claimed it was never more than an extended kiss. (She added the telling detail that the kiss always provoked a sneezing fit.) An innocent thing in comparison to the many contemporary examples of rank abuse that are regularly investigated by psychotherapy- and medical-ethics committees today.

I tremble that this chapter may turn into an act of confession: my own. I have always hated the oak-stark confessionals and I have learnt that confessions, even in the consulting room, while they can lead to temporary elation or excessive and immediate relief are not to be encouraged; or not the variety that is the equivalent of psychic diarrhoea. The problem with confession in therapy is that it can bring an instant, but temporary, relief if it is delivered before a foundation of trust and genuine intimacy has been established and that is no quick task. I encourage people to go slow as a confession is only a beginning and needs careful deconstruction and processing before it can trigger change.

I have grown wary of those people who arrive and, without having had time to measure whether or not we are a compatible therapeutic partnership, spill the intimate beans of their secret lives. I have discovered through experience that when a stranger comes into my consulting room and within minutes is displaying his or her 'dirty linen' as if it were whirling around in a washing machine, or when a serious disjunction exists between an individual's public persona and the messiness of their private life, the likelihood is that they will not return, post confession. On the two occasions when I have been left with a linen basket full of the dirtiest underwear, I have never seen the owners again. In one instance the vanishing person even rang the referrer to ask them to compliment me on my professional skills, which was not without irony. I have learnt, through repeated experiences, that the skill is to stop someone from vomiting out their shame or despair prematurely, before an authentic relationship has been created in which to contain and console the emotional volcano of shit.

My confession is a flight of gothic fantasy, or flatus; but it is a comparison I cannot stop myself from making. Yes, it is yet another of Proust's involuntary thoughts that appears in my associations with the word 'confession'. I remember that when an eminent colleague of mine, my supervisor, was approaching his seventieth birthday, I asked him if he was going to have a party. He replied that he thought not because the most interesting guests he could invite would be his patients. His answer related to the fact not only that some of them were successful in fascinating and interesting walks of life, but also that he was so used to conducting challenging conversations that the idea of party small talk had lost appeal. When I reflect on my death I imagine that some of the inspiring people who consult me will mourn and become my metaphoric pallbearers. That might or might not seem a disturbed, or inflated thing to say, but one of the requisites of therapy is that when somebody decides, or we mutually decide, that the time has come for an ending, in ninety-nine per cent of my cases it is an ending. The person disappears across the horizon. I almost never receive Christmas cards or information about people once our therapeutic meetings are over. There are thankfully a few exceptions to every rule…

In a chapter dedicated to the politics of friendship, I have somewhat perversely chosen to combine personal friendship with my professional life; but toss as uneasily as I will, the two interweave. As Proust twisted and turned between the values and distractions of friendship, so do I feel guilty that I am still glued to, or so passionate about, my professional work; my art. My life.

I end this chapter with a gesture towards the next one through my memories of the gutted pain involved in a friendship that was surrendered to a premature death. I had an enigmatic relationship with my friend, Roszika Parker, whose death has warned me never to forget another of Proust's adages that our bodies do not respect our agendas, our ambitions or expectations. Rosie had many strands of friendship in her public, private and presumably secret lives. We were never 'best friends' – of those Rosie seemed to have a surprising number, although some were better described as admirers or groupies. We were confidantes who kept a healthy and non-competitive distance between us. We were both passionate mothers of a son and daughter; we had also been passionate and then ambivalent about our psychoanalysts, our Jewish genes, the politics of maternity and culture. We were ambivalent, too, about our profession and almost everything else except animals; we could be flippant together. We loved to sit in cafés and indulge in Bloomsbury-type gossip. We were both driven to write and while we published books on different subjects we shared a passionate interest in the psychology of maternal ambivalence. Rosie was the author of two ground-breaking books, *The Subversive Stitch* and *Torn in Two: A Study of Maternal Ambivalence*.

Months would pass without our being in touch but when I heard that my son-in-law, Jay, had suffered grievous bodily harm and was on a life-support machine, Rosie was the only person I wanted to call to share my midnight terror. Whenever we met up, our conversations would focus on our children, our colleagues, anti-Semitism, my dog, her two kittens or her mother. We visited each other's homes in London, the countryside and France but almost always as semi-strangers. I had never looked inside Rosie's fridge until she was too ill to bother, and then I would bring her Italian sorbet ice cream, which was almost the only thing she could digest. When Rosie's mother, Miriam Rothschild, died at the age of ninety-seven in January 2005, we had no idea – and what an unspeakable idea it would have been – that Rosie would be dead five years later.

> Death came, death came
> And took you away from this
> Oh, I miss you so
> and I long to know
> Why death gave you his kiss.

LUCINDA WILLIAMS

Rosie invited John and me to Miriam's memorial service, at the conclusion of which everyone was given a packet of seeds from the wild flowers growing in Miriam's meadows. John came home and sprinkled them across our paved courtyard. I doubted whether, being watered daily with dog urine, they would ever bloom, but I was wrong. We have since been privileged to enjoy a seasonal flowering of Devon ferns, campions, and cornflowers. When the unthinkable thing came to pass, our wild blossoms also became unwanted signifiers of Rosie's death.

We decided to share private instruction in a series of Mindfulness classes. Each week we met at the now departed Carlucci's in St John's Wood High Street at 3.30 p.m. for our preliminary tea and gossip. It was the autumn of 2009. I would lament – in retrospect, I rather overdid it – that I could not share her chocolate brownie because of my chronic irritable bowel syndrome (IBS). Sometimes, we would try, unsuccessfully, to deconstruct the phobia that was preventing me from having a diagnostic colonoscopy. We had both suffered from absent mothers, which in my view, as discussed, provoke a disposition to hypochondriasis. I didn't much care for the Mindfulness classes but Rosie, who had a more punishing super-ego, took instruction and the homework more conscientiously.

Another Wednesday – and I thought little of it at the time – Rosie confided that she had a slight but stubborn ache in her left side that was waking her at night. When the ache had not improved a fortnight later, I suggested that she might like to go and see my female doctor friend. The preliminary diagnosis was of a mild infection, or virus, and over Rosie's constitutional brownie we continued to focus on the challenges of my IBS. All things change. Rosie's persistent pain was demanding an ultrasound. Her results left even the radiologist speechless.

Rosie died almost a year later. I was with her on the Sunday afternoon in November when the murmuring turned into a shriek of neural pain. I rang my medical friend who was caring for Rosie; she would never bother anybody on a Sunday. She was admitted into a hospice the next morning. Rosie, I miss you; I mourn your enigma, and your extinction beckons me towards you.

Loving will always be preferable to being-loved, as acting is preferable to suffering, act to potentiality, essence to accident, knowledge to non-knowledge. It is the reference, the preference itself.

JACQUES DERRIDA, *The Politics of Friendship*

5

GUTTED:
THE LONELINESS OF PAIN

You're on earth. There's no cure for that.

SAMUEL BECKETT

I HAVE BEEN WAITING SINCE MONDAY FOR IT TO BE Saturday so that I can begin this chapter. Yesterday evening I swirled around my consulting room like a dervish, 'Tomorrow is the weekend. Goodbye lovely room, goodbye grief, sadness, joy. I'm free as a bird on a wire.' A little manic, 'speaking a little wild' I am just relieved another challenging and stressful, but always passionate week of engagement is complete.

I wake to find the boring clock has not reached 5 a.m. Trying not to wake the dog or my husband, impatient as Juliet (although older than her Nurse) I reach through the dawn for my laptop. When I turn it on I can only see half of the font and a firework display is starting before my eyes, obscuring the other half. No fugue state, no warning chimes, only another swirling dervish, but this time of Catherine wheels, exploding into tracings of electric fields of mutating light. Damn!

Most times my migraines are without pain or nausea but manifest in ecstatic distortions of light. Today, I feel the ominous pressure of dull pain demanding to take up residence. The quality of this pain is never intense, it never incapacitates as it does with some unfortunate victims forced to take to their beds in dark rooms, but it can become insistent. Sometimes, its low-grade presence demands an inconvenient somatic accommodation for weeks. Migraines are notoriously protean and have dramatic energies that rarely follow any schedule. Mine procure visual changes to which I long to surrender in order to explore, except my fascination becomes fettered with anxiety. Reliably, these light shows last for twenty minutes, timed to the second, but with every visit their calligraphy is attenuated by a terrifying thought: 'What if this display never fades... what if my vision remains interrupted and distorted for ever?' The same question attends all pain and disease. If only Hermes, the messenger of the gods, could guarantee a benign ending in due course; if possible even supplying the reassurance with a specific date. I remember when I was going through the menopause wishing that a letter could be dispatched from 'on high' informing me when close of play would be called on hot flushes and night sweats. Proust's Narrator observed: 'It is illness that makes us recognize that we do not live in isolation but are chained to a being from a different realm, worlds apart from us, with no knowledge of us and by whom it is impossible to make ourselves understood: our body.'

Our bodies are extraordinary – 'What a piece of work is man' – and how horribly wrong it can all go! I have been fascinated, appalled and traumatized by the sight of blood in the wrong place since I was a child. There is nothing like the smell of fresh blood away from the context of the slaughterhouse. While warm, its smell is damp, cloying and tinged with a curdled sweetness.

Before continue on the subject of bodies, I will confess that I am a hypochondriac. I am not the type that doctors refer to as 'heart sink' patients, the sort they dread finding in their waiting rooms on Monday mornings. There are two principal types of hypochondriac: the patients who cannot wait to find a reason to visit their doctor, who like nothing more than being submitted to a battery of tests and investigations. They love to Google all their symptoms endlessly and some of them even enjoy being admitted to hospital for surgical procedures. When I meet them in my consulting room I am inclined to think that their hypochondriasis may stem from a failure in early maternal soothing mechanisms. In such failures, the mother, whose own anxiety spirals out of control, also fails to regulate her child's anxiety, particularly in times of childhood illness. In addition or alternatively, the mother, or parents may have failed to respond sensitively to childhood anxieties about illness and mortality. Such offspring may grow up seeking medical attention for themselves as an unconscious compensation for parental insensitivity.

The second group – while they are convinced that every symptom threatens their mortality – dread nothing more than having to consult their doctor. I belong to that club. I suffer from chronic and debilitating pain in the form of irritable bowel syndrome (IBS) whose origins defeat – in much the same way as does endogenous depression (which is a malignant depression that does not have a conscious external trigger), or bi-polar states of mind, or dreams come to that – current scientific research. The latest of which into IBS is more concerned with the brain, spine and neural pathways than it is with diet. The recommended diet regimes change with each decade and for the Harvard Fact Sheet diet is no longer the centrepiece of the IBS mystery. In terms of management, almost nothing relies on science; almost everything is subjective and widely there are conflicting opinions about the management of dysfunctional bowel disorders. One school of thought is committed to a raw-food regime, while another camp is convinced that cooked foods are best, and fermentation is the enemy. In one system a tomato is akin to poison, while in another it is a magic harbinger of digestive health.

I am the Chief Executive Officer of this latter group of hypochondriacs and it took me ten years of uncertainty, bouts of panic and prolonged periods of intense pain in my gut to overcome my irrational terrors (and with that amount of pain, any cancer would have killed me long ago) and more phobias to submit to a colonoscopy. I think the Holloway school-on-the-hill doctor, with his clubfoot and hands like grit, exacerbated my fundamental white-coat terror.

Bad reminds me of good and vice versa. I remember the first doctor I ever knew, Dr Colt, who had a mane of white hair and a soothing voice. He was kind. I also remember that the last time I saw my parents together was when he paid me a visit. They had summoned Dr Colt because they were worried about a tiny blur of blood vessels creating a mark on my face that is sometimes referred to as a 'stork bite' and is something that may last throughout childhood. I can still see the red blemish below my eye and beside my nose. It stayed with me until adolescence when one day it disappeared, and along with it a morsel of my identity. I remember Dr Colt listening to my chest and telling me to breathe in and out. I remember the sun shining through the open windows and the view into the garden. The springtime smell of lilac, which must never be brought into the house, filled the room while he told my parents that I had a small heart murmur. I had no idea what that could be but it sounded gentle. At that moment, in lilac time, my parents seemed to be loving and concerned. The next day, after a night of discordant sounds that seemed to come from the bathroom my mother disappeared. She never saw my father again.

Another particular memory, which demands prominence in my inventory of mortal terror, is also associated with Holloway Hill. I can visualize the floor plan of the first floor where the dormitories were situated, and where there was an enormous Edwardian oak armoire at the top of the 'back stairs' that reminded me of a coffin. The occasion was an autumn week-end when the days were getting shorter and the bedsteads were shrouded in darkness. Karen, a Catholic child – we were all labelled according to our religious affiliation and I was the only Jew child – had a bedside locker which displayed a cruel bronze crucifix. She was taken ill with a nosebleed. We all got nosebleeds from time to time but Karen's became a haemorrhage that caused all the curtains prematurely to be drawn. When they did not open again the next day, my mind flew into fits of terror. We were instructed to stay downstairs and preferably outside while Karen was removed from our dormitory into Matron's bedroom. When we crept up to bed an indiscreet spill of blood still travelled between the rooms. The corridors smelt of petro-leum disinfectant for days. There were only twenty boarders and the deserted building was haunted by the obstinate sweetness of blood. I cannot remember whether or not Karen died but I do remember that her crucifix disappeared.

This recollection of a dying child is what prompted my reflection that there is always something terrible about blood in the wrong place. That thought was confirmed later on by my experience of four bloody miscarriages and emergency-theatre scenarios. I have also found out subsequently, in various conver-sations, that surgeons dread, above all else, finding blood in the wrong place while operating in theatre. I think of phlebotomists, who can be rough-handed, as professional leaches who refer in portentous tones to blood as being 'the eye of the doctor'. I have been told that one reason a student may decide to become an ophthalmologist is that they do not have to manage blood flows. I have grown up terrified of blood emerging from any orifice. What will happen if the bleed, like the migraine, never stops?

Phantasy holds me more tightly in thrall than any reality, which can be a negative consequence of a too vibrant imagination. I live in dramatic terror of disease but when I am forced to submit, I become a model patient. It was the phantasy of Karen bleeding to death behind barred doors in a tidal wave of blood that traumatized the eight-year-old me along with the taut and secretive faces of the adults. Children need information. They need to be told the truth, or as close an approximation to it as is possible. Otherwise, their imagination can run wild and provide an even more terrifying scenario, one that may become attached to the unconscious and travel with them through life. I have grown up with an irrational terror, which must have started after my father's death, that there is something 'bad' inside me. I hate the idea of any scanner looking into my entrails and detecting a secret bit of 'bad me'.

I wanted to grow up and become capable of controlling my fragmenting universe and so it is not much of a surprise that I considered becoming a doctor. My education had never taken me near a science laboratory, so it was an unrealistic ambition. The thinking behind the idea was that if I became a doctor I would acquire healing powers to allay the terrors of my child-self who had been a helpless witness of pain, suffering and death. Throughout childhood I vacillated between becoming a doctor, with a leather case and stethoscope, or studying to be a vet. My small hands wanted the illusion of being able to take control of mortality. Instead, I trained as an actress, which is not altogether surprising as it provided me with another escape route from too much reality. I became an intense *tragedienne* with first-class escapist credentials.

In my early twenties, while I was waiting for acting jobs, I found myself working as a temporary medical secretary. I must have cost the Middlesex Hospital a fortune through my atrocious typing at a time when one still used carbon paper with Tipp-Ex. I had to provide six copies of every item of correspondence. One unforgettable morning, the secretarial agency called and shipped me off to Morbid Anatomy at Bart's Hospital. Naïve, I had no idea where, as the lift ascended, I was bound. I found myself in chilly surroundings where everyone looked messy and there was a nagging smell of formaldehyde. It was not until I was asked to take dictation that I discovered I was in the anteroom of the morgue. I found myself transcribing data about the irremediable organic abnormalities of a newborn infant. My horror at the pitiless description of this small being fuelled me with spectral terror about 'lost children' and my own future maternity. Without pausing to explain, I got up and left the building never to return. Dreams about that small and nameless boy, or perhaps he did have a name and not just a number, and the smoking incinerator into which his tiny body parts were cast, pursue me still.

In the same way that actors are rarely positioned to choose the roles they will play on stage, so therapists cannot choose what they will listen to. Sometimes there is nothing that has prepared them for the bloodbath that is sprung upon them…

The fifty-year-old man who is consulting me lives in New York and after recommendation from a London friend he has returned regularly over the last few years to consult me about his relationship with his twin sons. One had been successful in his entry to Harvard; the other had failed to thrive or to launch himself into university and ever since had been self-medicating with illegal substances. In March I receive an email from the father asking to come over to London to have a week of intense therapy. The wayward son had unexpectedly died at the beginning of the year. He has felt unable to find or speak any words to share his bereavement. The coroner's verdict was, 'Death by misadventure'.

He describes feelings of guilt along with traumatic images he cannot exorcize without help, if ever. His son's behaviour was increasingly disordered and addictive. After a violent argument, preceding a holiday, his family refused to remain at home with him. During that night, as a result of an intentional overdose, which was likely to have been a cry for help but which was accompanied by the complications of a rare and tragic haemorrhage, he died. Alone. His father, a divorcee, travelled upstate to support his grief-stricken family, to oversee the statutory forensic formalities and to await the inquest. The other family members refused to re-enter their home, now struck by this devastating thunderbolt. He arrived at the house to find a forensic cleansing team on site, who had been deployed to restore to order the despoiled place of death. As is so often the case with sudden death, it was the bathroom.

He described how the forensic team was visibly shaken and garrulous. The foreman, like the Ancient Mariner, wanted to rid himself of his 'story' and explained that in twenty years of forensic cleansing he had never witnessed such a bloody mess. Unsolicited, and without preparing the father, he handed over his iPhone's shocking evidence of the death scene. Not even the most brutal phantasy could have prepared the parent's mind for such a sight. He had become an unwilling witness to the unspeakable objectification of his son's lurid death. He returned to my consulting room suffering from post-traumatic stress and the burden of carrying an unspeakable secret. It took him until the last of our meetings to describe the extent of the bleed, and then the words were hoarse-whispered as confession. I could not protect myself from the bloodstained imagery that immediately entered into a visceral part of my internal landscape. To listen properly to another body in pain, to listen with engagement, is to be changed. Forever.

How to move away from such horror except into the hysteria of black humour? Gallows laughter often rescues medical and surgical teams in theatre. They laugh away their mortal terror as we laugh away Tony Hancock's apprehension in *The Blood Donor*. The body in pain, the gutted body, cannot be a comfortable body but it can, even in gravest despair, become a source of humour. If I were to attempt to write a humorous parody of the terror I sometimes feel in the grip of my intestinal spasms, its setting would be a bank trading floor where the currency was not fiscal but composed of aches, agues, diseases and pain. I imagine the scene, as I debate the currency I might exchange my IBS affliction for. I wonder whether I would swop it for an acute and potentially deadly bowel obstruction that required an immediate surgical intervention, if it carried with it the possibility of recovery. I ask myself whether I would prefer to have chronic arthritis or a weeping psoriasis.

A characteristic of my version of chronic IBS pain is that there are brief periods when I am released from its thrall. During such intervals of euphoria, my spirit soars, my energy flies – not that it creeps along the ground like a worm when I am stricken. The more intrusive the pain, the more I seek distraction through work. It feels as if this pain hates me to relax as it often plagues me at night. I sometimes think that I have such energy and mischief for life that I have created my personalized anchor to reality. The pain-free times, which I rejoice in, are also the times when the people closest to me want to believe that a Lourdes-type miracle has taken place; but the respite never lasts.

I must return to my trading floor to see whether any trading can be done with the pain merchants, whether any alchemy can be found to extend the painless times. I have learnt through repeated disappointment, that something, sooner rather than later, will trigger it back. I can never identify its precise triggers. One of the frustrations with the large intestine is that, unlike the upper stomach where people experience an immediate nauseous reaction to intolerance, the bowel is secretive, slow to announce its distress and even slower to recover from inflammation before the beast bites again. Although diet can exacerbate IBS, current research does not regard it as the cause. Along with acute and protracted attacks of gastroenteritis, it is being identified as a corrupted physiological response involving the gut, the spine and the nervous system. The suspicion is that it is the archaic footprint of repeated childhood anxiety as well the legacy of emotional trauma. The gut is often referred to as 'the second brain' and it is now known that it can, unhelpfully in this context, secrete more serotonin than the brain. The latest research is being directed towards faulty neuron connections between brain and gut or aberrations of the gut microbiome, with more than the suspicion that early trauma or sexual abuse, which often results in a hyper-vigilant child, may be key factors in adult causation. I fit into that category. As an adult IBS sufferer my characteristic vigilance has become fixated on predicting every movement of the involuntary peristalsis of the gut, which in the case of 'healthy' people happens without any awareness; for me painful contractions can at their worst mimic the contractions of childbirth.

I take consolation from knowing that I am not alone in my suffering and my complaint could be worse. I have a friend with chronic though benign vertigo, which I find more terrifying. Poor George Eliot often took to her bed for days with untreatable kidney disease; T.S. Eliot had terrible catarrh, while Virginia Woolf's mental torment persuaded her to drown herself. I console myself that I am alive and my friend Rosie is dead. I fantasize about ways to bribe the feral creature. I am by nature a chocoholic, but there is no Faustian pact to be made, no indulgences to be bought from Mephistopheles. When I am in exaggerated pain, my thoughts become vigorously colourful as I mutter, 'Buggared and beggared', in the face of the hideous realization that there is no escape from being broken thus on my personalized version of the wheel of medieval torture. My escape is to return to the trading floor and to remember that there are many mortals who have more debilitating diseases, who are in worse pain and who die prematurely.

Chronic conditions like IBS, along with endogenous clinical depression, belong to that side of medicine where there are many conflicting and speculative scientific explanations but there are still no guarantees of cure. Statistics tell us that one in four people suffer from IBS and that they are predominantly women. Our more complex hormonal make-up is possibly to blame. Once a physician, or surgeon, has seen scans of a bowel that do not reveal any physiological abnormality, they are as much at sea with regard to treatment as the sufferer. Almost everything that cannot be biopsied into a visible pathology is doomed to frustrate conventional medical practitioners. My own theory, which one famous gastroenterologist specializing in IBS imperiously denounced as myth, is that the gut thrives in the dark. It does not respond well to the light, or to being manhandled. Almost twenty years ago I had unrelated and minor pelvic surgery whose bloody complications took the surgeon by surprise. My traumatized intestines had to be exposed to unfamiliar rays of light before being shuffled, as best as was possible, unceremoniously, back into place. Do my problems stem perhaps from that rude intervention?

In a personal communication Adrian Searle, the writer and fisherman, speculates on the likeness between gut and worm: 'I thought about how worms recoil from the light when you try to lift them from a wet lawn at night (collecting worms for fishing!). After my operation, my bowels would often 'stick together' during the contractions of peristalsis for months afterwards. This was excruciating.'

I have also come to realize that *I am* my pain although my pain is not me. If my karma is to live chained to pain, as Andromeda was chained to her rock, there is no trading to be done and just the challenging tasks of acceptance and endurance to wrestle with. Pain is my gym! I live in thrall; it is *la belle dame sans merci* who leaves me withering on the lonely hillside.

Fear had stopped me agreeing to have the only procedure that can confirm a diagnosis of IBS, as opposed to cancer or inflammable bowel disease; the investigation is accomplished through a colonoscopy that will exclude organic pathology. Colonoscopy is a procedure that is feared by many individuals beyond any rational explanation. This screening process has the reputation of being the most successful test of all in reducing any cancer-related death. If I break my rule not to Google 'disease', I find there are many hysterical Internet reports that compare the procedure to the worst pangs of a difficult birth. When you

Google 'colonoscopy' and read some of the public accounts of the procedure you might think you were reading accounts of a medieval torture. Even when it is, as it is most commonly, accompanied by intravenous sedation there are irrational rants about the sedation failing to take effect. Inevitably, the side effects of any procedure will depend upon individual physiology (every bowel has an ordnance-survey-map of its own) and the skills of the medical practitioner. There is something additional however about a procedure that enters into tabooed areas of the body that can provoke a primitive response.

People are more willing to discuss endoscopy than colonoscopy, mouth ulcers rather than anal piles, because the mouth and stomach are perceived to be cleaner and less hidden in darkness. They have better PR ratings. In 1985 President Ronald Reagan's widely publicized surgery for colon cancer was responsible for a surge of individuals throughout the country seeking consultations and colonoscopy tests for symptoms of bowel cancer, which they had previously been too frightened or too ashamed to address. 'The taboo against talking about colon and rectal cancer, about the elimination of wastes from the body, and about the bowels in general has been broken.' said Irving Rimer of the American Cancer Society.

When the fateful day arrived for my colonoscopy procedure, which followed ten years of frightened procrastination, I decided to forgo the anaesthetic, or any other form of sedation, although I had no intention of watching the internal camera's journey on the screen, while the choice of whether or not to be sedated seemed to mimic the dilemmas of childbirth… how unspeakable to wake up and find one had delivered a ripe tumour.

I was fortunate to have a gastroenterologist friend and colleague who was not embarrassed by our intimacy and who was willing to perform the procedure not only with superlative skill, but also with compassion for my terror. William Osler was the first physician to introduce medical students to the importance of the now almost archaic 'bedside manner'. He wrote: 'The good physician treats the disease; the great physician treats the patient who has the disease.' I am convinced that the healing process, in any context, occurs most successfully when this is the case; when technique is accompanied by kindness. It is an insult to medicine that surgeons have earned the reputation that emotional intelligence is unimportant in comparison to their surgical techniques. I dispute this fact and would suggest that the emotional condition, state of mind and reassurance with which a patient enters theatre have a correlation with the state of mind and speed with which the patient recovers from the anaesthetic and their surgery.

I did not experience any pain during the procedure, no shame at wearing the silly paper pants with a hole positioned to allow the head of the scope to be inserted into the anus, no embarrassment that the procedure was being carried out by a friend of Apollonian good looks. I became fascinated by the oceanic camera vistas once the team reported that things were looking good. It seems strange but true that throughout this dreaded procedure we conducted the same tenor of a conversation that might have taken place over any cup of coffee. Many therapists are inclined to distain the art of small talk, but it has a vital place in the training of all healers. My body was being investigated because it was a body in pain but how marvellous for it not to have become an investigation hedged about with taboos of shame. My bowel scored ninety-nine per cent for visible health, or something close. Fate, on this occasion, was on my side. It is possible that I would have felt differently towards my surgical friend if he had become the Hermetic messenger of bad tidings. Except, there were bad tidings, because still nobody knows how to heal me.

My thoughts frequently turn to the mysteries of digestion. The gut is the second most secretive, flexible member in the body's hierarchy. Its primeval character and autonomous responses to emotional life mimic the eternal mysteries of our brain. I must stand to correct myself, however. While the brain's complexity and strangeness makes it mysterious and awesome, when it is healthy we live in ignorance of this complex, regulatory computer which controls every movement of our being. Whereas, even in good health, the bowel often makes a daily appearance and can cause anxiety; its presence is felt in myriad ways, while other healthy organs remain silent. The brain's subjectivity and its precise relationship to the gut remains uncharted territory, even to the new discipline of devoted and increasingly frustrated neuro-gastro scientists. The intestines, however, are the most primitive of our organs. They are situated within the cavernous, bloody and impenetrable pelvis that in female form also contain the mysteries of the universe. Their evolution began with the lowly worm. There is a paradox that whereas the engaged mother receives her child's faecal matter as a visible gift, there is probably nothing, with regard to the body militia, that any adult dreads more than the shaming of a public episode of faecal incontinence. I have come to the conclusion that the bowel's protean activities and mysterious narratives of transit and transport are best described as a subterranean hybrid, or the vaults of the Brothers Grimms' *Fairy Tales*.

I was intrigued by more anarchic thoughts and allegories on a recent visit, my first, to the garishly renovated Sistine Chapel in Rome; intrigued by Michelangelo's dismissal of convention in his depiction of God. In the panel *The Creation of the Stars*, amidst a glory of angelic naked masculinity, he painted a posterior view of an otherwise fully draped body whose buttocks remain defiantly bare-arsed. It turns out to be an image of God as described in Exodus 33 where God is talking to Moses: 'And I will take away mine hand, and thou shalt see my back-parts: but my face shall not be seen'. Michelangelo's image of God's naked buttocks defied the treatise of one of the most influential art critics of the fifteenth century, Leon Battista Alberti and, more oddly, the newly anointed Pope's immediate attempt at censorship. Alberti's treatise specified: 'The obscene parts of the body and all those that are not very pleasing to look at, should be covered with clothing or leaves or the hand.' Pope Pius IV, a year after Michelangelo's death, called in the artist Daniele da Volterra to provide appropriate concealment to the pre-eminence in all the frescoes, including *The Last Judgement*, of naked masculinity (which earned Volterra the nickname *Il Braghettone* – the breeches maker).

As I gazed upon the last remaining and defiant fresco, Jung's heretical thoughts about holy deposits of divine turds came floating across my panorama. After a visit to Basel Cathedral, when Jung was aged between seven and nine – his father was a pastor – the young boy had wrestled, like Jacob, with an angel (albeit in Jung's case, unsuccessfully) to repress his dynamic thoughts of God squatting above the cathedral's dome, releasing explosive turds into the holy of holies. In my experience most children, and some adults, whose thoughts are not too repressed, love to defile or ridicule convention with iconoclastic fantasies of their profane acts of defacation.

Preoccupied myself, I have found it easy to understand why so many creative, powerful and forensically disturbed people have become obsessed by, or driven by their bowel, and its ceaseless production line of elimination. Were there a Scatological Society its membership would be vast, and predominately male. Its high priest would be François Rabelais, its most notorious member Adolf Hitler. In the distinguished ranks would be Martin Luther, Samuel Pepys, Swift, de Sade, Freud, Darwin, Proust, Gandhi, Beckett and Dr John Harvey Kellogg. In love letters to Nora Barnacle, James Joyce enthused: 'You had an arse full of farts that night, darling… big fat fellows, long windy ones, quick little merry cracks and a lot of tiny little naughty farties.'

While I was surfing the Net in search of some obscure information about the history of melancholy, I came upon another bizarre tribute to the bowel's tyranny. The following morbid anecdote serves to remind me what a leaking piece of work the diseased flesh of man is and how the 'wonder' of the body becomes a malodorous mess when disease reduces it to incurable toxic matter.

I found reference to King Philip IV's fit of overarching melancholy at the death of his son. Confused by the long list of Spanish kings named Philip, my memory cantered first towards Velasquez's equine portrait but uncovered instead Titian's earlier portrait of Philip II who, while arrayed in exuberant armour, displayed an exaggerated pallor of complexion which was perhaps due to acute anaemia. I was intrigued to find out more. During his reign, Philip II was regarded as the most powerful man in the European world and yet he could not escape – as none of us can – the ways in which even the greatest Majesty, when stalked by death, is subject to the anarchic demands of a tyrannical bowel. According to a curious and anonymous historical document, Philip was dying of terminal bowel cancer. In the last weeks of his life, his illness demanded that while publicly he lay in his royal apartment receiving statesmen and family, a crude hole be cut into the royal mattress through which his majesty could void his uncontrollable gut. Unpalatable images these may be, but they remind us that disease operates without decorum, or respect for even a majestic title.

I have spoken about the bowels being the most demeaned part of our body because of the sense of shame and the related taboo that eclipses their physiological genius. As with so many aspects of life, when our bowels are functioning normally, we take them for granted rather than celebrating their efficiency. What is surprising about this taboo, which declares our brilliant bowel to be an outcast from its own body, as if belonging to an untouchable caste, is that it continues to be endorsed by society. Yet, paradoxically, nothing delights mothers of the newborn more than the arrival of another healthy poo. Almost all children will, during early childhood, go through a natural stage of development in which they are fascinated and delighted by the forbidden nature of their faeces. They are excited by the mysterious invisibility of the bowel and the variety of sensational sounds and smells that it produces. This healthy interest when too overt transgresses adult convention. In order to be fully enjoyed, it is an interest that must take place both behind the adult back, but also close enough for the scatology to risk being witnessed, which is an important part of ritual and taboo. Freud referred to this infantile preoccupation as the 'anal stage' and although, within the confines of his theory, he considered it to be natural, and in most cases, like the Oedipal stage, something to be worked through without psychological impediment, in certain cases he associated it with a rigid adult pathology and prejudiced intimations of homosexuality.

Every parent will remember times when their child has been delighted, if not obsessed, by 'bottoms', 'wee' and 'poo talk'. I can recall driving a clutch of eight-year-old boys to school and the back of the car being gunpowder – alive with ribaldry about farts, bare bums and rude couplets. The success of Windy Mindy, even better described as *The World of David Walliams*, pays tribute to this taboo. I have, by co-incidence, just finished reading a memoir by the father of one of my patients in which he writes of his schooldays in Chemnitz, Germany during the 1920s: 'I remember a bizarre practice in my last year at the primary school. A boy would raise his hand to tell the Master that someone near him had 'made a pong' [*hat gemodert*]. A group of boys would then be sent into the corridor to smell each other's bottoms. The one found to have farted would receive a mild punishment.'

Now, it is Bell's turn to delight me because she still perceives me to be her co-conspirator against the grown-up world (which I am), with conversations about her 'butt' and the silliest or, I should say rudest, of songs. She even dares to confide to me – with her hypnotic and subversive blue eyes fixed on me – that she likes the smell of her wee. It is Bell and not Botox that makes me feel young.

A dark and involuntary association between childish prattle and the unspeakable forces its way into my mind and directs my narrative. In the murky world of pornography, the aspect of female domination that has the most viewings concerns images of non-consensual, violent anal sex. I have known of and felt sad about this statistic for years. I have nothing against consensual pornography. I will recommend 'vanilla' porn as a useful tool to couples who have become bored with 'mating in captivity'. I have written about pornography in the media but recently something happened when I read an article that I have been unable to exorcize. I have been a contributor to the *King's Review*, which is an online academic journal under the auspices of some of the fellows and post-doctoral students at King's College, Cambridge. It brings together academic journalism with current affairs. Besides their online presence, they publish a print edition once a year that is also distributed to contributors. One languid afternoon I was browsing through these hard copies when I found myself reading an article on porn that disgusted me:

> Back in 2001, Martin Amis asked producer John 'Buttman' Stagliano why anal is so popular in porn, even when at least one of the players has a vagina. 'Pussy is bullshit,' he explained: the pleasure women show during vaginal penetration can be faked. The pain of anal sex – roughed up with the insertion of extra fingers, extra cocks, objects bigger than cocks – is reassuringly concrete. 'Extreme porn' isn't about shared pleasure; it is a cathartic display of ordeal and survival… Tellingly, Stagliano told Amis that women 'pushed to the limit' in traumatic anal sex showed their 'virility'; their 'testosterone'.
>
> KATRINA ZAAT, *Pornworld*,
> SEPTEMBER 2014

The idea that women's ability to fake orgasm has long frustrated men was commented on by Ovid, writing in about 1 BCE in his treatise on the art of love. In the *Ars Amatoria* he recommends that while ideally lovers should enjoy themselves, if they can't then the woman should do a convincing con job. He counsels the courtesan: 'Fake your sweet pleasures with a false sound' (*Ars* 3.798). And: 'Only, when you're faking, be careful that you're not too obvious.' (*Ars* 3.801).

The power to fake sexual arousal and climax that Stagliano refers to, is unique to women whose sexual and reproductive organs and energies are concealed inside the mystery of their bodies, which patriarchal religions like to assert are 'unclean'. Or 'smelly'. The hidden nature of female sexuality provides women with a possibility of choice, repetition and control. How often are men unsettled by a random or awkward erection? Men are liable to be involuntarily unmasked in the sexual act during which they can never be certain, let alone predict how their errant cocks will perform and what they will or will not agree to do. These fleshy appendages are notoriously unreliable in following instruction or responding to desire. Cocks refuse schooling and their owners will often, reluctantly or gratefully, take to medication, without regard for any long-term consequences of addiction. Faking it is not an alternative for men, and for many the first fumbling and premature experiences of adolescence may herald a lifetime of performance anxiety.

Freud, who became increasingly pessimistic about human nature, also originated many false conjectures in his clinical theories of sexuality. As a result he did men, as well as women, an injustice. While I have great respect for his philosophical writing and the way he brought the unconscious into popular nineteenth century idiom, I see him as a confused father of sexuality. Instead of reflecting longer on his own and society's unconscious envy of the indomitable Palaeolithic Great Mother's womb, Freud published his hypothesis, or phantasy, that women continued to be potential hysterics. Even if their wombs no longer 'wandered', willy-nilly as the Greeks insisted, he pathologised women as suffering from fears of genital castration and of penis envy, which also armed and alarmed the 'masculine' and turned women into 'predators'. Freud seems to have turned a blind (or ignorant) eye to the inevitable and primordial traces of primitive misogyny, or fear that the female genitals understandably arouse. In spite of his interests in ancient mythology and statuary he did not, as far as I am aware, make reference to the occult and universal symbolism of the *vesica piscis;* an ancient and geometric symbol for both the vulva and the symbolic origins of the fertile universe. *Vesica piscis* is a symbol of birth or regeneration that is recorded in almost all world religions since the earliest pagan times. In Tantra it was referred to as 'Yoni' and the words literally translate as the vessel or bladder of the fish, in itself a symbol of Christian iconography, but the symbol gathered accretions of misogyny because of the colloquial, denigrating associations that the vulva smells like a fish. In his poem about his mother *Kaddish,* Alan Ginsberg refers to his mother's body: 'the Monster of the Beginning womb'.

Freud's theory of fears of castration and penis envy were penned when few women were confident enough to challenge openly the ballocks of his myth, which then became a cocksure and quasi-scientific part of the nineteenth and twentieth century male *zeitgeist.* Freud's interpretations of female phantasies of castration do not take into account the violent genital mutilations of the labia still practised legally, not only across the majority of Africa but other parts of the world, and which were practised for many years before Freud wrote a word.

Why is it that for many males and an increasing number of competitive young females, non-consensual forms of cruelty which some porn sites revel in have become universally addictive? And now the menacing intimations of the Darknet provide an even more debased temptation to seek out twisted knowledge. What is it about our fallen, human and unkind nature that turns Wordsworth's infant at his mother's breast, who drinks in the feelings of his mother's eye, into a plunderer of the female body?

How apposite that the laptop I am writing on is named Apple, with its iconography of that mythic bite from the fallen apple. Who can predict the fallen depths of Tartarus to which the genies of computer technology and the Internet will deliver us? To what subterranean currents of dehumanization must our 'rough beast' still descend? Wallace Stevens, in his essays on reality and the imagination, in *The Necessary Angel,* warned:

> The mind has added nothing to human nature. It is a violence from within that protects us from violence without. It is the imagination pressing back against the pressure of reality. It seems, in the last analysis, to have something to do with our self-preservation; and that no doubt is why the expression of it, the sounds of its words, help us to live our lives. [1951]

What is happening to our minds? Our selves? I will leave it to others to answer and analyse, but the non-consensual porn world knows nothing of kindness and its presence is kindling a cataclysmic ending of mutual erotic engagement. The Internet inferno is being pursued by a younger audience, which now includes female teenagers who are becoming equally greedy for the sensational, and whose first passive experience of sexuality is often a porn site. The Internet provides its porn audience with ever escalating narratives of the degradation of pleasurable sexual intimacy. These viewers unwittingly become desensitized to other non-sensationalized experiences of Eros, which demand play, mischief, imagination, patience, intimacy and trust. While I do not want to condemn every action and thought that transgresses social conventions, these descending levels of plunder of the body, which so often focus on non-consensual humiliations seem to be infinite, as does the human appetite for corruption.

In the *King's Review* article there is another gut-wrenching discussion about what it means to society when men have become comfortable to witness, as entertainment, other men through acts of anal sex, transfer bacteria and the risk of e-coli infections directly from the women's bowel into her mouth or her cervix. Can such nonconsensual violations be an acceptable solution to the twenty-first century's viral affliction with boredom and addiction to crude sensations? Are there no limits to the wanton unkindness and humiliation that human beings will, unlike any other animal, succumb? Something is wrong with the world. Something is wrong with me. A rough and ravenous beast is not slouching but hurtling itself towards Bethlehem.

Humankind, human beings, kith and kin, kindred, mankind, kind, and kindness have been the weave and weft of my narrative and yet the semantic link, the umbilical cord between mankind and kindness has snapped. Perhaps it was ever thus, but today the awesome wonders and contributions to collective knowledge of Internet technology also provide us with instant access *ad infinitum* to the most ungodly deeds of humankind. It is important not to demonize our own times but to remember that the principle differences between 'now' and 'then' are the changes in the means of communication. The Internet has democratized both the process and the speed by which evil actions can be globally communicated as they unfold. One only has to read *King Lear* or other Jacobean dramas to know that demonic acts of evil have always perjured human nature, but they were transmitted through language rather than indecent and viral imagery. 'Hell is empty and all the devils are here.' [William Shakespeare, *The Tempest*]

The noun 'mankind', most likely, is related by philology to 'Godcund', or the divine. Job, of the Old Testament, is not alone in his experiences of the pitiless arrows of suffering inflicted by the divine. In Middle English, the adjective 'kind' or 'cynn', carried an implication of looking after others, or of being kind to one's kith and kin. 'Cynn' can be translated both as family and as behaving in a humanist, or humankind way. There is another metaphoric association to the family of 'cynn' being understood as a web of genetic life that is also expressed through DNA as a tangled ladder of associations. Boethius, the medieval philosopher who inspired Chaucer, pre-empted an imaginative equivalent of DNA through his metaphor of a 'Great Chain of Being'. He imagined the vertically linked and hierarchically connective web of humankind in a psychic premonition of what would evolve and grow into the Internet.

The body in pain, the gutted body, whether it is our personal body, the body politic, or the universe, is ravenous for human kindness. It seems as if the linked words of the kind-ness of existence, our being-ness in the world, not only risk becoming obsolete, but their meaning is falling upon a fatal epidemic of deaf ears. Man *must* be reminded that 'he jests at scars that never felt a wound'. [William Shakespeare, *Romeo and Juliet*]

> Remember in the forms of speech comes change
> Within a thousand years, and words that then
> Were well esteemed, seem foolish now and strange;
> And yet they spake them so, time and again,
> And thrived in love as well as any men;
>
> CHAUCER, *Troilus and Cressida*

144

6

DIDO'S LAMENT

Just then as Odysseus returned to his land after twenty years
Death came to his faithful dog Argos whose eyes closed in darkness

HOMER'S Odyssey

I SPENT MY CHILDHOOD RESCUING FLEDGLINGS THAT HAD
fallen from their nests and kittens threatened with drowning, and I often had a tame mouse concealed in my scratchy
school pocket. Watching chicks being hatched and cradling
them in my palms in the back yard, when I was 'outsourced' to
a Westgate-on-Sea boarding house during the summer holidays,
was like participating in the Eleusinian mysteries. Ever since that
Charterhouse afternoon, when I held a passionate armful of
golden cocker, I pined to have a dog. My mother had a detest-
able habit of dispatching anything I had rescued that was small
enough down the lavatory, or if it was too large of 'sending' it 'to
the country'. I did not acquire the dog that I pined for until I was
married and we bought our first Hungarian Magyar Vizsla, along
with a quorum of Eastern cats. Ali was a Vizsla, a Hungarian
pointer, who arrived at King's Cross Station in a twine basket –
not at Paddington like Paddington Bear. Incredulously, except
it was 1974, he travelled from the Hebrides chaperoned by his

breeder as far as Inverness Station, where he was deposited in the arms of a co-operative stranger. He arrived at King's Cross with an identity label attached to the basket, along with feeding instructions, which included a request not to be repelled when we discovered that Vizslas are by nature addicted to rolling in smelly, dead things.

To convey how much Ali transformed our family dynamic and fulfilled our lives, I need to speak not so much about his life, as about the effects of his death. Ali was ten and in seeming good health when he died suddenly and unexpectedly. Every night he would retire to the corner of our seven-year-old son's bed. They had become inseparable since Ali, while a pup, discovered Alex's highchair was a food source from underneath which he could hoover up all sorts of morsels. It was a winter's night in 1984 when I noticed Ali sink on to Alex's eider quilt with a plangent sigh. I thought nothing more until our reverberating house woke us past midnight. Victorian floorboards are vibrant things. Ali was in the throes of a major seizure, or epileptic fit, which Alex slept through. We did not know what was happening as our gentle animal turned into a snarling beast. After the fit and our terror had subsided, we hurried Ali well before dawn to our vet where it was judged humane to put him to sleep. The alternative would have been to subject him to a battery of tests and scans. Epilepsy is unpredictable, and an unreliable dog is not safe with young children. Perhaps we need not have acted so precipitately, but the impact of one fit had left us afraid of risking another. I heard from his breeder that on the same night, somewhere else in the country, his sibling had also expired, although more peacefully in a deep sleep and without fitting. Their allotted dog-starred-days were over.

Alex woke to Ali's disappearance from the end of his bed without preparation. He was tearful and very angry that we had failed to give him time to hug Ali goodbye. I am not sure Alex has ever recovered from the shock of Ali's nocturnal disappearance because it was his first experience of the permanent loss of a beloved 'object'. His forgiveness was not forthcoming. His relentless distress seemed to compound our loss. It was only later on, when we had finished grieving and acquired another dog, this time a sturdy and gleaming German pointer called Troy that Alex began to recover. Long past childhood, Alex remained scarred by Ali's unannounced disappearance, along with his harsh acquisition of knowledge of what can happen to change life between night and day.

By coincidence, only a matter of weeks after Ali's death my mother died almost as unexpectedly at the age of sixty-three. She had been suffering from chronic heart disease for several years. My mother dreaded going to the doctor as much as I do and had turned a blind eye to her symptoms until it became impossible for her to walk down the road without clutching a small bottle of Evian. Climbing stairs had become as difficult to manage as balancing on a tightrope. Problems with breathing forced her to submit to an examination, after which the cardiologist insisted she should at once be admitted to hospital. As she was not considered to be in any immediate danger her angiographic procedure was delayed until the following day, as her surgeon was required to perform emergency surgery elsewhere. Observance of our relationship, which was never enthusiastic, had become reluctant, although she had proved a devoted grandmother. I went to the hospital to visit her on what became the penultimate night of her life. I remember grudgingly buying some flowers on my way. I selected three gerbera daisies and recall now with shame that although they were then still exotic blooms they were not flowers, or even colours, that I liked. Gerberas remind me of carnations, which I find more artificial even than 'sunless dry geraniums'. There is a gaping morass between duty and engaged states of mind and this memory leaves a bad taste in my mouth and my conscience which cannot be eradicated. My mother choked and, as a consequence of asphyxiation, died while eating her supper that night.

The earth did not move, there were no shooting stars and tears did not fall after her death; neither were they frozen with grief. I returned to the hospital where I gazed on her emptied face and gave her a parting kiss. I wanted to cry out to the angels to take care of her, and of me, or to wail in what I always oddly think of as a keening lament of Sicilian widow-grief. My absence of tears brought back childhood memories of a time when I believed that I could not live without my mother. I was quite grown-up when even her brief absence caused me traumatic alarm. If we occasionally stayed in a hotel and she left me in the bedroom while she went downstairs to play cards, I would roam the corridors howling. Instead of grieving at her death, I was grieving for all the times when she had not been there when I wanted – no, not wanted but when I *needed* – her. I was startled to discover that the only tears I shed in the subsequent weeks and months were all for Ali. Ali's life had become a vessel which contained precious memories of escapades, ritualized walks on Hampstead Heath, high days and holidays filled with mischief, joy and sadness, which we shared during the time that he grew into a passionate part of Alex and of our family.

I have discovered that mourning is a privilege. When there are not enough memories of joy and engagement, nor of sorrows shared and soothed, grief may become replaced by lonely regret, or a melancholy for what might have been. I wish the world had been eclipsed with grief when my mother died, but nothing happened. I was spared the pain of loss but not of regret, which is a tragic but truthful indictment of our relationship. I have, I hope appropriately, sometimes shared these awkward sensations and thoughts with some other people whose landscapes also did not change in the face of intimate loss. I hope our consultations have helped them to understand and to be consoled to discover that an authentic experience of mourning has to be earned during a lifetime; it is not a biological given.

After our ten-year love affair with Ali, our family became addicted to Hungarian Vizslas. We adore them for their extravagant, russet-beech colours, and their amber eyes. Viszlas have resin claws and a nose that is colour-matched to their autumnal coat. They are the only canine breed whose gene-pool has coordinated its accessories from head to toe. Is it any wonder that Piero di Cosimo immortalized an ancestor in his painting *A Satyr mourning over a Nymph* in the National Gallery? They are themselves living works of art, with wilfully affectionate and sensitive natures, who have velvet ears, flopped as any bat's wing. Their athletic frames are lithe and powered with rippling muscles that can knock the wind out of you as they fling themselves against your calf. They were used in the days of the Austro-Hungarian Empire as carriage and retrieving dogs that ran with the hunter alongside the carriage in pairs. They were not reared to see the inside of any kennel but by a Habsburg royal decree, only their master's sofa, hearth and bedchamber. Or bed.

Before Hungary became a communist republic, Vizslas were, by royal statute, only permitted to be owned by the aristocracy.

All times change... Post the 1956 Revolution, when citizens wanted to broadcast the privilege of freedom, the ownership of the aristocratic Vizsla became an egalitarian if expensive statement. Their fate resembles that of the over-sized pedigree dogs purchased in Russia following perestroika; having lost their novelty, they were abandoned and now roam Moscow and St Petersburg in mostly harmless but hungry packs; some of them have discovered how to travel from park to parkland by the city metro. Hungarian cities and its countryside are now overwhelmed with starving Vizsla dogs. European animal charities, such as Vizslamenti, are hard at rescue work. The noble Hungarian Magyar Vizsla is capable of producing a litter of up to fourteen greedy, irrepressible and destructive pups. Inevitably, when their naïve and irresponsible owners discover these litters are impossibly challenging and expensive to rear and feed, they often abandon them to the highway. The same thing is happening to the refugee and migrant children in Europe, whom we are treating as highway litter.

When John and I were setting out on our careers, we were working at the Royal Court Theatre. There, we met an Australian immigrant couple who were older than us and had three adorable children. I have always been drawn to the company of children. The mother, Helen, was a charismatic creature who was capable of success at whatever she put her mind or hand to, while at the same time making it all seem effortless. She was already the Royal Court's casting director and a theatre producer in the making. I fell equally and differently in love. Russell was twice my age and worked as a behavioural psychologist at the Maudesley Hospital alongside Hans Eysenck; inevitably he was sceptical of my growing fascination with Freud and the unconscious. He had blue eyes that astonished everyone and which I found hypnotic. They are still vivid in my memory long after his death. Russell persuaded me, or perhaps it was his eyes that convinced me, that the panic attacks I suffered from were programmed by the autonomous nervous system, not my unconscious, which was a concept he refuted. I was too impressionable and adoring to argue. I used his unfamiliar words about autonomic systems as my mantra to fend off panic. They worked! Russell was a *bon viveur* who taught John about wine and set us both on our lifelong journey into the culinary arts via Elizabeth David and Michelin cuisine. Helen juggled silk kaftans, white truffles, pike quenelles, martinis, nappies and kitchen-sink chaos, all with equal panache; she conducted her life like a carnival. I was also in love with their children who looked as if they had stepped out of a fairy tale. The first time I felt grown up was when I took the oldest one, six-year-old Amanda, to tea at Selfridges. The moment when Amanda, wearing a tartan pleated skirt and Fair Isle jumper – she might have been one of the Cottingley fairies – emerged out of the Royal Court stage door and climbed into our VW beetle, I knew that I wanted to become a mother.

Our sense of privilege knew no bounds when an annual invitation to spend Christmas with their family became one of the rituals of our year. I have never been fond of Christmas, which had only ever amounted to an excuse for an even greater degree of neglect in my family. It was Christmas 1976 when something awful happened. We were gathered around the Christmas table and the chatter became an admiring silence while Russell carved the goose. I was in awe of the other guests, among them the playwright John Osborne and his wife, the critic Helen Dawson. Our host plunged in with his prized Tojiro knife, just as our inquisitive beast, Ali, lifted his nose above the tablecloth. The Tojiro sliced the nose. There was no blood but only a slicing of bone. Russell loved dogs and had two of his own; it was not intentional but I was speechless with indignation. Once more we moved precipitately and embarked on Ali's first nocturnal visit to Pimlico and the veterinary office of our eccentric friend Judith Iffey, who scorned the seasonal and almost everything else in life except for animals and her inheritance of Habsburg antique jewellery. With contempt for the human race and a sigh of despair, Judith prepared Ali's nose for midnight surgery.

Judith was an exceptionally glamorous divorcee and aristocratic migrant from Communist Europe, who lived and practised at 55 Elizabeth Street, Pimlico – an address which continues, forty years on, to house Central London's main emergency veterinary practice. Judith had disposed of her husband and lived alone with several Eastern cats and an amazing collection of jewellery, of which she once displayed one item when we took her to the theatre wearing a tiara to see Alex Guinness and Simone Signoret in *Macbeth*; it was not a successful excursion. Judith also disliked children, so once Tanya was born our relationship reverted to a professional one.

Judith had her own emergencies. The first floor of her Pimlico house contained not only her hoard of exotic jewels but also a settlement of crepuscular chinchilla rodents that were susceptible to heart attacks and at risk of falling off their perches at any unexpected sound or intrusion. I was impressed that balls of fluff had such sentience. When, some years later, Judith, having become increasingly eccentric fell into a morbid state of melancholy, we were no longer her confidants. She had deluded herself that she was suffering from a self-diagnosed terminal cancer. Now I wonder whether it could have been a form of psychosis triggered by the menopause. Seated at her consulting-room desk with two purring cats on her lap, wearing the treasured tiara and goodness knows whether much else, she administered a lethal dose of phenobarbitone to herself, and the cats… The post-mortem autopsy found no indication of any physical malignancy and recorded a verdict of death by misadventure.

I am blessed that John agreed to our home becoming a menagerie, for its inmates have saved me from my *lamenti* of being born into an uncomfortable and often disgusting world. When I am in my consulting room and listening to someone whose relationship is breaking up, or perhaps it might be someone who has a teenager suffering from untimely depression, or it could be anyone speaking about anything, they may comment: 'One of the things that would make me more content and be a consolation would be to own a dog, but the nature of my life makes it impossible.' I rejoice that the compatibility of my partnership has made it possible for us to share our home with a long inventory of animals. My being indulged in the matter of such demanding lifestyle choices may not have been coincidental in guaranteeing the longevity of our marriage. We have shared our bedroom with three wilful Vizslas, two Boxers and one German pointer. Twice, the Vizslas have been accompanied by drooling 'sibling' Boxers, which John, to counter my Vizsla obsession, has declared his favourite breed. Today, it is our youngster, the divine Dido, who rules our household with as many demands and rituals as a neurotic suffering from obsessional compulsive disorder. Foolishly, and at our peril, we celebrate every breath she exhales. Dido's imperiousness took us unawares. We thought we had grown into experienced Vizsla handlers, but she is a diva. No lament for Aeneas, her refrain is 'My will is thy will!'

Before I speak more of Dido's wild heart, or of her adored Vizsla predecessor, Lucy, who was a less entitled beast, I want to record John's indulgence of our farmyard-home. He was midwife and paramedic to litters of Burmese kittens and had to become adept at climbing, past midnight, over park railings to release inappropriate and overgrown creatures into the Royal London Parks. There was Jemima Puddle-Duck, whom we purchased as a wisp of fluff at the end of one glorious Suffolk summer holiday and who grew up to be an enormous white beast with a penchant for waking our neighbours at dawn. It became one of John's Twelve Labours to bundle Jemima into a twine basket, to clamber over spiked railings and to release her on to the lake in Regent's Park late at night.

In addition to the mice and hamsters that frequently went forth and multiplied, often in a child's mattress, our front hall housed a community of rabbits, in whom the rest of the family soon lost interest. Rabbits are intelligent creatures that are even receptive to house training, but they do not fare well with hunting dogs. Some bucks when threatened can become as aggressive as pit-bull terriers. One of ours did. Our vet told us there was a colony of rabbits in Kensington Gardens, which was led by a similarly vicious character. In the middle of another night John departed on another Labour, with yet another wicker basket of overgrown Oeyctolagus cuniculus.

Dido's predecessor was a Vizsla called Lucy who was the canine love of my life and object of my worshipful tutelage. It would be impossible for another dog ever to replace her. Yet here I pause to thank another dawn, to welcome the blue patch of returning sky, and to delight in Dido's energetic breath beside me. Her delicious wet nose nuzzles as we wake up to celebrate another day, but Dido is a restless sleeper and as insomniac as me. I think she suffers from bad dreams as her body shudders, her paws flex and clench, attended by small whimpers and snarls. She snores insufferably all night and lives in mortal dread of seeing a moth, which spooks her for hours; I demur to her neuroses in mindless devotion. Once you hit three score years and ten and have seen many oaks felled before you, it feels politic to thank Fate for allowing you to wake complete to the challenges of another dawn. Dido stretches languidly, but systematically, and yawns; I imitate her aerobics as I stretch out my spine.

Dido has gradually become the Queen of our Hearth, Home and Bed but inevitably her living presence is a reminder of Lucy's absence. Slowly, Dido has become as much a comfort to me as the nightingale was to Keats, except that she does not 'pour forth her soul in such an ecstasy'. She summons her voice – and I do not mean she barks – with complaint, joy, hunger, disapproval, and delight at hearing Bell come downstairs. We have never had such a dog, a beast with a vocal range from a plaintive whine to sublime crooning song, who uses her voice to alert you to everything she is thinking. Or so it foolishly seems to her Carthaginian slaves.

Dido arrived a year after Lucy dramatically died of a hemangiosarcoma. What a menacing word that is. It is the name of a symptomless tumour, which usually remains invisible until it becomes too late to treat; a trickster cancer that suffocates the heart – as relentlessly as does my trickster columbine bind the plant – until it implodes into seas of arterial blood. Lucy died, or drowned in her own blood, on the penultimate night before the Olympics in 2012, when she collapsed without warning. I vowed, as I watched Lucy dying, that I could never go through the pain of such Vizsla love again. So much for my resolve…

My adoration of Lucy was unconditional; she was without Dido's exasperating sense of entitlement. I invested everything into our relationship that seemed too complicated for me to deal with in human intercourse. Even the inconvenience of her acute fly phobia, which meant that we could never open a window or the garden doors in summer, was a privilege. We had no warning that one morning she would be bounding round Regent's Park nosing out scraps from the overflowing summer picnic bins, and by the evening she would be drawing her last breath. To the very end, Lucy was distracted by the scent of her quarry; that morning she chased, full throttle, from one side of Regent's Park lake to the other to empty a litterbin. Lucy, a divine part of myself for almost eleven years, was dying. She was not, as the vet initially suspected, poisoned by park litter, but was suffocating from an invisible sarcoma. For precision's sake, and death's measure is precise, her life was extinguished by an injection of phenobarbitone at 5 p.m. on Friday, 27 July 2012. John, Alex and I cradled her.

It is only in my love for our canine beasts that I have experienced the joys of a passionate relationship that has not been fretted with ambivalent interactions by my volatile nature. Lucy lived through her heart and fittingly it was her heart that stole the life force from her. No! Lucy lived life through nose and limb, a sassy, beautiful beast, who loved the scent of a small dead thing. Her special delight was to throw herself into a reeking heap of fox dung and then to hurl herself against our bruised shins. A born hunter and retriever, Lucy imagined Regent's Park into heath and highland. On her last day she ran the park like a gazelle and scattered the bone-scented-air with the remains of an Olympian picnic or two.

Inevitably, as I have accompanied many of our animals, at the close of their lives, towards a painless death, I have strong feelings about the virtues of euthanasia, or assisted dying, which for human beings is not lawful in the UK, and I campaign for Dignity in Dying. It is not the thought of dying that is to be dreaded but the hours or days of suffering that so often precede death. There have been advancements in the science and arts of palliative care but in reality the robust hospice-charity PR often falls far short of its promise of a pain-free death. Too many people, despite protest, will face extinction in unspeakable pain and terror, with their dying organs under stressful scrutiny. Cancer dances the dying without prohibition. Death's arrow or paintbrush, so busy in medieval imagery, has grown loath to challenge terminal suffering. Who can look at the triptychs of Roger Van de Weyden, with those terrifying eyes of judgement and the morass of tormented limbs, without dread? Dying is rarely an easy task but its course becomes impeded when intubation and the wanton use of antibiotics unite against an inevitable demise. We have no legal rights, or choice, as to how we die beyond the limitations of preparing a Living Will. Mine is ready.

To sit beside a dying animal that has come to the end of its lifespan and whose limbs have become immobilized by disease, and to watch the process of euthanasia being expertly administered, ideally in the tranquillity of home, is a poignant thing. During a marriage that has been serially enhanced by the companionship of cats and dogs, inevitably we have become accustomed to the practice of euthanasia. While writing this chapter another companion, John's geriatric boxer Danny Boy, has come to the end of the road. Boxers are not inclined to longevity but Danny Boy accomplished the grand age of fourteen. He possessed eyes like moist earth, with agate-band pupils, and devoid of any Vizsla entitlement. He was a rescue dog who never shared with us the secret of his unspoken beginnings. To sit beside a dog that is being 'put to sleep' is an ordeal, yet to watch Danny Boy's exhausted eyes and paralysed limbs slip from an induced coma towards the unknown was our privilege. Danny's eyes, so wide and distinguished, still haunt me. Because they did not close, even in death, they still follow me from beyond his opaque bourne.

Danny Boy, unlike Lucy, was privileged to die at home. When the palliative-care vet, who was a stranger, arrived for the consultation, her face looked tear-stained and it did not take much imagination to know why she had been delayed. She proceeded with her morbid task fastidiously while we, already agitated, felt assaulted by the rituals of paperwork and preparation. 'Please get on with it!' Later, I realized that while we were anxious for Danny Boy's inevitable end, the vet's needs were different. In order for a stranger to enter into the midst of our grief, someone who was going to leave our threshold with a heavy corpse, it was essential for her to proceed with a proper sense of dignity and pride in her work.

As we stretchered Danny Boy towards the waiting van with three pallbearers in attendance, for a dog of thirty kilos is a blind-heavy thing, I commented that his open eyes were following me. The vet explained that was where the custom of weighing down a dead man's eyes with pennies, so that they could no longer disturb the living had its origin. I discovered later that the Greeks, with whom she thought the custom had begun, had other more hopeful intentions. They placed gold coins on the eyelids of their deceased to signify to Charon the Ferrymen that money was no object in ensuring a safe passage. I expect the ancient Egyptians followed a similar fiscal send-off to their Land of Fields. It does not surprise me that the eyes are the focus of legend. While breathing is the first and last thing that *all* animals do, it is the eyes that communicate the soul's agony. The gut may continue to work posthumously, the nails and hair to grow, but, when the last breath is exhaled, the eyes relinquish their glow and a shroud descends on the living and the departed. It was not until I woke later that night to morbid thoughts that in Danny Boy's extinction I saw intimations of my own demise.

I cannot speak about eyes or the numinous, without reference to our feral beast, Zen, who is the smallest of cats and who adopted us on Christmas Day, 2015. During the previous autumn I had became aware of an echo of a mew in a piece of wasteland behind our garden. I tried to answer across the night. Nobody replied until Christmas Day, when Dido alerted us to a canine form so small, the cat had caught himself inside of our trellis. He's stayed ever since. Zen is wickedly black and more precious to our household than any motionless holiday gift. His eyes gleam out of another unknowable and mysterious past like emeralds beyond price.

I am aware that it is more characteristic for me to cry out to deaf angels than it is to write about celebration. The imperious beast, Dido, not without struggle, has become my canine consort in celebration. After an initial resentment that she can never be Lucy, I embrace almost every filament of her entitled nature, even when she is smothered in foxy dung. But, her presence – despite her fleetness of foot which strangely reminds me of the lame struggler left behind (or perhaps it is myself) when the lost children followed the Pied Piper into his cave – cannot compensate for Lucy's absence.

Whenever I returned home, I called out: 'Lucy, Lucy...' and she, like Odysseus' faithful dog Argos, greeted my homecoming.

Jane Haynes

Thus Nature spake – The work was done –
How soon my Lucy's race was run!
She died, and left to me
This heath, this calm and quiet scene;
The memory of what has been,
And never more will be.

WILLIAM WORDSWORTH, *'Lucy'*

7

BLOOD ON THE TRACKS

'It will have blood, they say. Blood will have blood.'

WILLIAM SHAKESPEARE, Macbeth

DOGS HAVING TAKEN A PRIORITY IN OUR FAMILY LIFE, there had to be some sacrifices, and any desire for frequent long-distance travel has been extinguished. My only exception has been my passion for India and an intuitive affinity with my deracinated Russian heritage that made me long to visit that country. I need only a headscarf to look like a Russian peasant. When an opportunity appeared, which later developed into the offer of working in St Petersburg on a regular basis, it was one of the holy and high days of my life.

I am not certain how many times I have visited St Petersburg over the years. My first professional visit took place when I was invited to participate in a London based training programme to bring Jungian clinical practice to the notice of the Eastern European Institute of Psychoanalytic Studies. St Petersburg is not a city of certainty. Built upon quicksand and marsh by Swedish prisoners of war, it upholds many versions of reality. It has an unruly and Dionysian heart. My arrival in St Petersburg felt like a homecoming and I sensed an affinity with even casual acquaintances. There were later times of daydream when I imagined relinquishing my identity, my responsibilities, my life and becoming a missing person under the city's buried quicksand.

I discovered St Petersburg not only has notoriously poor foundations but its landscape camouflages reality. You cannot be certain whether your experiences are reliable or even credible. My first visit coincided with the sinking of the *Kursk* submarine in the Barents Sea, some time in August 2000. Through circumstances which will unfold, I found myself, in a trance-like state of wonder, accompanied by Igor Brodsky to St Nicholas's Naval Cathedral on the banks of the Neva. Igor had recently been retired from his duties as technical captain of the *Kursk*'s sister submarine, the *Voronezh*. The mourners, mainly women with children, were wailing sirens beside the rows of open and grief-laden coffins. Eastern Orthodoxy does not conceal its dead from devotional or curious eyes. Shawled, and mistaken for a citizen, I felt privileged to be entering a hallowed space of national grief with a sub-mariner as my chaperone.

How foolish of me to have thrown away my old passport, deformed by so many officious visa appendages, which recorded the dates of my earliest visits. I shall not forget the moment when having not yet grasped the inflexible nature of a Russian visa, I extended the dates of my visit but not my visa and was arrested at St Petersburg airport. The experience of passing through Russian customs always makes me feel as though there is a chance of being dispatched to Siberia. There are so many computer buttons to be pressed, sullen sighs and an agitation of turned pages before the thud of the stamp. It was only when I was walking across the tarmac towards the welcome British Airways gangway that a fist descended. My visa was out of date. Immigration, who take pleasure in sadism of this sort, had allowed me, without comment, to pass through passport control, only to have the Airport Police pursue me. After interrogation and a significant dent of thousands of rubles in my American Express credit card limit, I was allowed to board the plane.

St Petersburg is nicknamed the 'Jungle City' by many of its inhabitants, despite being one of the most picturesque cities in the world. A city where citizens leave home after breakfast without any guarantee of a safe return, where trams run over pedestrians and policemen demand cash bribes on the spot. It is a city where I became as accustomed to hailing a random car, as do all the locals, and asking for a lift in return for a few rubles, as being chauffeur-driven in a limo. There were a few people still alive, of whom I had a salutary reminder at the end of my first lecture, who remembered the horror of having to eat their pets, along with the bodies of the dead, in order to survive the famine that accompanied the Siege of Leningrad. It is a city both cruel and sensual in its celebration of free-floating Dionysian ecstasy where friendship, generosity, secrets – not the disillusion of politics, or the frequently devalued ruble – are the staples of its indestructible citizens' premium economy.

I stayed at one of the most beautiful and historic hotels in the world, the Astoria Hotel. Built in 1912, it was where Hitler planned to hold a banquet to celebrate his Russian victory. It was in the adjoining Angleterre Hotel that the revolutionary and despairing poet Sergei Yesenin slit his wrists and scrawled his last poem in his own blood before hanging himself from the heating pipes on the ceiling of his room.

Oh, my birch-tree woods! Amazing pictures!
Oh, my dear land! My sandy plains!

In the face of crowds of mortal creatures
I'm unable to conceal my pains.

Poetry has always carried a higher status in Russia than anywhere else in the world. Throughout both the Revolution and
the Stalin Terror it was not uncommon for poets to commit
suicide out of an existential political despair, or to be murdered
by the authorities. The poet Osip Mandelstam, like so many of
his contemporaries who had not left before Stalin's purges, came
to a tragic end when Stalin ordered his arrest for a second time.
Osip was exiled to the insurmountable perils of Siberia and died
in a transit camp on his way to the Gulag in 1936. He wrote: 'I do
not know how it is elsewhere, but here, in this country, poetry is
a healing, life-giving thing, and people have not lost the gift of
being able to drink of its inner strength. People can be killed for
poetry here – a sign of unparalleled respect – because they are
still capable of living by it.'

Despite the Astoria's exotic history, its crystal-chandelier
gravitas and its unique view across St Isaac's square towards
the brooding mass of the cathedral, it is another location in the
'Jungle City' where anything and everything, even the unspeakable, happens before your eyes. Then, like the three wise Japanese
monkeys, nobody, *but nobody at all*, sees, speaks or hears anything – anything at all.

During my professional visits to St Petersburg I had experiences that took me beyond my focus of lecturing and training
students to become psychotherapists. I made astonishing friendships. I observed how my companions blanched, how every
voice was hushed, when we drove past the façade of the House
of Officers on Liteyny Prospekt, popularly nicknamed the 'Big
House' or Boshoy Dom. It was the local headquarters of the

NKVD the law-enforcement agency of the Soviet Union which was the ruthless instrument of the Communist Party bosses. (Later it became the local headquarters of the KGB, which has since been unsuccessfully whitewashed into the Federal Security Service, or the FSB.)

It is a city where I have drunk so many celebratory shots of neat vodka that to avoid becoming seriously intoxicated I often had to resort to emptying my glass beneath the tablecloth when I thought that my hosts were not looking. Alcohol has never agreed with me. I drank almost no wine or spirits until I worked in Russia, but there I found that it is impossible to spend time with Russian citizens without toasting Life and Fate with vodka shots. It is a city where I have stayed up until dawn breaks to enjoy the fabled White Nights. On one such night I was taken to Putin's favourite restaurant where knowledgeable diners select and fish, or in my case just fish, sturgeon out of a well-stocked lake. I watched Putin, surrounded by his myrmidons, jump into the water to secure a fist-caught meal.

St Petersburg can intoxicate you with its culture and terrify you with its violence. On a January visit, when the temperature was minus twenty degrees, I woke up with the novelty of a vertigo attack, which was so violent that I thought I was having a fatal stroke. I had spent a restless night feeling as though I was falling off my pillow, only to wake up and find I could barely stand up. In those moments of panic I could not decide whether to die alone in my guest room, or attempt to struggle down to Reception in my pyjamas. It was not the cold that had triggered the vertigo.

The evening before, I had been invited to a concert at the Philamonia where Shostakovich's son, Maxim, was to conduct his father's Eighth Symphony. I left the theatre with a mixture of elation and emotional awe. As we walked towards the waiting car,

I tried to avert my eyes from the cruel spectacle of the Nevsky Prospekt's tourist attraction – chained and dancing bears. In the biting cold, the animals were now freezing into statuary. As our car returned to St Isaac's Square, I heard a pistol shot ring through the frozen air, but assumed it to be a confused echo of the symphony still resounding in my ears. My companion's driver, a man better described as his minder, ignored my frightened uncertainty as he opened the door and seized my arm. He thrust me past a trio of expensive men who were crouched in the hotel portico where they seemed to be shielding something with their bodies. Snow tracks were changing before my eyes into rivers of what looked like cardinal blood. I was pushed through the revolving door and propelled myself into the cloakrooms where I threw up. In blind hysteria, I tried to return to the portico but a porter intercepted me and escorted me to the lift. A gloved hand pressing too tightly against my neck answered my protest. 'Everything is fine, calm down, madam. You seem distressed. Would you like me to call Room Service or ask our Medical Aid Team to visit you? A very good night, madam.'

When I had almost recovered from my frightening but transient attack of vertigo, I stumbled into my clothes and forced myself down to the foyer where, with a palpitating heart and dry mouth, I walked towards the revolving door. A starched maid was buffing brassware; the threshold was glorious with dazzling sunlight on the newly fallen snow. A smiling manager glided across the marble floor and commended, in impeccable English, the beauty of the unthawed snow, before he proceeded to alert me to a band of gypsies who had taken refuge on the cathedral steps. I asked what had happened on the hotel steps. His expression blanked as he answered with the warning gleam of his professional smile and silence.

I have a snapshot from my first visit to St Petersburg. I am standing outside the Hermitage gallery flanked by two shock-headed boys of about nineteen; the face of one is disfigured by acne. They have been assigned by the Institute, whose guest I am, to be my cultural guides. Max and Andre. They are first-year undergraduates at the Institute's Department of Psychology. As they are fluent English speakers, their Rector has chosen them to look after me during my leisure time. One passport to success – a way to stand out in any crowd in St Petersburg is an ability to speak fluent English. They were exceptional linguists and Andre's first question was: 'Which is the better English for us to speak, English English, or American English?' By the time of my next visit, six months later, Andre had disappeared into 'the Jungle' and nobody had knowledge of his whereabouts or why he had failed to enrol for the new semester. He was a war orphan and the existence he described, which moved between what his wits could provide and his impoverished grandparents' home, was scary and feral. He had made it to the Jungle City, but once there, like so many other young people, he did not have personal accommodation but slept on communal floors. Max and his family were more stable and became my precious friends.

One of the first things the boys confided was their sheer terror of having to do their National Service in the Russian army. Their age made it an imminent reality. Perhaps, Andre had been forcibly conscripted. Rumours of army brutality and alarming mortality statistics circulated in the city and promoted fear and terror as the names of Chechnya and Chernobyl were burnt into the national memory. I was ignorant of the horrendous legacy of the Chernobyl nuclear plant explosion and I realized too late that I had been rash in choosing the subject for my first

lecture on 'The Unspeakable'. I have since become better educated by the Nobel Prize winner Svetlana Alexievich's harrowing
accounts of the slow-burning physical deformations, infertility
and live exterminations through radiation of many Chernobyl
citizens after the explosion. Alexievich refused to remain silent.
Her book describes in first-person narratives the consequences
of the worst atomic accident in history on 26 April 1989. The
disaster contaminated as much as three quarters of Europe.
Approximately 2.1 million people including 700,000 children are
now living on contaminated land. 'The sparrows disappeared
from our town in the first year after the accident. They were
lying around everywhere – in the yards on the asphalt. They'd
be raked up and taken away in the containers with the leaves.
They didn't let the people burn the leaves that year because they
were radioactive. So they buried the leaves.'

My bushy-tailed young chaperones enchanted me in the execution of their duty; they told me they had a hired car waiting
and that today would be an opportunity for me to gather my first
impressions of the city. We made our way towards a battered,
blue Skoda. At that time the general population seemed to be
driving cars that would never have passed the MOT in England,
while the new elite travelled about in BMWs or chauffeur-driven
American limos. A man of about forty-five, whose handsome
looks were somewhat faded, jumped out of the Skoda and shyly
escorted me to the front seat, coughing painfully. Whenever the
three of us got out to visit a monument, the driver remained,
chain-smoking cheap Winston cigarettes beside the car, coughing
or gazing quizzically into a tangle of ancient mechanisms beneath
a rusty bonnet. The boys explained that he was employed as our
official driver because they knew he was a trustworthy man who
had a valid driving licence, a rare possession in St Petersburg. Max

gave their game away at the end of our first day when, amidst a long exchange in Russian, I picked out the word 'Papa'!

'Papa' was Igor Brodsky, former captain of the *Voronezh* submarine, who had been prematurely discharged, due to 'stress', from duty at the Northern Fleet submarine base at Murmansk. Following his retirement as a submariner he had been detained for a further two years at the base under the Official Secrets Act. Igor was not only suffering from a chronic cough but also from acute post-traumatic distress. I discovered from Max, who was still crimson with shame about the embarrassing deception, that his family had been forced to leave behind the wealth of their privileged Soviet home at Murmansk where Max had grown up in Soviet military luxury. Igor, with ruined nerves and sickly lungs, was now struggling to find his way back into civilian life in the beloved city of his birth, albeit with the reduced status of an unemployed engineer. He was, I soon discovered, married to the beautiful Natasha, as radiant as a Tolstoy heroine, who had worked as a broadcaster at the Murmansk radio station. They were, despite being worn out with financial anxieties over the calamitous change in their fortunes, as enchanting in their mutual affection and hospitality as any couple that stepped out of a story by Chekhov.

The boys were alarmed in case I thought they had deceived me by employing Igor as our driver. They need not have been. Igor was one of most courteous and modest Russian men one could hope to meet. His gentle spirit made it hard to imagine how he had ever commanded a nuclear submarine. Robbed of responsibility, he now had time on his hands, unlike Natasha, who was training to become a child psychologist. We became silent daytime companions. Sadly, he did not speak more than a smattering of English and my only contribution to our conversation was to repeat an exaggerated thank you, 'Bolshoe spasibo,' whenever appropriate.

Igor liked to conduct me along the Neva quay beside the N.G. Kuznetsov Naval Academy. With the aid of a dictionary and many gaps in our comprehension, he sketched his past as an ardent youth leader in the Soviet Komsomol, where he had dreamt of contributing to Soviet naval supremacy and marrying his childhood sweetheart, Natasha. Igor confided, using Max as interpreter, that Perostroika had destroyed his equilibrium. It had taken place, unknown to him, during the period when he had been isolated on the nuclear station in preparation for being dispatched on a secret command exercise for six months. When Igor resurfaced at Murmansk a year later, he was ill prepared and unable to reconcile himself to the astonishing socio-political changes that had taken place in his beloved Mother Russia following the Soviet Union's collapse. Communism had been his religion, although Natasha had always kept her inherited icons hidden under the mattress. Igor's blood pressure soared along with his dismay, or rather his incoherence, at the sight of a neon Coca-Cola advertisement which triggered a mental and physical breakdown. Unprepared for this rupture of his Soviet ideals, Igor was left not knowing what or whom to believe in.

It did not surprise me to discover that Igor preferred the painting collections in the Russian Museum to the Impressionist galleries in the Hermitage. He introduced me to the work of one of his favourite Russian painters, Vasily Vereshchagin, whose syllables spoke to me of enchantment. He and Natasha gifted me with catalogues of mystical paintings of ancient gateways leading towards mysterious and violent landscapes. Vereshchagin's desolate depiction of a pyramid of unburied skulls, *The Apotheosis of War*, made a deep impression on me. One day the three of us were in the Hermitage, where we had returned to explore the galleries which were crowded by Cezanne's work, when Igor turned to me and asked Natasha to interpret: 'Is the Mediterranean really so extraordinarily beautiful as it is said to be? I don't understand why the Impressionists' paintings are the most popular in the Hermitage, even though I do often dream about visiting France. Please tell me why these pictures are so important. I have only ever seen the Mediterranean coastline through my periscope.'

I have not felt the same towards the Hermitage – despite its stunning collection of Cezannes, many of which are stored unseen in the vaults – since I found out that thousands of slaves dropped, like mosquitoes, from its walls when Catherine the Great decreed that the construction of her Winter Palace had to be completed before her premature arrival. Chemical ovens were employed, without any regard for health and safety, to generate heat to dry out the damp plaster, while the workers fell like flies from their ladders. Similar stories are told of the thousands of lives lost in the construction of St Isaac's Cathedral. Life is and always has been cheap in Russia.

My social and professional lives in St Petersburg became intertwined. Freudian Psychoanalysis was outlawed in Russia from the 1920s until Gorbachev instigated important reforms between 1985 and 1991 under the umbrellas of perestroika and glasnost. These reforms included political pluralism, the establishment of non-governmental organizations, freedom of speech and the publication of banned texts, which included Freud's *Collected Works*. Until the brave initiative of the London Jungian Programme, Jungian ideas had only been secretly available to underground philosophers.

Towards the end of my perhaps immodest first lecture on 'Jung, Shakespeare and the Unspeakable' to a gathering of budding Russian Jungians, I became aware that a small and dapper figure with an imposing air of energy and the domed forehead of an academic, had entered the back of the lecture room. He seemed to be listening with approval to the Russian translation of my ideas. It was at the end of this lecture that one of the psychiatrists in the audience reproached me. To come to Russia and to speak about the *unspeakable* without reference to their famine during the Siege of Leningrad was both ignorant and arrogant.

The stranger at the back of the room turned out to be Professor Mikhail Reshetnikov, Rector and Founder of the Eastern European Institute for Psychoanalytic Psychotherapy. Reshetnikov is an ex-military general and a psychiatrist who, as a specialist in trauma, had once been responsible for the mental health of some of the military who had been at Chechnya and Chernobyl. Through some opaque processes, and the dynamism of his charismatic personality, on return to civilian life in St Petersburg, Mikhail Reshetnikov had persuaded President Yeltsin to permit psychoanalytic psychotherapy to have academic status in the national medical curriculum. During one of our later dinners, he explained how when he had worked in St Petersburg town hall at the same time as Putin began his career there, he had managed to access some banned microfiche texts of Freud's *Collected Works*. It became Mikhail's ambition to study and to share these texts without the political harassment of being in possession of samizdat literature. Mikhail Reshetnikov – who in 2010 received the award of Meritorious Scientist of the Russian Federation by approval of the Kremlin – has with irrepressible intellectual energy presided since 1991 over a stylish eighteenth-century building on Bolshoy Prospect. He persuaded President Yeltsin to gift him the elegant and valuable building as the first stage towards the accomplishment of his long-held ambition to provide a permanent home for his project of reinstating Freudian psychoanalysis in the academic medical curriculum.

At the end of my lecture, Reshetnikov crossed the room and invited me to step out of the Jungian programme and to become an independent visiting clinical consultant to the Institute. It was the beginning of an enduring friendship of mutual respect and admiration.

It is May 2005, the winter snows are receding and the excitement of White Nights approaches. I have returned to St Petersburg to give another series of lectures and supervisions. I have asked Mikhail if it would be possible for us to visit the flagship mental hospital in Russia, the Bekhterev Institute, which is not officially open to foreign 'inspection'. In the last few months, I have become interested in the clinical practice of hypnotherapy in the UK. I am intrigued by Freud's rejection of the technique when he was studying with Jean-Martin Charcot and Professor Pierre Janet at the Salpêtrière Hospital in Paris. I am now also curious to explore hypnotherapy's infamous reputation in Russia, where it was historically associated with the supernatural, witchcraft and more recently, brainwashing by the KGB. As the Soviet system, with its rigid and uncompromising thought systems began to collapse in the late 1980s, a widespread underground belief in magic and the paranormal that has always existed in the Russian hinterlands and amongst its aristocracy, began to flood into the mainstream cities of Moscow and St Petersburg. Hypnotherapy, in different manifestations, was practised before and throughout Soviet rule. Stalin is reported to have used it as a tool in state interrogation and even torture. After perestroika, in the height of the scramble for compensatory new ideas to replace the absolutes of Marxist-Leninism, its popularity peaked. A common feature of prime-time viewing spots on TV was the media hyp-notherapist Anatoly Kashpirovksy's hypnotherapy sessions. He achieved fame and then notoriety through exercising his psychic and charismatic powers over national television audiences and achieving record ratings. To the better informed, his hold over the masses was reminiscent of the monk Rasputin's charismatic control over the family of Tsar Nicholas II. (And today, it feels scary to me to observe the inflation of Putin's actions running amok, acquiring similar godlike proportions of a self-deified and omnipotent power.)

Meanwhile with the loss of Soviet ascendency, the conse-quences of economic chaos and family tragedies associated with wars in Afghanistan and Chechnya, and then the revolu-tions in Georgia and the Ukraine, the nation had once more become addicted to loss and the consolation of 'a quick fix'. Behind the facade of post-modern Russia there still exists, even in sophisticated Moscow and St Petersburg, a bizarre nether world, unknown to most Westerners. Marc Bennetts described, in an article he wrote for the *Guardian* newspaper in June 2010, a world where business people will turn to urban witches, or import Siberian shamans for solutions to their problems and it is reported that even sophisticated lawyers will consult psychics to predict the results of their upcoming cases.

During this visit I intend to venture into the Jungle and to find out whether in St Petersburg clinical psychology falls behind the national predilection to consult hypnotherapists or masquerading charlatans and quacks. Russian youth – with no certainty of the predictable future formerly provided through their commitment as Soviet Youth Pioneers to the compulsory Komsomol – has become vulnerable to quasi-religious cults that promise a certainty of sorts. Despite the official return of the

Russian Orthodox Church, a new-age occultism has become an alternative religion for many citizens. There are about twenty-five thousand psychiatrists and psychotherapists in Russia as opposed to three hundred thousand legally certified magicians and healers! There are more than one hundred state-licensed schools for magicians throughout Russia and it is a growing business that has been estimated to be worth at least fifteen million dollars in Moscow alone.

Among the intelligentsia of pre-revolutionary Russian society, belief in the paranormal was common. Freemasonry was popular along with table-raising séances, court orgies, and theosophical beliefs. There was the phenomenon of Rasputin, a Siberian peasant who like his contemporary Sigmund Freud, was fascinated by hysteria but, unlike Freud, exploited the power of hypnosis. It was Rasputin's manipulation of the female personality, in keeping with nineteenth century cultural concepts of female hysteria that was at the core of his control of high society women, including the Tsarina. Rasputin thought of himself as Christ like. He manipulated his followers, in ways that Putin now imitates, into the belief that his charisma was divine in origin.

Mikhail Reshetnikov does not know much about mass hypnotherapy which I am keen to witness, as these quasi séances are taking place all over the country but he has agreed to make arrangements for me to witness a hypnotic séance and also to visit the famous Bekhterev Psychoneurological Institute before I return to London. Today we are to meet with Dr. Rada, now a Consultant Psychiatrist at the Institute which was established under the pioneering psychiatrist and scientist, Vladimir Bekhterev, another medical army general. It was the august Bekhterev who first identified Rasputin as an expert 'specifically in the "arts of sexual hypnosis"'. His diagnostic perspicacity led to his untimely death after he was invited by Stalin to provide a consultation in 1927. He recklessly diagnosed Stalin with acute paranoia, allegedly having commented: 'I have just examined a paranoiac with a short, dry hand.' Surviving for only one day after this pronouncement, Professor Bekhterev was found dead in his rooms. The Kremlin physicians diagnosed food poisoning.

The Bekhterev Institute is still privileged to be the country's flagship psychiatric hospital. After my experiences of the emotional warmth, intellectual energy and aesthetic refinements of Mikhail Reshetnikov's Institute, I am not prepared for our visit. We arrive at an elegant but decrepit exterior. The building was completed in 1907 and there have been no visible refurbishments since. It is a building that I soon discover to be so environmentally hostile, so lacking in therapeutic energy that extended periods of incarceration have driven many of its patients to suicide.

Our host, Dr Rada, Medical Director of the Outpatients Department of New Technologies, President of the Russian Federation of Medical Psychotherapy, appears to be in his mid-forties. He sports a biblical beard very like that of the hospital's founder, and his eyes light up with passion when he speaks. Rada's eyes are beacons of hope in this ghastly location that is a desolate wasteland. We pause outside a locked ward where a notice dictates the rations that visitors are permitted to bring, but 'All forms of salt, homemade preserves and pickles are forbidden.' As we are admitted to the ward recreation area, through more locked doors, Rada excuses himself to attend another clinic. I am reminded of something I have read: 'The windows are disfigured on the side with iron bars. The floor is discoloured and full of splinters. The place smells of sour cabbage, unsnuffed wicks, bed bugs and ammonia, and this picture of smells at first gives you the impression of having entered a menagerie.' These words are Chekhov's description in his short story *Ward No. 6*.

The ward was designed, at the beginning of the twentieth century, to lull its occupants into believing they were being accommodated in a luxurious country dacha or turn-of-the-century Swiss sanatorium. Walls were painted like stage sets with *trompe l'oeil* windows opening on to now dilapidated landscapes that once conjured pastoral horizons. I fantasize the ward has become an uncensored space for a living performance inspired by Antonin Artaud and his Theatre of Cruelty. Patients mark dead time with obsessional pacings across the unswept floor. Odours emanate from blocked lavatories and there is a strong smell of cabbage stew. Psychotropic drugs and, I suspect, ECT have transformed the occupants into automatons as they wander between nothing and less than nothing. Other scarecrow figures lie on dirty and overcrowded bunk beds in catatonic rows. I experience a sadness that leaves me speechless. I turn, without words, towards Mikhail Reshetnikov, who tries and fails to reassure me.

Now, the ward psychiatrist makes a brief appearance from out of his locked inner office and explains, not without pride, that in-line with a recent policy change these wards in future are to be officially designated as 'informal dormitories'. Whatever they are called, these are dormitories from hell. I still haven't seen a nurse anywhere. While the ward psychiatrist is talking to us, I become aware of a woman flinging her weight in suspended agony against his re-locked office. This psychiatrist speaks impeccable English but his eyes are dead. His battered ears also seem indifferent to suffering. I observe that the one thing he and Dr Rada, and Mikhail Reshetnikov too, have in common is that all three are addicted to chain-smoking their Winstons. These Russian men – and the sea captain, Igor is another victim, they don't need to be psychiatrists – never tire of making jokes about their addiction to smoking and its associations with oral deprivation at the ruthless Mother Breast.

We shuffle into another 'dormitory' where the psychiatrist explains: 'These people are high suicide risks and need twenty-four-hour monitoring'. I cannot see there is anybody there to watch them. I have not seen one nurse, or anybody who might be identified as being on therapeutic duties, anywhere. The patients are too sedated to move. The only redeeming feature to be noted, as we pass an ancient electro-convulsive-therapy treatment chamber, is that that facility appears to be non-operational. The ferruginous equipment looks as if it has been there since the flagship hospital's inception. I exhale when the padlock is unlocked, and only then realize I have been holding my breath for minutes as we are reunited with and meet Dr Rada's quiz-zical gaze. We return to his office in another blanket of smoke for a constitutional lemon tea, heavily laced with cognac. I am consoled that Russia still has philanthropically motivated doctors like Dr Rada who, despite his thriving psychosexual private prac-tice in a designer suite in the prosperous city centre, continues against such odds to campaign for a reformed vision of state mental healthcare.

Tomorrow, Mikhail has arranged for me to continue my explo-rations into the mysteries of the national psyche by arranging for my translator and friend, Lara, to accompany me to a public performance of the Russian art and craft of mass hypnotherapy. Lara has been my translator since my first visit to Russia eight years ago. She lives in a crumbling tenement on the outskirts of the city. She has never spoken to me about her family background but she is the single parent of seven-year-old Misha who is already a precocious mathematician. Lara came to St Petersburg after she completed her university degree in Physics at Moscow State University during Soviet rule, and she has taught herself to speak and write fluent English. She has also become a Third Dan Black Belt practitioner in Karate and knows how to look after herself and me. Last year she visited my family in the UK and her current ambition, like that of so many of her contemporaries, is to leave Russia permanently and to find work in Germany.

Today, we are crossing over the most deprived area of the city to visit a former Soviet cinema called Prometheus, to witness the famous folk healer Marina – although it would be more accurate to say infamous – and her adept, Njura, hypnotize their audience into deceptions of health and prosperity. We enter a cinema to find about five hundred worn citizens gathered in expectation of physical renewal and even miracles. I am about to witness a threadbare community offer up their rubles in return for worthless baubles, which in the best interpretation might be called talismans. Lara tells me that in her opinion the performing couple are neither professional hypnotists nor folk healers but charlatans whose stage act is full of deceit. She warns me that this notorious couple knows how to manipulate the collective mentality of an audience whose lives are scarred by loss, sickness and economic betrayal. Most of the audience will have lost a son or a grandson here or there, to one war or another. I am taken aback by the absence of any attempt at a credible, or even 'theatrical', presentation, as the couple now appears in shabby tracksuits and mouldy fur. I expected there to be a charismatic fanfare of balalaikas from soulful Russians with smouldering eyes.

There are no lighting effects. Nothing to see except two drab individuals climbing on to the stage who are already receiving adulation and bouquets of flowers from arthritic and enfeebled men and women as they struggle up from their seats. I see a

youth and an older woman whose auras whiff only of deception. Without stage costume or props, the self-professed healer,
Lady Marina, begins to read her poetry. One idiotic ditty fol-
lows another until my embarrassed interpreter Lara, whispers,
'Frankly this is terrible poetry, let's leave.' I remind her that she
didn't bring me for the poetry but to witness a social phenomenon that everyone tells me gets repeated throughout Russia every
day among a neglected and deluded population.

Marina's companion announces himself to be the grandson of
the great holy man Gramma Njura. Not only does this impostor
promise to cure their audience of all ills, but also it seems he can
be of equal assistance to all the absent members of their families through the purchase of his talisman. 'Like our namesake
the great god Prometheus, I will bring the fire of health back
into your bones and change your destiny.' Njura's words carry a
common seduction in their promise of effortless gratification.
No one needs to do anything except believe in him because Njura
has access to the spiritual key, the secret of a bio-energy that will
make all things possible to all believers. 'Energy,' Lara whispers,
'is the second most popular national word after technology.' The
rhetoric becomes indefensible: 'If you haven't heard from your
grandson since he entered the army you need only sprinkle a
few drops of my holy water on to his empty pillowcase and he
will be returned to you by the end of the month. Or failing that
the end of the year.'

With an alarming electrical hissing, we are plunged into darkness. The polyester trickster Njura demands that we each gather
a citizen into our arms: 'All together now!' We are instructed to
rub away our neighbour's pain and to renew their bio-energy.
'Rub! Rub harder and harder!' The packed auditorium is alive
with the electrical energy of strangers rubbing up a tornado of

hysteria and hope. The light returns. I am amazed to see that the audience has transformed itself into an animated group of linked strangers who are looking towards these charlatans with the expectant eyes of the newborn. Can it be so simple to hoodwink and seduce? Are these brave and resilient citizens, who have endured so much suffering, so much hunger and passion for their Motherland, going to bite the bait of falsehood? Yes, the power and consolation of physical touch is contagious. In this derelict cinema, yet another wasteland, where the illusion is not on the screen but in front of my eyes, I see eager queues are forming. Hobblers that need hip replacements now appear quicker on the hoof. One group of the converted is waiting to be blessed with more poetry and baptized in dirty holy water, most likely contaminated. The other group, already baptized in collective deceit, is frantically competing to make their purchases from these unholy descendants of Gramma Njura.

Can it only be in Russia, whose elite used to be among the best-educated people of the world, that the dispossessed are deluded that doggerel and drops of dirty water will bring back their lost boys? Rubles are being scattered like cherry blossom as, emotionally drained but not financially ruined, we exit. Corruption is now resounding to a *Eugene Onegin* chorus. During our long walk back to Lara's home to eat blinis and pickled mushrooms – and yes, pickles are everywhere – we calculate that in the course of one hour Marina and Gramma Njura's young descendent have filled their coffers to the equivalent of one thousand, five hundred US dollars.

It is early evening by the time we return to the Institute and the building has warmed up with activity. Startling paintings of nudes line the walls along the extravagant marble staircase that leads student and patient alike towards Reception. Perhaps the presence of these images, which seem a bit incongruous, are to alert all brave enough to enter the lobby that their task, in contrast to national characteristics and habits, will be to unmask and reveal their naked thoughts. Something contrary to the average Russian's psychic portfolio, traditionally schooled into confining secrets to memory and not by the risk of the written word. I think of Goya's famous *Maja* portraits, whose sitter is represented both clothed and naked. I also think of Leonard Cohen's lyrics from his *The Secret Life*: 'I smile when I'm angry. / I cheat and I lie. / I do what I have to do / To get by.' In Soviet Russia, secrets and 'getting by' were normal and now, once more under Putin's iron fist, are becoming daily chores which are essential for self-preservation. Putin does not believe in individuation, except for his own.

The corridors are alive with the buzz of post-graduate students who have come on from daytime employment to develop their new passion for psychoanalytic psychotherapy. Fashionable-looking individuals spill out of the building and on to the pavements to enjoy the lingering May sun. White Night's fever and blossom hang on the dusk. Everyone is smoking. Only now, after two intoxicating but disillusioning days, do I reflect on the extraordinary purpose and philosophy of this institute; on how much its founder and Rector, Mikhail Reshetnikov, has contributed to the development of national psychological understanding. He has also become a traveller between St Petersburg and the Kremlin, where he is Consultant to the First Chamber of the Russian Parliament. It seems, in Russian politics, you are either regarded as a national threat or absorbed into its elite.

We join Mikhail who is now obscured by a halo of cigar smoke and seated beneath a photograph of Freud's notorious Monday Club. He offers us vodka and explains: 'I was never a conventional military man and my friends were surprised that

I served for twenty-five years, but my contribution was to the psychology of trauma and terror. After I left the military I was invited by the Mayor of St Petersburg, Anatoly Sobchack, who was a very popular political leader, to work with him as the Chief of his Analytical Department. Putin, who was a poor but ambitious young man, worked in the mayoral office. It was that appointment which inspired me to set up an independent training institute but I was only interested if it was exclusively dedicated to the development of psychoanalytic studies. The idea emerged out of a dream; it was 1991 and a period of intellectual intoxication, when great ideas were still in the air. However, when I said that I wanted to establish a Russian Institute of Psychoanalysis, I was told it was impossible. To begin with I was forced to compromise and it was established as the Institute of Medical and Psychological Problems. Later we changed its title to the Eastern European Institute for Psychoanalytic Studies. Fifteen years ago psychoanalysis was ignored by Russian psychologists and psychiatrists but now it would be impossible to have a psychology conference without its presence as an academic discipline.'

Other colleagues explain that it is no longer the authorities that pose a threat to the expansion of psychoanalytic psychotherapy in Russia but the collective mentality, which has become addicted to the idea of 'a quick fix'. Psychotherapy, in contrast, requires discipline and patience and is without any promise of instant gratification. Sometimes, they admit to finding it difficult to reconcile themselves to classical European techniques of psychoanalytic psychotherapy which do not take into account either their national psychology or the importance of a culture which has been constructed from famine, oppression and constantly changing crises of identity.

I arrive back in St Isaac's Square to pack and prepare to confront another ordeal at Passport Control that I cannot face without a strong fix of Valium. I do not want to leave the intoxicating city just when the fabled White Nights are approaching. The only compensation, apart from returning to my family, work, and Lucy is that I will stop smelling of Russian Winstons. I shall also be released from the appealing habit of avoiding infection by cleaning my teeth in vodka.

The view from my window stretches towards St Isaac's Cathedral. Despite the late hour, the unsleeping sun has not set. I do not know whether my experience is common, but I shall carry its imprint of metamorphosis on my astonished retinas forever. My gaze moves towards the lingering pinks of rosy sun that beckon me across the shade of the square. The gloom of the building's granite south portico has acquired an unearthly translucence; a wash of Tiepolo's pink. I imagine, as I know nothing of geology, tesserae of crystal to be embedded in the melancholy of these massive blocks. Or, could it be the fitful glinting of souls of the convicts buried under mudslides as they perished inside of the building? I see a pink nimbus of spiritual energy unfold which perhaps belongs to those slaves who were harnessed into forty years of grinding toil to construct a holy building on the Neva's shifting sands.

8

PROUST'S ANACOLOUTHON

T WO DESCRIPTIONS OF THE TRICKSTER WORD:

> In speaking, he [President Trump] is prone to *anacoluthon* – sentences whose grammar collapses.
>
> *Trump's rhetoric: a triumph of inarticulacy,*
> SAM LEITH (*Guardian*, 13.1.2017)

> *Anacoluthon*: ending a sentence with a different grammatical device from that with which it began. It is both a vice and a device with which to demonstrate emotion.
>
> *Style: An Anti-Textbook*, RICHARD A. LANHAM.

For many years I had no interest in Proust. I knew nothing about him or his mind-altering novel, *In Search of Lost Time*, let alone that such a fabulous noun as *anacoluthon* existed. I eventually discovered, rather like Proust's infamous and prick-teasing heroine Albertine, that I am also liable to speak or write in sentences that collapse into discursions with too little coherence or respect for where they began. Albertine is the heroine of the book until her untimely death in volume 6, *The Fugitive*. She is one of the young girls Marcel, the narrator, observes playing with her friends one unforgettable summer when sexuality is pricking into his young and fragile body. He spies on her playing on the beach with her girlfriends, who have their own volume in the novel: *In the Shadow of the Young Girls in Flower*. Albertine is the high priestess of the *anacoluthon* and she deploys this rhetorical beast syntactically, strategically, and ruthlessly. She will grow up to torment her lover Marcel, with partial details of where and with whom she enjoys her secret assignations, or provoke him with the exasperating gender fluidity of her sexuality. On the occasion of one row she starts to offer Marcel an explanation for her absence, or some detail of her ambiguous relationship with one or other of the 'girls in flower', only to bring her incomplete sentence to a tantalizing full stop: 'The cruelty was turned on me. Not as a refinement of style, but to cover her [Albertine] careless lies she used unexpected leaps of syntax which resembled what grammarians refer to as *anacoluthon*, or something like that… I wished I could remember the beginning of her sentence so as to decide myself when she shifted ground what the ending would have been. But as I had been listening for the end I could hardly remember the beginning… '

The tease of the *anacoluthon* is its predisposition to form a sentence or construction that lacks grammatical sequence. Its Greek root *akolouthos* means 'following' and the prefix *an* negates that intention; the term literally translates from its Greek root as 'not following' or 'it does not follow'. Such tactical deceptions are also deployments that I have, independently of my delayed discovery of the word, been familiar with in my consulting room, when someone may intentionally, or unintentionally (unconsciously), wish to deceive or distract me. The *anacoluthon*, although now being used as an image rather than a phrase, also frequents the landscape of dreams, and poetry too, where the dreamer or poet experiences travelling along one highway, only to find herself suddenly beside an unrelated landscape. It seems extraordinary to me now that for so many years I resisted, without any good reasons except perhaps out of laziness and fear, to follow John's enthusiasm to read Proust, which has belatedly become an alternative source book of the mysteries and vagaries of the unconscious.

John became intrigued with *In Search of Lost Time* over forty years ago – when it was more commonly known as *Remembrance of Things Past* – through his admiration of French cuisine and culture. It took John another ten years to finish the novel, while I was still immersed in washing nappies. I thought Proust was a bit of an old fart, an elitist drone, and when I heard John discussing him with fellow travellers on *Swann's Way,* the first volume, I thought they were members of an exclusive male club for snobs. Oddly, I never overheard a woman participating in their discussions.

Many years after I became a registered addict, and like the initiated even dared, in a nonchalant way, to refer to the novel as *A La Recherché.* John explained, and this fact would have delighted Proust, that his first encounter with Proust had taken place in the lavatories at the Everyman cinema in Hampstead. He had returned from fulfilling his National Service in Malaya and moved into a Hampstead house-share. It was a Victorian house that sheltered the bohemian young manager of the Everyman as well as a female impersonator renowned as a pantomime dame who also ran a cleaning service called Happy Housewives. One of the men immediately set John to work with a mop, and the other provided him with free access to the awe-inspiring films of the early sixties, directed by Antonioni, Fellini and Buñuel that have accompanied him along his way. It was in the Everyman's loos that John came upon an item of graffiti: 'They were all faggots', followed by a list of the names of famous gay men; the list began with a faint scribble of Proust's name that someone had tried energetically to rub out. It was 1959 and John claims that he still had no concept of what constituted a faggot, neither had he ever heard the noun 'gay' used. The heinous escapades of the Baron de Charlus have since enlightened him, although it was not until many years later that he bought his first copy of *Swann's Way*.

Since that time there has been endless dissection and argument in the groves of academe over the title of the first volume. A more precise translation has since been decided upon by Christopher Prendergast's team of translators for the Penguin Modern Classic as *The Way by Swann's*. I continued to regard Proust as a yawn. These somewhat ignorant distractions came to a timely end when my close friend and reading partner, Christopher Potter, was living between London and New York. We compensated for the distance between us through investing time and intimacy in convening a reading group of 'us two'. It was December 2007 when Christopher suggested that we think about a shared reading of Proust. I confess that it was not until I met Christopher, and we read Tolstoy together, that I became aware of the importance of translation in literature. Now I received another challenge – the unthinkable idea of reading Proust. As much research and preparation went into choosing a translation of *In Search of Lost Time* as I would have spent on choosing a wardrobe to board the *Queen Elizabeth*. I was entirely out of my depth. In a former role, Christopher was publishing director of Fourth Estate. I entrusted our search to him, while I relegated myself to the lower deck, a little intimidated and still unable to make sense of the competition.

We, rather he, settled on the new Penguin translation edited by the Professor of French at King's College, Cambridge, Christopher Prendergast, who controversially had employed a different translator for each of the seven volumes. Christopher Potter had briefly wobbled at Volume One being translated as *The Way by Swann's*. Such detail still bewildered me. I have, since leaving novice-hood, discovered that the earlier Scott Moncrieff translation of the title as *Swann's Way* fails to convey Proust's literal intention of a pathway literally passing by Swann's house. After copious preparation we began our shared journey. My life was now additionally occupied, enriched, consoled, astonished and transformed by Proust's genius. A year later we decided to complete an entire rereading of Proust's transforming work, which has not only changed the ways in which I think, but also, I like to hope, the tenor of my syntax.

∾

Our family is spending part of the summer with Dido in a secluded Norfolk village. Dido is still pining for the loss of her companion, Danny Boy, while I am fretting about whether I can find the confidence to make a coherent beginning at writing my way into this chapter about Proust. I do not mean that I want to imitate him, but I do want to learn from the infinite ways that Proust astonishes and admonishes the reader's brain and heart. He uses his vision like an autopsy, which can expose elements of a stone edifice as transparently as the caprices of a salon full of inflated literati, bores and aristos in the Faubourg St Germain. I do not want only to write about Proust but into him; I also want to telescope landscapes present, past and involuntary. I want to celebrate his influence on my mind's eye.

The modest Norfolk village we have arrived at is a village without a future, which mirrors the anxieties I am feeling about my unfinished manuscript. We discover there are irreversible cliff erosions that threaten local livelihoods and homes. Stark notices everywhere warn us to beware of falling rocks and record the recent statistics of accidental death to dogs and their intrepid walkers. Other notices deter those bold enough to consider the cliff descent with their warning of deposits of a noxious palm oil that dogs find irresistible. Very little else seems to happen here beyond the perils of the North Sea.

The coast exudes the melancholy of chronic and irresolvable loss. It is named Happisburgh, which is more appositely pronounced 'Hazebru' as the village has, along with the centuries, migrated into a sea-changing haze. Once, Happisburgh was situated some distance from the sea and separated from the coast by the parish of Whimpwell, but the parish has long since been eroded and wailed itself away into history and the ocean's maw. Historic records indicate that over two hundred and fifty meters of coastal land were lost between the years of 1600 and 1850. It is both fable and truth that in the year of 1845 a hapless farmer ploughed his field at dusk only to wake to find that invisible ocean currents had claimed his furrows. Waves continue to swallow their prey at around fifty meters of coast every decade.

The Norman church with its curmudgeon tower, like Proust's tower at Combrai, dominates the landscape, but nobody knows for how much longer. Rebuilt once in the fifteenth century, its existence is now that of an everlasting supplicant in dialogue with ocean minerals and currents. The cemetery gardens are neglected except for pots of either plastic or withered flowers. The church, furnished in local flint and dash, which has been bleached into sediment, assumes a sacrificial destiny. It remains as the last monument between a hazy landslide and the North Sea.

We stop while Dido pursues a butterfly into the hedgerow. I notice that our seat is dedicated to Thomas Jordan who died aged twelve. The hedging beside Thomas's empty seat is strangled with bindweed; my weed and one that makes no apology for a parasitical energy. Ever since childhood I have been supplicant to its ethereal glow. As a child I was spellbound, then frustrated by my many attempts to carry it away from the vegetable gardens before the pearly bells shrivelled between my bitten fingers. Columbine, and how could it not be a 'she', has always fascinated me with her exquisite malignity, her tireless tentacles, which she disguises as love-hearts of sweetest green. The whiteness of her vessel, with its lambent beginnings of yellow stamens, beguiles. Throughout my life this Columbine weed of strumpet love has seduced and drawn me towards more understanding of my obsessions with ephemeral beauty and its extinction, obsessions I willingly share with Proust.

Involuntary memories of lost landscapes break through my thoughts in stone flashings of alchemical gold. The unrelenting flint of the church is crumbling into a livelihood of pink dusk that glows into other sun-dying tones. Pink is my favourite colour. It always has been. Pink does not only belong to fairy-tale princesses and little girls like Bell, who do not at all like slugs and snails, let alone puppy-dogs' tails, but who adore pink. Vascular shades of pink speak to me about life and love; they pour in and out of Lucien Freud's tumescence, and soothe Auerbach's remorseless eye. Pink for Matisse and rose for Picasso. Proust's eye seized upon Titian's palette of violent pink until it was Bacon's turn. Rudolf Steiner believed that colour reflects the spirit realm, which is infused with (and, in a sense, consists of) colour. Pink is associated with birth, healing, love and life. Hokusai dreamt in pink. While Philip Guston was perhaps the pinkest.

It should not surprise anyone that Proust loved the pink, as did his first mentor, John Ruskin. Its quartz and lambent hue, which in his vision stretched beyond the cherry trees at Combrai to the basilica on St Mark's Square, was engraved on Proust's soul and climaxed when he transformed the colours of his adored Venetian basilica into his vision of a Fortuny *haute couture* gown which the Narrator bought for Albertine: 'And the sleeves were lined with a cherry pink which is so peculiarly Venetian that it is called Tiepolo pink.'

In the half-light, I sense that ambergris souls are embalmed in the ancient yew-tree trunk. As we follow Dido's chase we pass a modest hillock hallowed in more bindweed, which I discover is an unnamed memorial to local sailors who lost their lives in the hazardous North Sea. The lost stones entomb one hundred and nineteen sailors of *The Invincible* who were on their 'way' from Yarmouth in 1801 to join Nelson. Happisburgh seems destined to the same twists of fate. Proust was fond of sailors.

To enter Proust's world is to enter a sea-change of matter where he supplies us, through many versions or narratives of 'truth', with the lineaments of what it means to be a human being. Far too much important criticism has already been written about Proust for me to want to attempt a critical study. I have screamed with laughter, turned emotional somersaults, become insanely bored at the snobbish salons, grown green with envy at Proust's genius and the way even a paving stone, let alone an emotion, spire, swallow, wave, or perspective, like Orpheus's lyre, animate beneath his gaze. I have been changed for ever, which is not an exaggeration, in relation to my mortality, after reading the notorious satire on extinction, the *bal des têtes* sequence in *Finding Time Again*. Proust was a connoisseur of love, desire and jealousy, Phèdre, lift-boys, bell-boys, waiters, nature, birds – especially swifts – hawthorn, fabrics, architecture and cathedrals, spires, music, the sea, sunsets, jealousy again, family, fruit trees, salon gossip, Racine, politics, the self, the face, the voice, the olfactory, scatology and sleep erotica. Dreams, music, art, history, *The Thousand and One Nights,* medicine, perversion, the Dreyfus Affair, Madame de Sévigné, *more waiters*, love, death, more jealousy, homo-eroticism, the effete and still more scatology. I think he preferred the whiffs of the latrine in the Bois to the linden fragrances of *tilleul* or Françoise's hollandaise sauce. Even the 'Madeleine' offers no competition to his love of scatology. Proust does not often do tenderness: he is as ruthless with his readers as he is with the unmasking of his characters. Proust is a creative, if deadly sadist and sceptic. The nearest he comes to tenderness is through his observations of Nature, but all the time Proust is undertaking his ruthless autopsy of matter and unmasking the indulgences, foibles and perversions of his characters, *himself,* or of society.

He explored perspectives that move between microscope and telescope; he looked forward as well as backwards and towards changing political horizons and inventions like the telephone and aeroplanes. He described his work as a telescope fixed on time. He was a satirist who never stopped ridiculing pseuds but he *knew* that it takes one pseud to recognize another. Whatever his eye happened upon has provoked awe and devotion in me in the ways, like a palaeontologist, he uncovers past layers of meaning. Miriam Rothschild referred to him as the first urban naturalist. He was also a nocturnal magician who, in the enchanted half-light of the shadows of dusk and dawn, never forgot the influence of his earliest childhood gift from his parents of a magic light lantern.

'True books', reflects the Narrator in *Le Temps Retrouvé*, 'must be the product not of daylight and chitchat but of darkness and silence… an atmosphere of poetry will always hover around the truths that one has reached in oneself, a gentle sense of mystery which is merely the remains of the semi-darkness we have had to pass through, the indication, as precisely marked as on an altimeter, of the depth of a work.' These comments resonate with my own practice.

Sometimes, it feels as though I directly transpose some of these ideas that I am reading and reflecting on into the work I do in my consulting room. It often happens in therapy that the therapeutic 'couple' need to move away from coherence and reason towards a vital kernel of being that cannot be articulated except through the poetic idiom of uncertain ambiguity. I never encourage people to equate their feelings with poetry unless they are already at ease using metaphor. While I want to tease out the unconscious, I do not want to promote self-consciousness. It often happens that an important shred of psychological discovery will have equivalence to the ambiguity of poetry. It can be tantalizing that such discoveries often repel the light of reason and seek to return to, or become lost again in the unconscious, in the same way that a dream often cannot be captured even after it has been recalled. 'What on earth was it that I (or maybe you) just said that felt so important and I cannot now remember?' the person asks. I am liable to become equally dumbstruck by memory loss, although we can usually claw our way back towards a vital component that has again taken flight from the rational light of our dialogue. The same process is true of many dreams that, unless captured on paper or present in the form of a waking nightmare, will obstinately recede from consciousness and logical expression before dawn breaks. It is in such instances that the grammar of my sentences might intentionally collapse and I will find myself using the rhetorical device of the opaque and incoherent *anacoluthon*. In this instance my intention is not to confuse or deceive, but in the hope that the other person will, through free association, know how they want to finish my sentence.

Proust was not interested in the medical treatment of neurosis and he claimed not to have been influenced by the publication of Freud's *The Interpretation of Dreams*, which was published in 1899, but he did see himself as a 'radiographer' and a 'magician'. He also recognized himself as a 'thief' who picked the flesh off the bones of unsuspecting friends and acquaintances. He told one potential publisher that there was no point in anybody trying to uncover the inspiration or models on which some of his more notorious characters like Swann, de Charles or Albertine were based. Proust insisted in every case there were at least 'ten keys' of identity he had 'stolen' from his observations of himself, strangers, family and friends, to inform and immortalize any of his characters. In *The Captive* the Narrator captures Swann's enchanting dilettantism which becomes the key to his immortal reputation:

> Although Swann was a remarkable personality with a great aesthetic and in spite of the fact that he had 'produced' nothing of worth in this world he had the good fortune to survive a little longer. Ah, my dear Swann whom I have known since I was young and whom you must have regarded as an idiot but you were already nearing your grave, I have made you the hero

of one of my novels so that people are beginning to speak the name of Charles Swann again and that your name will perhaps become immortal…

The desire of artists to achieve immortality through their imagery or narrative was also one of Proust's preoccupations. In another of the novel's most famous passages which reflect on the relationship between art and immortality, Proust allows the Narrator's thoughts to pause on Bergotte, the fictional author, who has a heart attack while he is sitting in a Parisian gallery and gazing at the yellow patch of light in a painting by Vermeer. The Narrator comments, but not without irony: 'He was dead. Dead forever? Who can say?'. Bergotte has been immortalized in Proust's portrait of an internationally esteemed novelist who was privileged to die while seated in front of what Proust described as: 'The most beautiful painting in the world', Vermeer's *View of Delft*. The reader witnesses Bergotte's suffocation as he expires from a heart attack. This mortal collapse is perhaps a mimesis of Proust's experience of the sensations of acute asthma. He pens a fictional collapse that is soon to become prophetic of his own premature death through pulmonary failure and suffocation. I cannot think of any final breath, my mother's or my own included, without recalling the breathless and disinhibited death of 'Grandmother'.

> Her eroded face also seemed diminished and terrifyingly expressive, it seemed now like the rough and purple, ruddy coloured and desperate face of some unknown guardian of a prehistoric and primitive sculpture. The cruel work was not yet complete and later the sculpture would, having been smashed, have to be lowered into the tomb which hitherto had been so painfully guarded by her now harshly contracted features.

My sensation of the extinction of flailing limbs, and a sense of suffocation, and Proust reminds his readers that remembering facts and sequences is less important than experiencing sensation – *reality lies hidden beneath the surface of small things* – refuses to fade. Grandmother's death has, like my earlier traumatic memory of the bloody misadventure of my patient's son's death, and its resonances to my mother's death, become an involuntary part of my visceral interior. Proust never ceases to remind the reader of the sinister and undesirable splitting between the ambitions of our mind and the actions of our body on our journey towards extinction. He returns again and again to his vision of our bodily demise and the ways in which it can become a foreign country which we are forced to inhabit, or are rather bound into, and yet all the time it is maliciously preparing for our extinction.

I recovered from Grandmother's morbid extinction only to be inducted into another remorseless satire of time's indifference to our protest against physical degeneration, in the passage notoriously referred to as *Le bal de têtes*. Long before I reached this section, or even the final volume where it is situated, the phrase was quoted to me by other more advanced Proustian neophytes as many times as Proust's description of his involuntary memory and associations to the iconic madeleine. The madeleine has become immortalized in Proust's recollections of the unique baking smells that permeated his childhood home under the housekeeper, Francoise's watchful eye. In life, as well as in fiction, it was a version of Francoise who continued to attend on Proust until her death. Whereas, almost everyone, whether or not they have read Proust knows about the aroma of these madeleine, I was now growing intimidated by constant and learned referrals to *bal de têtes*, always with such intimacy and, worst still, always in French: 'And what do you make of the *bal de têtes*?'

At last, I reached the notorious passage where the Narrator stumbles across a threshold of broken paving stones into the psychic crevices of another involuntary memory, at the same time as his physical entry into an afternoon tea party is announced by the footman. 'To begin with I did not understand why I was slow to recognize the master of the house and neither of the guests nor why everyone had seemed to put on make-up, in most cases with powdered hair, which changed them completely.' When I first read this passage I took the narrator, Marcel, literally and thought he was describing a masked ball, but I was mistaken. Every one of the guests, who have already become the reader's familiars in their youth, has grown older and uglier. '"You think I am my mother", Gilberte had said to me.' The narrator goes on to provide the reader with a list of other guests who are all now presented in scorching satire as if they had discovered home recipes for Botox: 'Only perhaps Mme Forcheville, as if she had been injected with a liquid, something like paraffin, which soaks into the skin and prevents it changing, still looked like a coquette from the old days but now stuffed.'

When I first read the notorious masquerade I dumbly over-looked its satire. It took a second reading for it to dawn that this was not a masked-ball celebration. I was confused by the re-appearance, forgetting that time passes, of these Faubourg salon familiars, whose vanities had been ravaged by the havoc of time. Their rheumy eyes, tumid features and lichen-tint noses had grown into the real thing. I have become someone who also fears catching an involuntary sight of myself in the mirror in case I see my mother's sad smile, or find that I have disappeared. Death, Proust might say, has also taken up a tenancy in me. The flexibility of youth mutates as we get older into the physical carnage that becomes our geriatric age. Advanced age does not take kindly to deceit. Beauty, as Proust's narrator knew well, is the most effective disguise of all. Its mask is often mistaken as a messenger from the soul.

Proust was preoccupied, even tormented by the inscrutability of the self; the tantalizing state of our human solipsism. His narrator frequently returns to descriptions of his frustration with the human condition, how the face, while revealing emotion, is equally capable of concealment. Facial expression may speak one language, while all the time the mind, or self, is capable of clothing itself in another. Marcel is tormented, as is almost every Freudian psychoanalyst, by his inability to read Albertine, or anybody else's mind: 'I could take Albertine on my knees, hold her head in my hands, I could stroke her, run my hands all over her, but just as if I had been handling a stone enclosing the salt of immemorial oceans or the light of a star, I felt that I was touching only the closed outer casing of a being which on the inside was in touch with the infinite. How I suffered from the position, which careless Nature placed us, when it instituted the separation of bodies from each other, and forgot to provide for the interpenetration of souls.'

He is persecuted by Albertine's erotic secrets. Every breath of her independent existence torments him: she is either his prisoner or a fugitive. Albertine is the twentieth-century mistress of literary concealment. She does not use language to articulate thoughts but to tantalize, conceal and provoke her listener. Her sentences, which often disappear before they are complete, are designed to provoke doubt in Marcel; to rouse the green-eyed monster of jealousy. She speaks, Marcel complains, like someone desperate to escape capture, with sentences that are full of ambiguity. Facts are ruptured, disguised, or both, in her maddening syntactical style. Her grammar collapses in endless diversions, which leave the listeners stranded on a linguistic island of detour. Proust's *anacoluthon* device is as mysterious as any freak tide.

I continue to be drawn towards and intrigued by *anacoluthon* because it mimics both conscious and unconscious processes that so often take place in the consulting room. There are occasions when it is to my advantage to leave the destination of my sentence unrealized, or confused. In therapy there are gains to be had in the therapist pausing, or even hiding inside an incomplete sentence or hypothesis, and waiting for the 'other' to produce an independent ending. *Anacoluthon* is a device that is as useful to the therapist as it is to the poet. It is a subtle rhetorical tool that can be employed when either speaker does not want to finish the sentence or thought with which they began. I will often use it in this way.

One purpose of such employment is to use its intentional disruptions as a preliminary signifier to a topic that I suspect is still too dangerous or painful to approach; to observe whether or not my listener will accompany me towards a topic that might provoke shame or distress. One example of my employment of the treacherous *anacoluthon* might be when I suspect (generally, my suspicion will sadly be confirmed, if only months later) that someone's partner is having an affair. The speaker addressing me, despite providing several small give-away clues over the weeks, still shows no conscious signs of the fact. I have to remain in a nebulous dialogue with their unconscious. They may return to each session to report, or brood over another unexplained absence, or the conspicuously and repeated delayed return of their partner, as a result of which they might also report finding themselves absent-mindedly drinking a third glass of wine, or finishing the bottle. Then, they try to satisfy themselves (if not me) with some spurious explanation. I might reply with something bland: 'I think you are beginning to ask whether you are self-medicating with your glass of wine.' (Pause... longer pause.) If the person does not respond to my hint, I may end by continuing my unfinished sentence: 'The end of the day is always tiring with the demands of fractious children.' It is not my habit to draw attention to something that although becoming evident to me, the speaker is not yet ready to hear.

While many readers will develop an allergic reaction to Albertine's prick-teasing ways, they are a wise reminder that deceit is an all-pervasive human attribute. Acts of deceit happen everywhere. Often the person seeking my help has a greater investment in avoiding, or concealing their shameful thoughts and actions, than in risking the horror of rejection. Society lives in fear of war and many individuals live in fear of rejection, which is also true in the context of therapy, where there are often people who seek out the confidentiality of the consulting room, but who are still too afraid of my rejection to face the deceits of the self.

I recall historic winter afternoons at around four p.m., when a man in his mid-fifties, clad in a dark overcoat and always carrying an impressive umbrella with a Parisian label, Guy de Jean (it was so impressive I once peeked at it when he was in the lavatory), would ring the bell. The only advance information that had been given to me by his medical referrer was that he had a tendency to obsessional compulsive disorder (OCD), which had recently spun out of control. His need continually to wash his hands was inconvenient and disrupting his schedules. I had an open copy of *La Recherche...* behind my chair, which his attention clamped onto. He told me that he was devoted to Proust. To begin with I thought his knowledge and impressions might become another entry point through his resistance to focus on his problems. He insisted that his doctor had exaggerated his OCD and provided the example that although my door handle must be a reservoir of germs, he had no difficulty touching it. He preferred instead to discuss whether or not Albertine was one of the most unpleasant and shameless heroines on record: 'I have always been intrigued by the feelings Albertine arouses in me, I cannot decide whether I admire her audacity or think she is a sadist, *anyway* I am having difficulty in deciding whether it would be selfish to the family to invest in a new and faster car.' Frequently, I have discovered that the adverb 'anyway' will precede someone's intention to distract or to deceive me.

I asked him to tell me what it was about Albertine that seemed to get up his nose and he replied without taking breath, 'The way she leads the Narrator such a merry, or rather a deceitful, dance.' Our own waltz continued for several weeks during which time he would reluctantly refer to the fact that he was a believing if lapsed Catholic, who would love to find a way through our conversations of ridding himself of guilt. After several consultations, and some gentle probing, we were no closer to the ingredients of his guilt, or hand washing. He liked to emphasize that in addition to his prominent public profile he was a privately devoted family man.

Our weekly sessions were interrupted after about three months when he did not arrive at his usual hour and I was subsequently unable to reach him. His doctor was unable to provide me with any information until he was later informed that the man had suffered a fatal coronary driving to an unknown destination on the French AutoRoute. It was only when it came to the complex funeral arrangements that I discovered, again from the family GP, that in addition to his legitimate family, this stranger had another clandestine family of small children who resided in ignorance of his polygamy with their mother in Paris.

Proust also knew all about fears of rejection. He suffered from a lifelong fear of misunderstanding about his ambitions, first by his father and later on over his repeated failures to get his novel published. He was forced to finance a part of it himself as a vanity project. The important literary publisher Gaston Gallimard boisterously rejected it during Proust's lifetime, although his firm would later become its admiring publisher after Proust's death. All the publishers that Proust initially approached responded with confusion, boredom, or in the notorious case of André Gide, revulsion. One reader to whom the publisher Fasquelle sent an early manuscript of the first book reported: '712 page manuscript... one has no notion... none – of what it is about. What is it all for? What does it mean? Where is it all leading? It is impossible to know. It is impossible to say.'

How recompensed Proust would be that this work, the meaning of his life – which to begin with could not find favour among his contemporaries – and which was still incomplete by his dying breath, finally inspired Gide, with another dying breath, to lament that one of the greatest mistakes of his life had been to reject Proust's manuscript. On 21 November, 1922, three days after Proust's death, his past lover and lifelong friend, the composer Reynaldo Hayn, made a prediction: 'Proust's book is not a masterpiece if by masterpiece one means a perfect thing with an irreproachable design. But it is without a doubt (and here my friendship plays no part) the finest book to appear since 'L'Education Sentimentale'. From the first line a great genius reveals itself and since this opinion will one day be universal, we must get used to it at once.'

I cannot imagine my life without Proust. Proust has become another best friend. Boethius found his consolation through philosophy and mine has come through Proust; both living and learning to die with him as my guide. Proust's work is a testament to the poetics of the unconscious and the vagaries, conceits, deceits and perversions of being and becoming a human being, which is the oldest and most difficult pursuit in the universe.

I began my chapter 'The Politics of Friendship', with a quotation from Proust about friendship. His novel has, by chance, also become the catalyst of a late flowering but enduring friendship, which as a corollary has also enriched my understanding of Proust. I have already written about some of the close friendships of my youth and how as one grows older there is less time left to make new friendships, with the exception of the easy familiarity of shared interests and the frequency of contact between inspiring colleagues. In addition, there are people who can be counted on a single hand, whom I regard as true friends and who have changed my life in different ways, but I have grown too old for lists. A welcome act of serendipity has been that my passion for Proust also provided me with an opportunity for friendship which began on Thursday, 9 December 2010 at the European Commission in Smith Square, when the Royal Society of Literature hosted an event: 'What's so great about Proust?'

The same Christopher Potter with whom I set sail on our Proustian Way had emailed me from New York to ask if I would be a participant in the Royal Society of Literature's forthcoming event on Proust. I would not. Any public appearance provokes ambivalence: a conflict between narcissism and my desire to remain concealed. I find the amount of adrenalin that is consumed in preparation for any performance is disproportionate to its worth and exacerbates my insomnia. Christopher remonstrated with me. With my passion for Proust, 'Why?', he asked, would I turn down an invitation that meant sharing a platform with someone who, as a professor of French at King's College

Cambridge and the General Editor of the Penguin Modern Classics translation of *In Search of Lost Time*, knew as much about my hero as any living person? I accepted.

I imagined Professor Christopher Prendergast to be an airless gentleman, liable to rival Proust's character, the uber-bore, Monsieur Norpois, whose interminable lectures I confess to skipping. The event coincided with the December 2010 student protests when Parliament Square came to a standstill with rioting students. The drone of patrolling helicopters uncannily recalled Proust's descriptions of enemy planes over Paris in 1916 during the blackout. I was the only speaker who was not delayed. What I did not know was that Christopher Prendergast and his companion speaker, the poet, Ian Patterson who had translated *Time Regained,* had not been delayed by their Cambridge journey but had to restrain themselves from joining the student protesters in Parliament Square in sympathy.

When the two 'Fellows' entered Smith Square, where an impatient and anxious audience mainly in formal wear had assembled, my phantasy ruptured. Both men were wearing muddy trainers and jackets that were inclined more towards a Fenland hike, although Prendergast had surrendered to something that looked like a tie. I was unprepared for his modesty, his playfulness and his intellectual generosity towards a novice. There was an immediate alchemy in our riff on ideas, in our smiles, our play. Inspired beginnings come easy while friendship demands a slow burn. Not only did I meet a brilliant polychromatic mind and commentator on Proust, European literature and aesthetics, but also I made an important emotional connection into something rich and strange.

I took an absurd and impertinent exception to Prendergast's nickname 'Chris', which was how he introduced himself. He seemed to me to be neither a 'Chris', nor a Christopher. Later that evening, imperiously and without any knowledge of his subsequent email to me, I spontaneously announced that forthwith I had decided to address him as Kit. I cannot imagine now what provoked me to do such an odd thing. He seemed agreeably taken aback and did not take offence. He told me that on his return to Cambridge he would explain in a letter:

Jane,

In haste: the explanation of my first name is historic. On my birth certificate I am 'Christopher'. But the reason for that is because of 'Kit', as I was always called as a child and still am in my family (siblings, cousins, etc.). Who was 'Kit'? He was Kit Conway, an Irishman, friend of my father's, who died alongside him fighting in the Battle of Jarama during the Spanish Civil War. My father was seriously wounded (shot in the back), but survived and invalided out of the remainder of the war.

As I believe I've told you, as I grew up I became more and more self-conscious about this name, not because of Kit Conway but because, idiotically, I saw the name as 'cissy' (made me think of 'Kitty'). So I discouraged its use outside the family and ended up as 'Chris' (a flat, weak thing). I now do what I can, by asking some since our meeting (within reason, I can't go round asking everyone to switch to Kit) to honour what I abandoned… So all is not lost.

Tanya tells me that I have a reputation for being a difficult or a challenging woman; I do not especially think I am. Kit has a reputation for being a challenging man. Regardless of our reputations, neither of us finds the other difficult but a source of mutual inspiration and intellectual trust. We share gratitude to Proust that we have each discovered the other's friendship. Kit, unlike most 'Fellows', inside or out of academe, has an undemonstrative ego and rarely talks publicly about his accomplishments.

In 2013 he published a book on Proust: *Mirages and Mad Beliefs: Proust the skeptic*. It was published by Princeton University Press and did not get reviewed by the broadsheets; neither did it get a review in the *London Review of Books*, which is sad because the book would have brought pleasure to a 'lay' readership. The truth will out; not only was Kit then honoured by inclusion into the American Academy of Arts and Sciences, but this 'invisible' book has since been awarded the R.H. Gapper Prize by the Society for French Studies for a scholarly work of outstanding merit in French and Francophone studies. Kit, I nosed out, is the only author ever to have been twice awarded this prestigious prize. He might be expected to have an ego as big as the Kremlin but his does not extend from King's College as far as Proust's beloved Ritz.

Monsieur Proust, your sublime book, my family, my work and knowing there are people in the world that I love more than myself, have enhanced my soul.

9

APOLLO AND DIONYSUS: THE DOUBLE BIND

Love's mysteries in souls do grow,
But yet the body is his book.

JOHN DONNE

MY LIFE IS DISGUSTING. MY LIFE IS GORGEOUS. MY life has amounted to a combination, or a 'bouquet', of 'necessary mistakes', whose consequences I hope will lead me towards death having accumulated a few drops of Athena's mythic wisdom along his Royal Highway. I have been masticating mouthfuls of guttural words for months, which sometimes choke, sometimes console me. I wonder if classy body tattoos might not be an easier alternative to writing one's life, which can feel raw as any flaying. Yet, writing continues to be an imperative of my existence and helps me to resist my fears of extinction.

I saw Him yesterday, or perhaps it was his doppelgänger, wearing an astrakhan collar as he patrols 'the Gardens', as the police like to designate our leafy, garden-lined north-west area of the city. Other days he favours identical routes to those we share with Dido. John sees him from the wheel of the car. 'There he is again, across the street.' Our mapping extends between the London Business School in Park Road, through the Inner and Outer Circles of Regent's Park and across to St John's Wood, where he loiters among fragments of Victorian gravestones before he moves on past Lords and disappears once again into the Inner Circle. His gestalt has a stern motivation, which distinguishes him from other rough sleepers. Could he, wrapped in his Cossack coat, be Pavel Ivanovich Chichikov doing a brisk trade in the city's dying soul? His vagrancy has cheeks of distinguished weather-beaten bone. His shoes impress; they are impermeable and sometimes polished. There is a proud lift to his arch. Almost concealed, his frayed jeans have a discordant whiff of Armani. His posture aggressively stoops towards the future, while his hands are clasped behind his back; hands, not palming for litter, but for fingering reluctant bones. His appearance astonishes. If I have an ambition for my book, it is also to astonish with my random accounts of foibles of human nature and the caprices of Fate.

As I reach, if not cry out, to my wordsmith angels for nouns that might help me to metaphor breath into imagery, I have an involuntary memory of how my mother choked to death on nothing more than air – suddenly, like Hamlet's father's ghost, 'When I to sulphurous and tormenting flames/ Must render up myself...' I see an uninvited apparition of my father's death certificate rise before me, which I have not thought about since childhood when I secretly 'rendered' it from a locked drawer. The cause of his death was registered as 'Asphyxiation'. A word I did not, could not, understand.

I have come to associate the threat of asphyxiation with the processes of writing and its block. I was having dinner with the co-author of our book about medicine, *Doctors Dissected*, when

I was overcome not by audible choking but into the paralysing and mute sensations of acute 'dry drowning'. I could not speak, I could not cough; my breath was suspended. I was fortunate it was a doctor sitting beside me who at last, after what seemed an eternity, noticed my declining consciousness and came to my rescue by performing the Heimlich procedure. Instantly, as it now seems, my recovery was accompanied by the onset of writer's block. We had to delay publication of that book for two years. It feels as if a connection exists between writing a sentence and the involuntary processes of breathing in and breathing out. The critical pendulum of existence, or creation, happens when the peak inhalation of air changes into exhalation, as the word also becomes a sentence, or ceases to be.

I sat in an Intensive Care Unit for many hours beside someone whose life means a great deal to me. I found myself involuntarily breathing in time, except there was no reliable time to be had in their gasping suspensions. I waited; waited helpless for signs of a dying breath to turn towards the living. My body mirrors these processes when I am writing. I experience a process of breathless inhalation in the crag of every sentence, every paragraph, until its abortion, or exhalation becomes another page of existence. As Nietzsche knew long before the science of neurobiology became fashionable, our bodies are our mind:

> Behind your thoughts and feelings, my brother, there stands a mighty ruler, an unknown sage, whose name is self. In your body he dwells; he is your body. There is more reason in your body than in your best wisdom. And who knows why your body needs precisely your best wisdom?
>
> *On the Despisers of the Body*

If I were asked to choose not three fairy wishes, but to list seven words that I have burnt into my manuscript, they would be: ambivalence, humiliation, privilege, reciprocity, Apollo and Dionysus. As the tales of 'The Sleeping Beauty' and 'Pandora's Box' remind us, there is always hope, although hope can sometimes turn out to be heartless and cruel. My seventh word would not be hope but love.

I don't recall being introduced to Nietzsche during my studies at Bedford College; it was not until years later that my 'patient' Max introduced me to *The Birth of Tragedy*, and its anti-twins Apollo and Dionysus. I found Nietzsche's dynamic metaphor for the binary system of emotional life to be a life-changing concept. An attempt to reconcile these warring opposites – whose twinned existence is another example of the Columbine double bind knot of the impossibility of resolution – has preoccupied me personally and professionally ever since.

I imagine Dionysus and Apollo as symbolic elements of internal psychic conflict: twins who are occupied in a civil war of emotional energy. They battle between convention and individuation, conservation and extinction. I imagine Helen of Troy's betrayal, Paris's sexual appetite and the destruction of the two great civilizations of the Achaeans and Troy as being under the command of Dionysus, who hates order, conservation, the habitual and marriage, and who champions libido, individuation and chaos. I have also heard it muttered once too often by older men, oft-times thrice married, and hitherto without the benefit of any inter-regnum counselling, 'I might as well have stayed in my first marriage as my romantic life has turned out to be nothing more than a fatal merry-go-round.' The twins are locked into what feels to be an irreconcilable existential dilemma. Possibly, its resolution could be achieved through negotiation and a commitment to mature compromise, but Dionysus has only contempt for compromise. Yeats' image of Helen of Troy who was a Greek queen, married to King Menelaus, who eloped with the handsome youth Paris, often comes to mind in these situations:

> *A shudder in the loins engenders there*
> *The broken wall, the burning roof and tower*
> *And Agamemnon dead.*

> W.B. YEATS, *Leda and the Swan*

I compare someone's mature commitment to the vicissitudes, pleasures and inevitable compromise of a stable partnership to the example provided by ancient Greece, with its Apollonian love of order and symmetry, the maintenance of hearth, home and an undivided financial economy (although I take exception to its patriarchy). Marriage, or partnership, as I never tire of repeating, is an inevitable compromise, which requires a dessert spoon of reality and a large dose of Apollonian control. It is a relationship that requires maximum thoughtfulness and flexibility; a long-term project which changes like the delicate fruits of the seasons. References to 'good enough mothering' have become commonplace but we might also apply the concept to marriage or partnership. Plato had a metaphor for this civil war of emotional life, which he imaged in *The Phaedrus:*

> Let our figure be of a composite nature – a pair of winged horses and a charioteer. Now the winged horses and the charioteer of the gods are all of them noble, and of noble breed, while ours are mixed; and we have a charioteer who drives them in a pair, and one of them is noble and of noble origin

and the other is ignoble and of ignoble origin, and as might
be expected there is a great deal of trouble in managing them.

In my idiosyncratic interpretation of Plato's concept I see the
charioteer as an equivalent of the Freudian 'Ego' and the horses
as equivalences of Apollo and Dionysus, or of the 'Id' or unconscious. This does not mean they are polarities of good and bad
but rather they represent the conflicting impulses that occupy
the human adult mind. All the medieval tales about knights and
their quests are soured by the rivalries and forgeries of jealousy
between these two deities.

I cannot think about the metaphors of chariot and charioteer, or of Dionysus, without returning to the enigma of Ronnie
Laing and why, despite his compulsive and latterly self-destructive
behaviour, it is his Glaswegian brogue that so often I continue to
hear in my inner ear as a supervisor. I do not have any satisfac-
tory answer, except to observe that should Dionysus enter into
your personal space, in any of his incarnations, his flaying will
be life changing. Ronnie was both Apollo and Dionysus, a man
of brilliant intellect and, when he chose, of immense personal
discipline, who respected the vagaries of the unconscious rather
like the complex music scores he often practised daily and for
hours on end. Tragically, or perhaps this is my presumption, his
premature international fame and notoriety – he was thirty-three
when he wrote *The Divided Self* – caused him to lose control of his
chariot whose energy was fuelled by bloodied childhood hounds
of humiliation and early failures of attachment.

Dionysus not only revels in carnival and excess. He also strikes
upon timid and unsuspecting natures, whose lives have become
habitual, for one reason or another, and where the instinctual
has been relegated out of orbit. He attends on lives that fall out

of balance. His unsuspecting 'revellers' are of either sex and Madame Bovary is a prominent literary example of a victim. A man comes to see me reluctantly because he cannot, without help, make sense of a chapter in his history that although concluded continues to haunt. He hopes that I may be able to help him untangle the knot. If, in our first meeting, I had used the proper nouns of Apollo and Dionysus as metaphors, he might have accused me of speaking in tongues. He is dressed in stern suiting but a flaunt of pink flashes from his tie and pocket, which suggests that beneath his stern mask is a welcome and captivating streak of flamboyance. And the feminine. He has kind eyes. He is not looking for a long-term therapy but wants to see if I can help him to make sense of a historic scar that has refused to heal.

He was born into an isolated, rural family of which he was the first member to go to university. His father died before he reached secondary school and his mother, who was ambitious for her son's future, was forced to work as a dinner lady in his school, which he found humiliating. He was far more than just a bright spark academically. His intellectual superiority, which was combined with a willingness to work hard like his mother, meant that he held a senior position in a major university by the time he was in his mid-thirties. His career was stellar. He was married to another successful academic whom he met when they were both gauche students. They had a family of young children. Both were super-ambitious professionals working in the public sector for modest remuneration whose lives turned into a *bind* of impossible demands to meet their children's needs as well as their own needs for time and intimacy at the same time as they were ascending their respective ladders to even greater heights. By the time his children were early teenagers his marriage had become stale, any spontaneous attempts at intimacy neglected, and mutual sexual desire had withered.

This mock edifice of Apollonian order came crumbling down when the 'Professor' met an exotic and sexually sophisticated post-doctoral European research student whom I will refer to as the 'Scarlet Woman'. She seized upon her unsuspecting 'Fellow', who was at once seduced. Their illicit sexual lives became a Dionysian carnival of flagrant desire and unaccustomed international extravagance. Undoubtedly, if she were in my consulting room I would be listening to another version of this story...

My 'Fellow' lost all sense of marital fidelity and paternal consistency, although he was too burdened by ambition and responsibility to allow his golden career to suffer visibly. Within a few years he was divorced, alienated from his children and married to the 'Scarlet Woman', who bled him dry until she became serially unfaithful and demanded a traumatic divorce. He still cannot understand what happened to him but in a shy, boyish breath he tells me that to begin with – and even post divorce – he found this woman, who wreaked devastation on his life, the most desirable, exotic and exciting figure he has ever met. She was and will always be *la belle dame sans merci* who, despite his recent third and seemingly successful marriage, still holds his imagination in thrall.

We spent a few sessions deconstructing these events and then I told him the story about the twin energies of Apollo and Dionysus. I told it to him exactly as I might tell a child a fairy story. I did not offer any explanation, or an interpretation. Being such a model student he did his homework and returned with a merrier twinkle in his eye. He was able to suspend his scientific scepticism and agree with me that in a life that was devoted first to his aged mother's care, then to professional duty and later on to interminable international responsibilities, but which had grown emotionally stale, he had become a prime risk. Taken aback, he realized that he was now almost grateful that the god Dionysus had visited him. He had found his answer. In spite of the pain and the expensive processes of two divorces, he was at last, and before it was too late, learning not more intellectual facts but acquiring more knowledge about his repressed emotional needs. Dionysus had exacted his price and it had been high. His principal regret was that he had had to sacrifice a good enough first marriage and his children's happiness in the process, because neither he nor his first wife knew how to privilege their needs for intimacy, play and an emotionally literate marriage.

When I am wrestling with the complex challenges of any couple's relationship, whether personal or professional, I have found these warring anti-twins to be a helpful paradigm. I use it in my consulting room to explore the virtues and discipline of relational commitment to monogamy versus the weathercock winds of desire and change. Although I have no constant position on which is the better alternative, I know that a marriage or relationship that grows habitual and flat, or which does not have enough oxygen for the couple to grow, will take a heavy toll on the children's emotional lives. I also know, through listening to every combination of relationship that the most important dynamic in any successful partnership is emotional intimacy and that requires time, patience and variety. Parents, I firmly believe, should try not to sacrifice their primal needs for continuing intimacy and mutual engagement to the daily rituals of their children's busy and competing lives. A little and occasional neglect may not be a bad thing if it is in the service of privileging the parents' essential needs across time for continuing intimacy. The roles of parent and partner are always a challenging balancing act but one that needs to be taken seriously. I listen with a wry smile when I hear women complain: 'I wish I could take my husband to a garage to be serviced weekly!' What is too often absent from their partnership is time, intimacy, foreplay… and play.

I do not believe (not a word I generally care for *and* there is no scientific basis for this lack of 'belief') that men are genetically designed for monogamy. I have sympathy for their predicaments, which are hormonally and instinctually different from those of most women. Until the twentieth century, when there were such dramatic improvements in infection control, along with a reduction in female and infant mortality, as a result of advances in obstetrics, it was rare for women to survive beyond the cycle of female fertility.* Marriages were often short and tragic. Historically people did not have so much time, leisure, or the distractions of social media in which to make comparisons or become so quickly bored with their sex lives. Today, many of the people I see have become addicted to variety, which they may confuse with passion, or their idea of it.

I do not consider that passion, which feeds off the illicit, or desire which always enjoys an obstacle, are reliable predictors of sustained marital longevity. Move their status on the chessboard from the illicit into the respectability of marriage and the habitual, and they may freeze before dawn breaks. I have sat and listened to stories of mercurial attraction, incendiary affairs that have sometimes left me privately feeling envious of accounts of these burning towers of physical alchemy. Who could guess

---

* In 2011 life expectancy at birth was almost double what it was in 1841 at which time the average female girl was not expected to see her forty-third birthday. A newborn boy was expected to live to 40.2 in 1841, compared to 79.0 in 2011, whereas a baby girl was expected to live to 42.2 in 1841 and 82.8 in 2011. (Figures from the Office of National Statistics, 2015.)

that within months or, at best, brief years, the narrator would awake like Titania to the appalling notion: 'Me thought I was enamoured with an ass… '? A sad but wise observation was recently made by a well-known divorce lawyer on television that but rarely has he found sexual desire, love and marriage to be frequent long-term bed partners.

Recently, I was working with a magnificent elderly lady who had travelled through the perils of a malignant disease as though she were a nineteenth-century traveller visiting Europe. Married once, a divorcee, there was also evidence of a gallery of exotic lovers. We still did not know each other well. During one conversation I refer to my husband. 'Oh!' she said, 'Oh, my dear, you don't mean to say you have been married to the same man all your life?' She looked so openly flabbergasted that I thought she was going to declare me unsuitable to be her therapist. Marriage is a word that is beginning, as more and more people are regarding their lives to be a series of unrelated chapters or even short stories, to become unfashionable. (I find it difficult not to sound imperial when referring to 'my husband' and prefer to say, 'My partner'.)

When I apply the influences of the twinned divinities to my personal life, their presence plunges me into a labyrinth of confusion. By nature I am drawn to Dionysian carnival, wounds and subversion, but this rebellion now mainly exists inside my mind as an intriguing debate. The chaotic disorder, fractures and unpredictability of my childhood and precocious adolescence have been compensated for by a more cautious and consistent adulthood. Even so, the unleashed forces of murder and loss have played a vital part in forging my identity and awareness that Fate, like the body, has no respect for our personal agendas or ambitions. If I could be granted some more foolish wishes, I would choose to come back as a vodka-swigging, sun-worshipping and gender-bending courtesan who could sing in tune. With a ribald sense of humour. Such wishes will not be well received by my family but I cannot eradicate them. I feel some regret that I have over-compensated for the ravages of childhood by trying to take control of my life in a doomed devotion to Apollonian symmetry, beauty and discipline. There have been earlier times in my life when I experienced and celebrated Dionysus' subversive revels, albeit in modest form, and when even if my limbs were not flayed, others were.

I was sixteen when my first cousin, to whom I was close, was a first-year undergraduate and scholar at Cambridge. David was something of a prodigy and achieved a double first in law before he was twenty. Males in our family, for the first time, were expected to be educated. He was sent away to public school to board, albeit in a Jewish house, Polacks at Clifton College. David's education did not cost anything as he won one scholarship after another. By contrast, I was expected to learn shorthand and typing and to make a good Jewish *shidduch* and marry a wealthy boy with a fast car. Nobody was going to supplement my university fees and as they were means-tested anyway, it was not even a possibility. I had run away from school at fifteen with two GCE's. David was destined, or doomed, to graduate from Cambridge straight into a 'magic circle' city firm as partner. He was not twenty-one. Before he was thirty he had escaped from selling his soul in the city to Portugal, where he gratefully committed himself into the permanent guardianship of a charismatic practitioner of bio-energetics who has maintained a parental role of mentorship ever since. David's childhood had been as empty of culture, and any focus of engaged parental attention as mine. The only difference was his had been as emotionally bland as mine had been fractured. We were both brought up in homes that were barren of cultural influences, without books, without music, without spiritual or political interest. I don't think either of us ever heard the word 'Holocaust' mentioned by our families as we grew up.

The first time I visited David at Cambridge was in 1960. Already obsessed with Jean Cocteau's writing and his talk of opium pipes, I discovered the existence of a society convened at Trinity, called *The Heretics*,* which had been resurrected that year with an exciting incognito visit from William S. Burroughs. My cousin, who preferred Union debates, politics and May Balls, did not accompany me. I met a brilliant Math undergraduate from Darlington, called Ian Sommerville, who was a Scholar at Corpus Christi. He acquired local notoriety by becoming the lover of the counter-culture writer Burroughs. Ian spent the summer vacation, before his third year began at Cambridge, living in Paris with Burroughs who he met while he was working at the Mistral bookshop. He was then employed by a mutual acquaintance of Burroughs. The acquaintance believed Ian, an Apollonian beauty, a flame-haired youth, as tantalizing as Ganymede, with a complex-ion of androgynous desire, might be able to assist the Dionysian Burroughs' drastic recovery from an addiction to the prescription drug Codeine by treatment with Apomorphine: 'I can't tell you what it's been like, man, it's been fucking unbelievable… I never want to go through this again, man. Hallucinations, convulsions,

---

* The Cambridge Heretics Society was a group of Cambridge students and other intellectuals who challenged traditional and religious authorities. Founded by C.K. Ogden in 1909, the group continued to meet until 1932. Many prom-inent modernist intellectuals, from Bertrand Russell to John Maynard Keynes to George Bernard Shaw, were associated with the Heretics Society and gave lectures for it.

freakouts, the edge of insanity. I had to hang on to my sanity by my fingernails, and they're bitten down to the moons. But it's worth it, man, Bill's getting better.' [quoted in Barry Miles, *Call Me Burroughs*, 2014]

Ian, who was the authentic progenitor of Burroughs's and Brion Gysin's famous dream machine, became my first partner in the Dionysian delirium of love. Corpus Christi was still an all-male college and very 'gay'. A randy and lonely Fellow with rooms immediately below Ian's would interrupt our romance. He was in the habit of pounding floorboards, and hopefully Ian's attention too, with a broomstick handle powered by carnal desire. The Fellow's frustrated appetite turned into malevolent revenge when he discovered my nocturnal presence. The sixties was still a time when it was Dionysus and not Apollo, with his sense of decorum and justice, who ruled over the unruly appetites that stalked the all-male Cambridge colleges.

Ian had an extraordinary undergraduate friend who was commonly recognized by dons and students as a prodigy. David Bonavia was reading Modern European Languages at Corpus, in which he would be awarded a double first *nonpareil*. David spoke more than twelve languages fluently. He had taught himself Chinese at school and later he returned post-graduate to Cambridge to study Russian. David suffered, albeit invisibly, from the black dog of depression but equally he could be a Dionysian celebrant of Bacchus when Dürer's winged angel released him from melancholy. We shared a Dionysian May weekend when Gala, who was now a notorious emblem of sixties psychedelics, the film-maker Ken Russell's muse and most of the time off her head on LSD, accompanied me to Corpus to celebrate the end of 'finals' with the two bacchants. None of us had an inclination for May Balls but at the end of a stoned evening Ian and David thought it would be 'a lark' for us to break into the Master of Corpus's private guest room. 'A traitor' had misinformed Ian that it was listed on the Fellows' notice board as unoccupied.

We none of us quite knew who loved whom that night until we were disturbed by the Master of Corpus who, having also wanted to escape the hurly-burly of another ball, had returned late with his guest. Rudely discovered and literally uncovered, Gala and I were frog-marched, wrapped only in sheets, by college porters across a midnight quad. Ian and David were sent down before they received their Finals results, and were grudgingly grateful, after the decision of various humourless committees, not to have been permanently disqualified from graduation. David's black dog – despite his genius, his professional success as Foreign Correspondent for *The Times* in China during the Chinese economic reforms in the early eighties, and his later celebrated expulsion from Moscow – bit him once too often; once too hard. Ian died in a car accident aged thirty-six. Neither of these golden celebrants was destined to grow old.

～

In September 1985, I had another meeting with 'the twins' when I accompanied John, who was working with the National Theatre, to the Odeon of Herodes Atticus in Athens. Ian McKellen was in the role of Coriolanus and our friend Greg Hicks was playing the rival warrior Aufidius. After morning rehearsal had finished some of us, who were not involved in the evening's performance, decided to set off on a challenging expedition to Apollo's shrine at Delphi. Greg whose life, as far back as can be recorded, has been divided between the conflicted desires of the sacred twins, insisted he was coming. As our taxi was departing, Greg was physically hauled out by Stage Management, who were afraid that, seized by the seductress of Apollo's Oracle, the serpentine Pythia, Greg might not be back in time, or in a fit state, for the evening performance.

Coriolanus was performed in the moonlit arena of the Herodes Atticus Theatre below the Acropolis in front of an audience of five thousand. The original acoustics are so remarkable that you can indeed hear the clichéd pin drop. As the play surged into the field of visceral drama there were gasps of collective astonishment; it seemed that Ian's body had morphed into a spirit which soared beyond and above the ramparts. The tension of the fight scenes between Coriolanus and Aufidius threatened each other's mortality with every thrust. The performance did not bring the relief of catharsis but the very real terror that there would be a mortal injury. I became a twentieth-century witness to the birth of tragedy. The *anagnorisis* of Coriolanus' sob: 'There is a world elsewhere,' provoked a collective shudder. As the shaken audience departed we ran towards the ramparts where Ian, in a state of emotional collapse, was being carried towards his dressing room: 'During the final show I drank five litres of water and a jar of Greek honey that I filched from Greg Hicks. Even so, after it was over I leant against the backstage wall unable to move and I was half-carried back to the dressing-room and an ouzo. That is the day I first felt mortality as an actor.' [Ian McKellen, writing in *The Stage*, 2003]

We woke to Greg knocking at our bedroom door. 'Follow me, I want to make it before sunrise.' We were still high on the performance and ouzo. He refused to reveal our destination. We set off towards the sacred ruins of a Greek theatre built in Dionysus' honour. Any entrance to its portico was prevented by barbed wire and a notice warned us that access was forbidden on health and safety grounds. (The space was not publicly reopened until 2009.) We had arrived at a vast arena, situated halfway up the Acropolis hill, along the Areopagitou Dionysiou, which had been concealed from public view by the dense undergrowth of rusty wire covered in bindweed, if not asphodel. Like a goatherd Greg leapt ahead of us, while we inched our way gingerly down the crumbling cliff. Companioned by the rising sun, we found ourselves entering a forbidden and sacred *temenos*. Greg had trespassed us through the dawn into the ruins of the Theatre of Dionysus. Historians estimate that its original audience would have numbered close to seventeen thousand of Dionysus' worshippers.

Do I remember or did I dream it? Greg was already familiar with the spirit of the place and he led us towards the remains of three Hellenistic thrones, restored by the Romans, whose marble forms were catching the rays of sunrise. He drew us in, closer to their ruined calligraphy. These thrones were dedicated to the fathers of Greek tragedy who had once occupied them – Socrates, Euripides and Aeschylus. Alone with their greatness, seated upon marble, we saluted the glory of another day rising over the Doric remains of Dionysus' spiritual home. Tragic narratives that recorded the fall of Apollonian family dynasties had consumed each of these Greek masters' dramatic imagination. All the while, Dionysus had directed their dynastic extinction.

'Extinction' is another word embedded in my text. It is a word admired by Proust but one not otherwise often used except in relation to the extinction of animal species. It carries a gravitas that is often missing from contemporary idiom when referring to death and the processes of dying. I bristle with allergy when I observe that so many people cannot say: 'He died.' The euphemism 'passed away' seems to have evolved, if that is possible, into more bland versions like 'passed on'. Just 'passed', I am told, is now most common of all in America and is quickly becoming the acceptable and impoverished lingo in the UK. If only that 'on' indicated any belief in the speaker in a non-temporal, non-material universe but it rarely does. It exudes a strange and repellent mix of evasiveness on the one hand and coarseness on the other. Its passive tone, if not tense, is used like a breastplate to protect the heart and stop the mourner thinking. Otherwise, they might be tempted to question the destination their deceased has been 'passed on' to. Our twenty-first-century deceased have barely issued a dying breath before they are 'passed on' from bed to van, to refrigerator, to incinerator. Nobody much cares to imagine that.

I like to imagine dying while I am lying and sedated in my own bed; watching the tree outside my bedroom window sighing like an Aeolian harp in the wind. I have discovered it is called a weeping pittosporum. I have treasured its presence, on which I have unfailingly focused my waking sight, as a living Calder mobile, for the last thirty-seven years. Some years I am privileged with the miracle of a blackbird's nest almost concealed within its boughs. I remember planting the tree as a frail sapling, with Alex standing by. We had no idea that it would grow to be taller than our four-storey house. I am grateful that its roots, unlike those of the wayward yew, or the spirochete, do not incline to burrow into the foundations of our home. I also like to imagine that my death would not frighten or disgust my family, but they would keep and care for my body until every cell had turned cold, before I was pitched out onto the undertaker's bier. 'Have pity upon me, have pity upon me, O ye my friends; for the hand of God hath touched me.'

I cherish Poussin's painting of the *Extreme Unction* in his series of seven deathbed scenes depicting the sacraments of the

Catholic Church. The giving of 'The Last Rites' – for which I have prepared no secular equivalent – is part of a sociable bedside farewell as 'community' pays its respects to the extinction of life. It is only at this stage of my life that I experience a sadness that, in cauterizing my relationship to Jewish community and culture, I have forfeited my entitlement to the consolation and comforts of Jewish mourning rituals and the *Shiva*, which is the ceremonial of bereavement.

When I think about mourning and grief I find myself involuntarily reflecting on the *business* of Poussin's sacraments. How death was then far more familiar to society than the hitherto sacred mysteries and dramas of childbirth, which today have become a free-for-all with programmes like *One Born Every Minute* that now parade on our television screens. I cannot help wondering what will be the future consequences to some of the neonates, whose births are publicly, and to my mind, brazenly broadcast at prime viewing time. I have not cared to investigate whether the parents are financially remunerated for agreeing to participate in these serial and degrading spectacles. Nietzsche's unspeakable predictions have become a living reality, or deadly virus, for our society of media slaves, where Dionysus cracks his whip and Apollo has lost his lyre. Today, when there are so many variables over which we have no control as to the ways in which we may be conceived, gene-selected and delivered, and where the long-term consequences of these intrusions on nature remain perhaps the only mystery, the impact of Laing's question of 'whose womb?' becomes an even more compelling and tantalizing counter-factual.

In my earlier list of seven trigger words I included 'privilege'. When I come to elucidate and contextualize my definition of privilege, I cannot do so effectively without also examining my idiosyncratic interpretation of its shadow energy, 'failure'. (I am aware that a better antonym would be deprivation.) Before I deconstruct my eccentric twinning of 'privilege' and 'failure', it feels important to identify, even at this late stage, what I mean by psychotherapy. I find that nothing has surpassed the descriptive statement that I offered in my first book, *Who Is It That Can Tell Me Who I Am?* It was the psychotherapist and writer Adam Phillips, whose statement mirrored not only my own experience, but also brought with it professional enlightenment as to the *meaning* of my own experience. It is unusual for me to refer back to a previous work and not feel that several years later I want to make an adjustment, add a codicil, or even to experience faint nausea, but today my opinion remains unchanged:

One day – sometime in 1990 – I read an article in the *London Review of Books* by a psychotherapist and writer whom I had not then heard of, Adam Phillips. It provided me with another lens with which to understand what was taking place in my consulting room between patients and myself. I have since come to look on that day as a moment of clinical transfusion when what I most valued about the therapeutic process, which was the experience of dialogue and the relationship in and for itself, was reflected back to me with new meaning. Phillips observes how easy it is to go through life denying the origins of psychic pain: *People organize their lives to avoid the imagined catastrophe of certain conversations; and they come into analysis, however fluent they may be, because they are unable to speak. But some people have had unspeakable experiences, or experiences that have been made unspeakable by the absence of a listener. [Phillips 1990]*

I was thrilled by Phillip's observations. The image of Coleridge's Ancient Mariner rose, unbidden, before my eyes:

'O Wedding-Guest! This soul hath been / Alone on a wide, wide sea.' I recalled how when I began psychoanalysis I was astonished that I had found someone, my analyst, who was prepared to enter into relationship, argue and laugh with me, and with whom I wanted, and was also afraid, to have a dialogue that I had been waiting to have forever and which could not take place with family or friends. A dialogue with someone who could help me to understand more about the hidden roots of my suffering. I felt as though I had been playing a game of hide and seek for years and that at last there was someone there who knew how to find me. In order for any dialogue to begin there has to be two people who are meeting each other with openness and equality that will facilitate a culture of trust. This model of relationship where there is equality – although not symmetry of purpose – could not be more different than the psychoanalytic ideal of a blank screen where the analyst's role, in the service of the patient, is one of personal anonymity. [Haynes]

It feels like a 'no brainer' not to acknowledge that the role of the specialist *listener* Phillips describes is privileged, and 'privilege' is a word that I have frequently used in these pages to describe the work that I am trained to do. Such privilege does not prevent thoughts crossing my mind about the presumption that is also required to set up shop as a psychotherapist. I was reminded of my arrogance at the time of my first lecture in St Petersburg, when I blithely felt entitled on my arrival to lecture its brave citizens – whose history is one of intellectual and physical violation, yet whose hospitality and courage seem boundless – on 'The Unspeakable'. The memory makes me cringe. While I am able, if requested, to produce certification of years of training and professional development, it is impossible to produce any accreditation that will guarantee my patients access to funds of wisdom and compassion.

I have become allergic to the ways in which the concept of empathy has come to be an overused buzzword. I prefer an out-of-fashion noun, sympathy, while compassion is the *sine qua non* of my daily bread. Empathy signifies to me a process of emotional and psychological projection. More specifically, outside of over-enthusiastic therapeutic jargon, it can refer to the concept of *Einfühlung* – literally, the activity of 'feeling into' – that was developed in late-nineteenth-century Germany, in the overlapping fields of philosophical aesthetics, perceptual psychology and art and architectural history, to describe an embodied response to an image, object or spatial environment. While examples of projections into inanimate objects feel appropriate, when it comes to one person feeling, or still worse, projecting their way into another person's psyche, I come unstuck. I feel the best we can do is to steer society towards an empathetic attitude, which I understand to mean caring about one's neighbour. I am comforted by Jung's position, echoed by many of the greatest thinkers in various disciplines, who are preoccupied by our solipsistic fate: 'Philosophical criticism has helped me to see that every psychology – my own included – has the character of a subjective confession, even when I am dealing with empirical data, I am necessarily speaking about myself.' One of the most problematic aspects of the claims of psychotherapy is the danger of us therapists overestimating our powers of empathy when, in reality, we are often speaking at some unconscious or even conscious level of ourselves. Jung went on to insist that we can never know what the other is thinking and the best we can ever do is to respect their difference.

I can appreciate the therapeutic value of an empathetic attitude, so long as it does not imply permission to enter into another person's mind but only intimates a subjective estimation of another person's emotional inscape. Otherwise, I am content to work within the confines of a *sympathetic* attunement or engagement. I wonder why the idea of sympathy, despite its therapeutic origins and metaphor of wounds and healing, has become so unfashionable.

Maybe, because all the people who come to see me do so at the behest of either their GP or a psychiatrist, or, less frequently, hear of me by word of mouth, I have never been questioned about my qualifications, or what kind of therapist I am. There are a few exceptions, such as when someone comes for a consultation after having completed a course of Cognitive Behavioural Therapy, whose limits they have found frustrating, and they now want to know how the work we would do might differ. There are also many people who arrive disillusioned with the formal processes of psychoanalysis and wanting to be reassured that I will be a visibly and audibly active co-participant. I have never been questioned at the initial interview about my theoretical orientation, although that may become of interest during the course of therapy as the person becomes more intellectually intrigued by the discipline.

These experiences take me back to the thorny question about the alchemy between two people where one becomes privileged to listen to thoughts and feelings that have hitherto been experienced as unspeakable. I think the verb 'becomes' is important; I have already indicated how dangerous I believe unmediated confessions can be, whereas for something to 'become' indicates a passage of time and a shared process. I have also learnt, across time, not to confuse parts of a narrative, a shared confidence, or the unlocking of a secret, with the whole. It is easy to become seduced into thinking that the story shared is being communicated in its entirety, only to discover maybe weeks, months or even years later, the kernel of meaning was being withheld. The genius of Proust's construction of Albertine, one of the most despised of literary heroines, is that she mirrors all the despised deceits of the self that we are all heir to, and to which I am often 'privileged' to listen.

As I do not practice in the NHS I know that another limitation to my work is the financial constraints of some of the people who consult me, and the fact that a long therapy can be the monthly equivalent to a short-term mortgage. While there must always be a symbolic exchange of currency, I am well aware that for people who are struggling to make or to maintain a living, less often equates with more, and it is the people at the bottom of my fee scale who will find it hardest of all to pay them. I try to exercise a mindful concern of flexibility in my fee structuring. My practice not only contains people who are at the top of their professional lives but also young men and women who are still exploring possible directions for their lives to take, and who are beset with limited and uncertain financial resources. At the risk of repetition, it feels an exceptional privilege to be trusted by vulnerable young people who are often in a process of reaction to conventional authority figures. Sometimes one of them will leave my room and I have to catch my breath; I feel as though my spirit has swallowed an elixir of trust which is derived from their confidences. Therapies that occur at an earlier life stage can sometimes become lifechanging in ways that become more difficult to achieve as time goes by, which in itself provides me with a rich reward. I further provide myself with modest comfort about the unfairness of the scant availability of affordable therapy in that I have never refused, or stopped working with, anyone who has approached me with commitments because they could not afford my fees. Although there has to be a limit to the number of 'reduced fees' patients that I can accommodate, I have never refused the opportunity to work with somebody with whom I felt a sense of 'enjoyment' and mutual compatibility at our assessment meetings.

'Enjoy' may sound a strange word to use in the context of therapy but for me is a vital one, despite the intense suffering and shame that is often involved in speaking the unspeakable. By 'enjoy' I mean the mutual and involuntary sensations of pleasure that occur when I open my door in the repetition and ritual of greeting. This involuntary and sometimes fleeting pleasure exists spontaneously at the moment of a return when I open the door in welcome, even if the previous session has involved anger, disappointment; or both.

The only 'deprivation', to return to the correct *antonym* to my concept of 'privilege' that has occurred through my work, appertains to Gary Indiana's statement at the beginning of the book that any good novel is more revealing than a memoir. It is a possibility that I might have attempted to become a novelist, but it would not have been compatible, even if I possessed the application and talent, with my work as a therapist for two reasons. The first is related to the fact that I spend my day absorbing and remembering – I disdain note-taking except in circumstances where I need to record a crisis, or deteriorating health – the narratives and genograms of so many lives. I do not have any hard drive left for even an attempt at constructing any additional fictional narratives. As I wrote in my first chapter, so many of the narratives of therapy concern the thorny matters of early attachment, of love and its shadow, or of tales of family revenge, which have their beginnings in our families of origin, or relationships that we have created later on in adulthood. The same is true for the novelist. History, whether domestic or royal, begins with the ancestral roots of every individual. I would find it difficult to focus on fictional families when the living branches of 'the family of man' preoccupy my mind. The second reason, if I were to write fiction, would be the danger that someone who has consulted me may, however mistakenly, think that they recognized themselves.

While I request permission from everyone I write about, this ignores the quandary of the unknown feelings of the people I have not referred to, which to my surprise are not always those of relief. With three exceptions, everyone I submitted these vignettes to gave me their permission without requesting any adjustment. But, what about those people who consult me whom I have not written about; how will they feel if they happenstance upon the book? In most instances, there will be gratitude at being invisible; from our beginnings, we have had a pledge that I will never reproduce a syllable's-worth of our dialogue. And then there is the sacred: 'Whereof we cannot speak, thereof we must remain silent.'

But, I know from past experience there were some people who told me that they felt disappointment not to find themselves amongst the pages of my previous books because they assumed their lives were too bland to have left any mark. There is more discourse about the rights and wrongs of including verbatim material than the consequences of unwittingly inflicting a further wound on someone's self image through exclusion; through unintentionally making somebody with whom I have shared a sacred journey once again experience a familiar feeling that they did not matter, that they were always destined to remain the invisible journeyman. It is not without the risk of committing damage to request permission and then to present someone with my objectification, or pathology of their experience and feelings, but for some other people the wound of not having a speaking part can be even more painful. To return to Wittgenstein: 'If only you do not try to utter what is unutterable then *nothing* gets lost. But the unutterable will be – unutterably – *contained* in what has been uttered!' Who has put the dilemma better?

I am still reflecting on why I chose to make my corrupt binary between privilege and failure, instead of privilege and deprivation. It is because unlike privilege failure is hard to live with and while it has been possible to describe untold instances of the privileges of my work and the satisfaction it has brought me for so many years, it is harder to find a way of talking publicly, or outside a professional context, about professional failures. It is the consumer's voice of complaint and debate that needs to be heard and that is a challenging option within these pages. If I have failed serially to understand somebody's 'cry' the relationship will have terminated. Or, someone may give an excuse prematurely to end the therapy rather than to admit failure. Even trickier to decide is what amounts to failure. I find it more frequent in contexts outside my consulting room, as a partner, parent and grandparent, to identify distressing failures of communication and absences of sympathy that I may be responsible for inflicting. My training as a therapist, or the routes I travel and explore in my consulting room, sadly do not exempt me from such failures or familiar defensive manoeuvres, in my domestic life where I am too often, unlike in my consulting room, in a hurry! I do comment to the people who are consulting me that many of the phenomena we discuss are easier to explore in words and dreams in the therapeutic hour than to accomplish as considered actions outside of it. Change takes patience, time and practice. And more time.

It may only be retrospectively, after many years, or even a lifetime, that someone is positioned to know whether or not the therapy was effective. Dissention, or unresolved conflict, can turn out to be as creative as collaboration but, inevitably, it will, like the oyster's pearl, be born out of an uncomfortable inflammation of self. Rarely does any session pass by without containing an element of failure. As I remarked about Mrs Darling's annoying obsession with cataloguing her children's underwear, nobody likes to feel that they are transparent. In the same way that parents will inevitably fail their children, so will the therapist be responsible for misunderstandings and even inadvertently causing harm along the thorny way. What becomes an important sign of mature therapeutic health is whether or not that misunderstanding or unintentional wounding can be revealed in a subsequent session; whether it can be shared without defensiveness and become mutually understood, even forgiven.

It is only while I have been reflecting on some private examples of failure that I realize the final section of this chapter owes its existence to a failed but meaningful therapy. The summer break had ended and autumn was approaching when a man whom I had been seeing for maybe three years returned from Trani in Italy, with a small gift. He had snapped and then printed a photograph for me of a piece of graffiti scrawled across a delicatessen door in a remote village. He had no idea why it should have been written in English:

In the end what matters most is how well did you live
How well did you love
How well did you learn to let go…

Along with the delicate and faded origami bird, which has LOVE written across it, that my grandson produced for me when he was a teenager, this scrap of paper shares a precious place on the Georgian mantelpiece in my consulting room. The therapy was a failure because I could not help this man, who was approaching his mid-sixties, to let go of the depression that had haunted him for half his life, or more. He held a responsible position as a permanent under secretary in the Civil Service. He had joined the service at a time when there was still a taboo about mental illness being recorded in personal files. This meant that he had conducted his career without ever applying for medical leave, regardless of the intensity of his depressive episodes, which at their worst led to severe panic attacks. In spite of the illness, he was a bon viveur and active traveller who would return with marvellous accounts of spring hikes with his wife in the mountains where their hobby was to study the counterpane of alpine plants. He had been sent away to a boarding school at a young age where he often suffered from an abdominal version of migraine, which is not uncommon in children and which added to his misery the humiliation of the occasional public vomiting.

While we had many 'enjoyable' meetings and animated conversations during which I like to consider that we both learnt more about his illness and each other and I felt that I was his trusted listener, none of them did anything to ameliorate his great suffering during the three years in which he consulted me. He was a natural classicist who had been mistakenly influenced by his father to go against his inclination for philosophy in search of security and to read mathematics. His successful marriage was unintentionally childless. We became able to talk about intimate feelings. I also shared some details of my life with him when it felt helpful. He was the person whose descriptions persuaded me to take my first tentative steps into opera. He also urged me to read the early Greek philosophers, whom he found to be a source of consolation. None of our conversations improved his clinical state of mind for long and he would sometimes say that his therapy was a financial luxury that it was hard to justify continuing. He had been under the care of two psychiatrists and a handful of therapists during the years before he was referred to me and had been prescribed a variety of anti-depressants and cognitive behavioural therapy, with the threat of electro-convulsive-therapy always in the background.

One day he arrived in such an acute state of physical panic and terror that it was hard for me to understand how he had managed to survive the tube journey and get himself to my door. I felt helpless and seriously alarmed. His shirt was dripping wet, while despite the heat he was shivering with terror. I was at a loss and frightened. We both knew there are so many different reasons for and origins of clinical depression. We had explored every backwater and cul-de-sac of his developmental history. Although there were inevitable frustrations and disappointments, his life was meaningful, his work fulfilling and successful, and his marriage content. We were left feeling helpless in the face of this mortal terror. My final and desperate attempt at a partial solution was to persuade him, with some difficulty and without any delay, to consult an alternative psychiatrist to the one who had originally referred him to me. This psychiatrist, who was a trusted colleague and an expert pharmacologist, took his time to arrive at a diagnosis, which required a new type of drug regime that slowly resulted over time in a moderate improvement of his mood.

Reluctantly, we had to agree with regard to the 'cure' that he had arrived still hoping to find, there was nothing else I could offer. He could not justify continuing to pay for therapy as a crutch and he reluctantly began to accept that his depression, while being a heavy burden to bear, had not destroyed his marriage, his refined cultural sensibility or his career. Even in his darkest days he had managed to avoid the extreme of electro-convulsive therapy. We had reached the stage where we could both see that his illness had attached itself to him like a shadow. Our therapy, while meaningful, had failed to make any clinical difference to the quality of his life. There was nothing to be done except for him to let go, not only of the therapy, but also of any expectation – although some healing had taken place – his psychological health was going to be 'cured'. Whenever I think of the inevitable, I never tire of quoting a passage from Hilary Mantel's unforgettable *The Giant, O'Brien*: 'But finally, here's why he is lying on the floor. No fancy reasons. Forget philosophy. He's lying on the floor because he's realized this, that there's nothing to be done. There's simply nothing.'

Sometimes, there is nothing more that can be done other than to work towards 'letting go' of the wretched and suppurating psychic ulcer that refuses to heal. How ironic that it was this man, whom I failed, who had brought me a holiday photograph of a random aphorism that contains the philosophy and mantra of my old age. It is a destination that I am still struggling to reach myself, while at the same time I am beckoning, when appropriate, some of the other journeymen along that way.

Because his gift of a scrap of graffiti was essential to this chapter, and because he had been so anxious about his 'black dog' ever escaping into the public forum, it felt necessary for me to approach him in advance for his permission, or refusal, to contextualize his gift's existence. I wrote the following email after a distance of about four years.

Dear C,

First of all, A Happy New Year. I see from Google that you are still listed at Chambers, and with commendations which must carry some positives.

I am writing to you because I am finishing the last chapter of my book, 'If I chance to talk a little wild, forgive me' [taken from *Henry VIII*] and the last section of the final chapter, which I have taken a couple of weeks off consulting to overcome my resistance to completing, is forming itself around 'Letting Go' and the little piece of paper you gave me which still sits on my mantelpiece and informs my practice. I should very much like to make that aphorism you brought to me from Italy the ending of my book and to contextualize it within an anonymised version of our meetings. I do not refer to you as a QC but as a senior civil servant. I wonder how you will feel about this. Naturally there are not any identifying details at all and of course if you did not want me to contextualize the way in which I have made such meaning out of the gift I can do so without providing any references to the giver.

By the end of the week I expect to have a first and completed draft of the final chapter that I should be happy to send to you once it has percolated a bit.

I do hope life is treating you well enough in this mortal world. I also record how you, or this person, urged me towards opera and loved the Ancient Greek philosophers.

I hope the meds are still doing their work. Sadly, I have found nothing at all to remedy my IBS pain, which holds me in tight a thrall as Andromeda to her rock! In spite of that I am still practising full time and still in a 'Passion' about my work.

With many good wishes,

Jane

The following morning I woke up to this email, which took me by surprise:

Dear Jane,

What a charming letter to welcome me into 2018! I am so sorry that you still suffer; it seems cruel when you do so much to help others that you should prove unhelpable. But I am delighted that opera gives a little consolation

About the little 'In the end' piece from Trani I could not be more delighted that you should let others ask whether it does not give them some of the compass points you led me to see in it, and I do not have the least difficulty in you referring to me as a barrister. People are becoming so much more open that after chambers had had a very good lunchtime talk on coping with pressure I wrote a roundrobin to all members of chambers telling them that I had been fighting the black dog all my career and saying that if it could be a real problem it could be overcome; you will be interested to know that about 10% took the trouble to write back and thank me for telling them because they felt it had helped. So to me a bit of openness is a way I can repay the debt I feel to people like you who have helped me so much. Incidentally if you refer to Trani remember that the cathedral there has in my view, some claim to be the most striking building in all of Italy, perched as it is in all its Romanesque glory high on the sea wall where the Crusaders set sail.

I am seeing Stephen tomorrow for the first time in over a year (largely because the DVLA are working out whether to renew my licence!) and you will gather from that that he has with his drug regime got me to the best of my knowledge into a state of contentment and stability. Of course the black dog barks from time to time... So between the two of you you have scored an awful lot of marks and E and I never cease to give thanks for our good fortune in having come under your care.

With renewed thanks to you for contacting me and with every good wish for 2018.

C (and E too)

PS. Some general thoughts on the black dog. The Black Dog is certainly not a lap dog, and is I think probably a mongrel of the first order, unlike Dido, unless you can have a pedigree mongrel! The oddest thing is that others cannot see him as he trots along beside me on our occasional walks, and he seems better at biting me if I offend him than others who do not know how sensitive he is! And you know from Dido that hounds need their exercise, so even the black dog needs a quick walk from time to time, and can even be on occasion a good companion.

I have omitted one or two facts from this email exchange, like the name of his chambers and changed the initial of his wife's name. Despite the comment about their joint care, I never met his wife with the exception of a fleeting occasion when our paths almost crossed at the opera. Yet, in some therapies, as in this instance, it turns out that the patient's partner also becomes an active but absent, or invisible participant in the work and sometimes it can feel as though we are all collaborators. (I find it far more difficult to conduct a long term therapy where I do not feel any sympathy towards the partner.) I also decided not to change my previous masking of him as a civil servant, because it was with the intention of disguise that I approached him. What sent a shiver of pleasure down my spine was the fact that he had – after a lifetime of shame – gone public as a highly respected QC and declared his mental illness to his colleagues. It was not something that I could have imagined happening.

When I reflect on the process and meaning of 'letting go', it is likely to be Dionysus wearing his creative mantle who enters 'centre stage', because Dionysus hates the predictable and the habitual. Unlike Apollo, he understands that the journey of individuating from received social conventions and daring to challenge the repressive and habitual super-ego of society, or what Jung called 'Individuation', while risky, even dangerous, is also instinctual and life-affirming. It is Apollo, and not Dionysus, who is responsible for the daily routines of my work as a psychotherapist for which an essential requirement is constancy. It is also Apollo who watches over my grammar and tries to reign in my unpredictable punctuation, unwieldy discursions and wild parapraxes, which I still insist on displaying. Yes, it is Apollo who has become the spine of my book.

In my many private reflections on the meanings of 'letting go' my initial association was the importance of 'letting go' of those lifelong grudges, which often originate in failures of attachment and parenting. Such grudges, or barnacles, which may be conscious or unconscious, are then at risk of being projected in patterns of repetition onto future relationships. In the case of the QC, it was encouraging him to be brave, to accept his debilitating and at times devastating illness as a meaningful part of himself, rather than fighting it in the psychic equivalent of the High Court. There is no justice to be found in either the families we are born into, or the bodies we are forced to inhabit.

While so much of my work centres around the broken attachments of childhood and youth, an addendum to these thoughts has emerged relating to a new phenomenon of attachment anxiety. Because of the dramatic increase in life expectancy, many of the people who consult me, who are in their fifties and even early sixties, still have parents who are alive. As someone who lost both my parents at a relatively young age, I find it a challenge to overcome my first unhelpful impulse, when I hear of such delayed bereavements, to exclaim, 'But they have had their three score and ten!' These impetuous thoughts are incompatible to the feelings of people who are experiencing late parental loss and to the consequences of what it means to live most of your life, rather like Prince Charles, in the presence of parental 'authority'. To be parented at some existential level means one is still a child, and by extension that there is still an open umbrella of protection from one's mortality; from being the next person in the firing line.

In a situation which is very different from that of the helpless child, these overgrown children can, after the remaining parent's death, find themselves feeling dread about their own mortality, or falling into melancholy, for many reasons, around their ambivalence and the harsh exposure towards the processes of aging, sans eyes, sans teeth, sans everything. Some of the bereaved are emotionally overthrown by the death of geriatric parents with whom they may have at last become best friends and confidants. There are other cases where the people who consult me are still alarmingly, and often unconsciously, dependent upon their parent's reflections; and when death is no guarantee of release from archaic parental criticism and the reprimanding internal voice of 'the Critic.' When historical attachments are not of love or respect, but rather through a clump of overgrown thorns, then it may become necessary to find a way to perform the delicate, if not impossible and overdue surgery of 'parentectomy'.

If somebody is in therapy who still has *living* parents, even though they have become estranged, I regard that as a gift. There may still be some time left to make reparation. Regardless of their historical feelings, I try to encourage these overgrown children, if there are any shreds of possibility, to find a resolution to their differences and disappointments, their fears that they have never matched up to their parents' expectations.

I regard the process of not merely reconciling oneself but of becoming able to let go of a historic grudge, a contemporary disappointment, or rejection – all of which can suppurate as an unhealed wound – as an essential step in the journey of healing and individuation, which is sometimes ignored in psychotherapy. Being aware of these restorative powers does not necessarily make one an adept in the practice. I am often aware in my domestic life of a narcissistic wound, which, unless I maintain great self-control, will gnaw away at my psyche like a rogue toothache. I have also become aware with each decade how pernicious and reductive a fear of rejection can be to the psyche. It is not only conscience that does make cowards of us all, it is also rejection, or that has been both my observation and experience in my earlier life. When I reached fifty I made a covenant with myself. I decided that I did not want to treat the fear of 'rejection' as though it was a tool with which to castrate myself. If, after careful reflection, there was something in the world that I wanted to pursue, I would do so. Likewise, if there were to be somebody in the world that I wanted to approach, if it were possible to do so without a gross intrusion, I would, without being afraid of rejection. Such occasions do not happen often but when they do I have felt as if I have taken possession of a 'golden fleece' of authorship.

I was not sure how to 'let go' of this book until a recent incident with my little granddaughter Bell showed me the way. I cannot think about the child becoming the father, or leading the way, without also thinking of Prince Myshkin's words in Fyodor Dostoevsky's *The Idiot*: 'The soul is healed by being with children.' So often, it is children who can restore our sense of direction, if we care to listen. I referred in my first chapter to a pearl reliquary in which I have collected the first teeth of my children and our dogs ever since Tanya was born. Not a month passes without me wanting to open the box and reminisce on its minuscule contents. Ever since Bell became aware of the box she has been intrigued and fascinated. She loves me to tell her imaginary stories about the different owners of the teeth. Sometimes she will volunteer me a story. I have to explain that there are none of her teeth in the box because they are too precious for her mother to relinquish. She does not find this explanation to her satisfaction. At first she was too small to reach the box, which is high up on our mantelpiece. Then it became possible for her to stand on tiptoe and to admire the container. Now that she is six she is both dexterous and tall enough to reach up, remove the box and explore carefully its mysterious and miniature contents.

Bell is a careful and truthful child who, despite having access to everything in our home, has never abused her privilege, or our trust. A few weeks ago, while I was still searching in vain for my conclusion, I absent-mindedly walked past the mantelpiece and reached out for my pearl reliquary. There was nothing suspicious about its position on the mantelpiece, the pearl and glass container were intact, except on opening it, there was not a tooth to be found. Everyone who has access to the mantelpiece knows that I regard this small box as the *summum bonum* of my possessions. It would be inconceivable that anyone would remove the teeth. They are the only collection that I have from my past and they were the bounty of my maternal life. The signs pointed towards Bell. I knew, although I knew not what, that something extraordinary must have taken place and that I must approach her cautiously. I did not want to shame or humiliate her. In response to my bland inquiry, Bell replied in an uncharacteristic and oblique way. 'Yes, I remember, but it was all such a long time ago when I was still little. Dido and me needed to protect the teeth, but I don't remember at all what happened to them. Maybe Dido put them under the couch. They were there once. I saw them.' Her hyacinth eyes, full of exquisite mystery, enchant me.

As the falconer says to the wild eagle, 'I will let you go, everything has its end.' So I have let go of the pearl reliquary, let go of my history of childhood.

Acknowledgements

I WISH TO THANK NAIM ATTALLAH, WHOSE ETERNAL PAS-
sion for the Word shines 'steadfast' as John Keats's bright star.
Thank you to all Naim's dedicated team at Quartet Books who
have been engaged, creative, and supportive: Grace Pilkington
is as special as her name; gratitude for my editor David Elliott's
sensibility and discrimination.

I am grateful to Hilary Mantel for reading and re-reading my
manuscript as 'work in progress' and whose thoughts always
imprint the air – my air. I want to thank Camilla Nichols, who
was my first 'safe' reader and Robert Wilson for smoothing out
some early knots of unruly syntax. Mikhail Reshetnikov's devotion to spreading the dialogic 'word' against resistance persuaded
me to become a regular visitor to SPB and 'his' inspiring Eastern
European Institute of Psychoanalysis.

To Christopher Kit Prendergast who inspires me and without
knowing it gave me the courage to dare to write about Proust. To
Adrian Searle, for opening my eyes to new 'concepts'. I also want
to thank my colleague, Dr James Arkell, for being close beside of
me, and of some of my 'patients' whenever 'the talking cure' has
required more than just 'words'. I could not have written this book
without the contributions to my thoughts of all the people who
have shared, or continue to share, a professional dialogue with me.

To Christopher Potter, who provokes me to go further: to think more, read more, write better and always to play more, and his inspired 'eye' which spirited the cover image out of my husband John's Rome archive. And my constant gratitude to Annabelle, my 'Bell', who gave this story an ending and finally, to Gala, my life-long muse.